Chief "Red Cloud" and
Freddie Davis
son of- July 4, 1904
Dr Davis. Chadron
Nebr.

AFTER COLUMBUS

The Smithsonian Chronicle of the
NORTH AMERICAN INDIANS

Herman J. Viola

Smithsonian Books Washington, D.C.

Orion Books New York

Author's Dedication To American Indians everywhere,
especially those who have enriched my life
by allowing me to be a part of theirs.

Herman J. Viola

THE SMITHSONIAN INSTITUTION
Secretary Robert McC. Adams
Assistant Secretary for External Affairs
   Thomas E. Lovejoy
Director, Smithsonian Institution Press
   Felix C. Lowe

SMITHSONIAN BOOKS
Editor-in-Chief Patricia Gallagher
Administrative Assistant Anne P. Naruta
Senior Editor Alexis Doster III
Editors Amy Donovan, Joe Goodwin
Assistant Editors Bryan D. Kennedy, Sonia Reece
Senior Picture Editor Frances C. Rowsell
Picture Editor R. Jenny Takacs
Assistant Picture Editors Carrie E. Bruns,
Juliana Montfort
Picture Research Ann Monroe Jacobs, Anne P. Naruta
Picture Assistant V. Susan Guardado
Copy Editor Karen M. MacKavanagh
Intern Gwendolyn Moodispaw
Production Editor Patricia Upchurch
Assistant Production Editor Martha Sewall
Production Assistant Kathy Kim
Business Manager Stephen J. Bergstrom
Marketing Director Gail Grella
Marketing Manager Ruth A. Chamblee
Design Phil Jordan and Associates, Inc.
Typography Harlowe Typography, Inc.
Separations The Lanman Companies
Printing R.R. Donnelley & Sons Company

Page 1: Oglala Sioux Chief Red Cloud and young
Freddie Davis, July 4, 1904, in Chadron, Nebraska;
pages 2-3: *Visions of Yesterday*, by William R. Leigh,
1944; pages 4-5: *Earth Knower*, by Maynard Dixon,
c. 1932; pages 6-7: *The Mirage*, by Thomas Moran, 1879;
page 9: buffalo, deer, antelope dance, by Awa Tsireh,
c. 1930; pages 10-11: *The Emergence of the Clowns*, by
Roxanne Swentzell, 1988.

Distributed to the trade by Orion Books, a division of
Crown Publishers, Inc., 201 East 50th Street, New York,
NY 10022. Member of the Crown Publishing Group.
ORION and colophon are trademarks of Crown Pub-
lishers, Inc.
ISBN O-517-58108-6 (Orion Books)

Library of Congress Cataloging-in-Publication Data

Viola, Herman J.
   After Columbus: the Smithsonian chronicle of the
North American Indians/Herman J. Viola.
      p. cm.
   Includes index.
   ISBN 0-89599-028-8 (alk. paper)
   1. Indians of North America—History.   I. Title.
E77.V56 1990
970.004'97—dc20   90-9990
                                                        CIP

Manufactured in the United States of America
First Edition
10 9 8 7 6 5 4 3 2 1

Contents

Introduction—*George Horse Capture*   12

Encounter   14

  Real Americans   16

  Landfalls   40

  Cultures in Collision   66

  End of the Beginning   90

Inheritance Lost   102

  A New Nation   104

  Indian Destiny Sealed   126

  Loss of the West   156

  Era of Internal Exile   186

Fighting for Rights   226

  Red Power   228

  Horizons   250

  Index   280

  Acknowledgments   284

  Picture Credits   286

Introduction

When the Welsh, Irish, English, Spanish, and other European immigrants fled their countries to settle in America, they were escaping governments that allowed religious persecutions, excessive taxation without representation, and other vestiges of the feudal system. To sever ties with their unsatisfactory past, upon arrival in the new land they jumped into what came to be known as America's melting-pot mud and reappeared as Americans, and, therefore, have only brief traditions, if any at all, and do not understand those who do have them.

Beginning in the Caribbean, then working northward and west, the clash of values between the European invaders and the Indian people grew. Expanding from their homelands in Europe, the whites were feverish for a new land, which meant wealth, for from wealth came stability and power. Only one thing stood in the way between them and their "right": the Indian occupants.

Much of our culture and religion, which are the basic components that make us a distinct people, were savaged and destroyed by both the good and bad groups of the white people. This destruction was nearly fatal to our race because we are more of a homogenous people than any other and therefore suffer as a group together.

Soon the original inhabitants of the land were assaulted by the newcomers, using all means at their disposal, and the Indian people had to flee or die. Once the land was cleared the invaders could come and take over forever. Today only two percent of the original land area in the United States remains in Indian hands, but the raids from the outsiders have not ceased. The ranchers continue to seek Indian-owned grazing lands to feed their cattle, miners and oil companies desire what is beneath their earth, the sportsman desires the game and fish, the farmer their water: the siege is unending.

By 1900 a lot had happened to the native people of the New World since its "discovery" by Columbus over 400 years earlier. The combined foreign forces had cut the estimated American Indian population from perhaps five million when Columbus arrived to only 250,000 by the beginning of the 20th century. Diseases, "Manifest Destiny," government policy, greed, missionaries, and many other destruc-

tive elements focused upon the Indian people, and all took their deadly toll.

Since the early 1900s, the Indian population has been increasing. This could happen because the Indians were no longer a threat. Once our numbers were sufficient, leaders emerged as we became discontent with our status. The occupation of Alcatraz Island in 1969 and other aggressive actions increased our rate of self-awareness and self-determination, and today we number approximately two million. Although the days of overt genocide have passed, the Indian people still face immense problems and challenges—again the problem is ignorance. In spite of being the first occupants on this land and surviving our holocaust over the last 500 years, only a tiny percent of the non-Indian population knows that American Indians still exist and are surprised to learn we do not wear feathers and scalp people. The schools are severely deficient in teaching about the American Indians. By being relatively unknown, our many needs are seldom addressed by others outside of our communities.

History clearly demonstrates that the loudest squeaky wheel always gets the most attention, but since we constitute only half-a-percent of the population, our voices are seldom heard. The power brokers, insuring their own continuity, focus their attention solely on the non-Indian voting majorities, and the Indian people are ignored.

As more Indian people leave the reservations and interact with the non-Indians, conditions have somewhat improved as others know we exist and realize that all is not well, but there are just not sufficient numbers of these native "diplomats" to have any effect on the problem. When an identifiable Indian person is among the general public he or she is subjected to overt stares, rude comments ("Look Edna, there's an Indian!"), war whoops, and, sometimes, awe. All of these actions are at the very least embarrassing: they reinforce the walls between races and keep us close to home.

Because the Indian voices are limited by numbers and geography, the only way to reach mass audiences with the story of our tragic history and present depressed situation is through non-Indians. Although white people tend to feel ill at ease with real live Indians and may suspect their messages, they warmly welcome the same messages from one of their own.

For various reasons, many white authors write about Indian people. They may be historians, sociologists, hobbyists, religious people, and, our favorite—anthropologists. One of the most successful types to reach a massive audience with the educational discourses is the popular author. This sort of author may or may not come from a scholarly background, but he writes in a manner that is knowledgeable, easily readable, and readily understood. The content of his work is not esoteric and structured for a few, but addresses the wide sweep of the subject to allow the reader a full understanding.

In recent years the Indian people have been most fortunate to have a number of such authors spread the word about them. It is believed that the more the outsiders know about them, the better are their chances of surviving as Indian people. One of the most well-known authors in this category may be Mr. Dee Brown, author of *Bury My Heart at Wounded Knee*. Another prominent author is Mr. Alvin Josephy, Jr., whose most recent work, *Now That the Buffalo's Gone*, is very informative about the history of the Indian. Their enlightening works about American Indians have reached many thousands of people in a positive way. I consider myself fortunate to personally know each of these authors and they are good men. This volume is such a book, and falls into the same category. It is written for the general audience, deals with the Indian situation, and I know the author quite well.

When Dr. Herman Viola and I met many years ago, he was the director of the National Anthropological Archives of the Smithsonian Institution and had established a tribal-historian program. This needed program provided funds for Indian people with a strong interest in history to go to Washington, D.C., for a period of time to research their tribe's history and culture. In those days, this was the only Indian access to this prestigious institution and its tremendous resources. Many Indians from across the country enrolled in the program and traveled east to the nation's capital. I was one of these tribal people. We all found a treasure trove of relevant materials and more and we copied everything and took the information home. Once home, the data was used in school lessons and college courses, and it even helped to create a few tribal archives. We are grateful for that rare opportunity.

Since then, Herman and I have kept in touch with each other and visited often. As time passed I learned he was a family man, scholar, and a nice person. It soon became apparent that he was also a jogger and devout Christian, but I liked him anyway.

Over the years, his studies have usually involved historical Indian subjects, but he has a large number of living Indian friends as well. They are from many different tribes that are spread across the country. He is one of the few Smithsonian scholars so inclined. After many years I considered him a special friend and invited him to attend the last of my four Sun Dances in Wyoming. As with most endeavors he wholeheartedly threw himself into the effort and could be seen jogging across the prairie in the morning and slogging waist-deep in the slough cutting reeds for the ceremony in the afternoon.

This grand adventurer is a good man and has written a good book. It is subdivided chronologically and geographically and seasoned with his personal observations and anecdotes. His prominent status among many Indian people allows him a unique access to the Indian world. From this exposure, his extensive academic background, and his experience as an educator, he can process the information into a distinctive grasp of Indian history that the reader can enjoy.

Traveling along with him in this book I found myself enjoying the experience. The easy writing style enhanced the literary journey and the contents made it worthwhile. As one who has studied Indian history for most of my adult life, I found myself learning more than anticipated as we moved into areas other than the Plains region. If I can be educated by this work about my own people I am confident others can as well.

So come along on an adventure into Indian country, past and present. You will enjoy the outing and will learn much about the Indian people. Such education is the key to our survival.

George P. Horse Capture
Cody, Wyoming, 1990

Encounter

Real Americans

For Indians of North and South America, the Columbus Quincentenary will not be a time of celebration. Some individuals plan to wear black arm bands in 1992. Most echo the sentiment of George P. Horse Capture, a member of the Gros Ventre tribe and author of the preceding introduction. "For America's Indians," he observes, "1992 means we will have survived as a people for the 20,000 years before Columbus and the 500 years since." Roots run very deep, and no matter how acculturated an Indian may appear, he or she has unbroken ties to a past, to a land, to a religion that neither white man's education nor other forms of external pressure can transcend or destroy.

Pragmatic and utilitarian, Columbus and other newcomers possessed two goals that changed Indian life forever: first, to establish tight control; and second, to recreate the subjugated Indians in their own image. The conquistadors conquered the Indians. The colonists colonized them. Epidemics of introduced European diseases decimated them. Missionaries, reformers, and a host of others Christianized them. During two centuries, the federal government of the United States tried to Americanize them. Whether Spanish or English, French or American, those of foreign heritage systematically worked to eradicate "Indianness" from the Indians, if not to eliminate the Indians altogether.

It almost worked, but not quite, and the victory

Overleaf: Kutenai hunter canoes in Columbia River country. Arapaho Sun Dancers honored the painted buffalo skull, below left. Ojibwa veteran of three wars, Leroy Fairbanks dances at a Minnesota pow wow.

represented by Indian survival gives this book a theme and a reason for being. Further victories from the Indian peoples are expected, especially now that the United States Government and the Smithsonian Institution have formally pledged their support for continuing cultural resurgence among the far-flung tribes.

Despite the best efforts of countless white interlopers, Indians have managed to survive their long ordeal. Today they retain much of their traditional culture and many of their beliefs—the legacy that defines them. It involves a feeling and attitude that few non-Indians can comprehend or appreciate, and it often includes an uncommonly profound spirituality.

Most outsiders prefer to think of native peoples as suspended in time, living artifacts of the 19th century. We hope that the following narrative will help shatter this and other long-held misconceptions. Certainly, no Indians live as they once did. They do represent something of a mirror image of the Europeans whose culture came to dominate the New World. Outward appearances are much the same, at least for everyday, with eagle feathers and beaded buckskins worn only on special occasions. Yet deep differences express themselves, and often in surprising ways that touch the heart. For instance, many if not most working cowboys today are Indians, particularly in the movies, because, as one producer noted, "The white boys don't know how to ride crazy anymore."

On and off the reservations, Indians live much as Americans do everywhere; they are represented in all professions and trades. Women are a force in government and education as well as in maintaining the cultural and spiritual life of the community and the home. Indian men and women have distinguished themselves in the arts and sciences, in the classroom and the courtroom. The men have long excelled on the athletic field and the battlefield.

Warrior traditions survive and Indians maintain them by serving with pride and distinction in the armed forces of the United States. The men actively seek out combat assignments during wartime. Commanders want Indians in their units because they improve morale and increase fighting effectiveness.

Arctic
The last Siberian wanderers to reach America, ancestors of the Aleuts and Inuits probably arrived starting 5,000 years ago, and ranged from Alaska to Greenland.

Subarctic
Nomadic hunters of the taiga or northern forests, Carriers, Crees, Dogribs, and Kutchins pursued such big game as caribou and moose, and small fur-bearing animals.

Northwest Coast
Premier woodworkers, the sea-faring Haidas, Kwakiutls, and Tlingits crafted totem poles, boats, and elaborate dwellings from the region's giant evergreens.

Plateau
Fishermen, foragers, and hunters, the Nez Percé, Spokane, and Yakima Plateau tribes lived in underground, pit-house villages in Columbia River country.

Plains
The horse and the gun transformed the Arapaho, Cheyenne, Sioux, and other Plains tribes from farmers into nomadic buffalo hunters.

Northeast
Three great confederacies—Powhatan, Iroquois, and Miami—occupied settlements on the coast and in forested uplands, where they farmed, hunted, and fished.

Southeast
Skilled farmers, the Creeks, Chickasaws, Choctaws, Cherokees, Yamasees, and Seminoles built their villages in river valleys.

Southwest
Pueblo-dwelling Hopi and Zuni lived on rugged mesas and, along with such desert-dwelling agricultural tribes as the Pima, fought Apache and Navajo hunter-raiders.

Great Basin
Making the most of scarce, seasonal resources, bands of Paiutes, Utes, Shoshones, and Bannocks roamed a land of arid basin and snowy range.

California
In a bountiful area smaller than today's state, a dense but diverse population of hunter-gatherers lived in tribal bands and spoke hundreds of different languages.

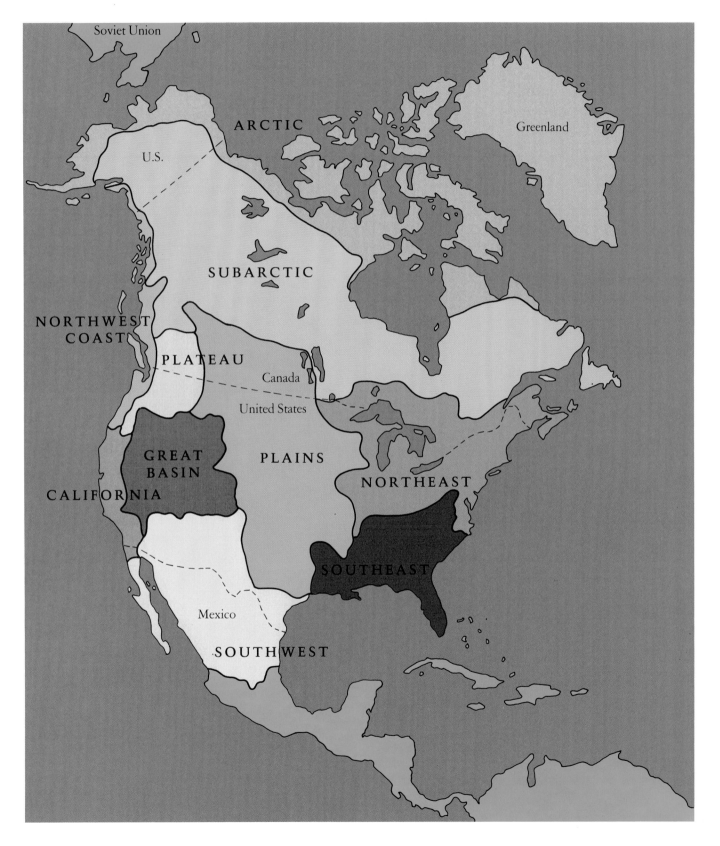

Crow tribesmen, below, meet in 1989 to recount their war experiences; from left to right, Andrew Bird-In-Ground, Carson Walks-Over-Ice, Joseph Medicine Crow, and William Stewart. Andrew Bird-In-Ground joined the 1944 Allied landing in Normandy, earning the Bronze Star with three clusters. Carson Walks-Over-Ice was a paratrooper in Vietnam. Joseph Medicine Crow, tribal historian, fought in Germany, Austria, and Italy. William Stewart saw action at Christmas Ridge in Korea. Wearing a war shirt and carrying a fur-covered coup stick, Carson Walks-Over-Ice, opposite, re-enacts his exploits. Women in war bonnets portray Viet Cong soldiers, right.

As a Ute friend once joked, "We Indians are grateful that the United States became such a militaristic country because it has provided us with an acceptable way to continue our warrior ways."

Visit almost any reservation and one is struck by the number of American flags and VFW (Veterans of Foreign Wars) posts. All Indian people take special pride in their veterans. The women actively promote and participate in commemorative events, including traditional dances as well as parades and honor guards. Not only are Indians intensely patriotic, but they are prouder still to wear the uniform and to openly celebrate those who wear it, because military service reinforces age-old traditions that unify the entire community. No better evidence of this is needed than a check of the records of Indian men in the Vietnam War.

Although thousands of American boys went to Canada to escape the draft, few if any of them were Indians. In fact, there was an opposite movement on the part of Canadian Indians. Many crossed the border into the United States so they could enlist in a fighting unit, preferably infantry or airborne. As

men in uniform, Indians in Vietnam often behaved as did warriors of times past, even to keeping track of their "war deeds" or "coups," which are personal battle triumphs or honors.

Carson Walks-Over-Ice, a member of the Crow tribe and a combat veteran of the 101st Airborne in Vietnam, counted many coups. He also took what he calls "symbolic" scalps from the Viet Cong soldiers he killed by cutting finger-thick strands of hair which he tied at one end. Among the Crows, warriors traditionally could earn four types of coups: leading a successful war party (which meant its objective was accomplished and no member of the war party lost his life), touching an enemy in battle, taking an enemy's weapon, and capturing his horse.

Although he tried, Carson Walks-Over-Ice failed to get a Viet Cong horse, but, as he noted, "I did get two elephants. That should count for something." On one occasion he even reached out and touched a North Vietnamese soldier who was rushing past him trying to escape. Carson explained matter-of-factly, "I didn't hurt him. I just wanted to count coup, but I can tell you he was one surprised fellow."

Carson Walks-Over-Ice is probably typical of Indian veterans of Vietnam. A librarian in Hardin, Montana, he earned the Bronze Star and still carries a Viet Cong machine-gun bullet in one leg. For the Crow Fair in August 1989, the tribe selected Carson to relate the exploit that earned him the Bronze Star by participating in an honor dance traditionally reserved for warriors who had distinguished themselves on the battlefield. He wore a beaded buckskin shirt decorated with ermine tails made for him by his mother according to a design revealed in a dream while in Vietnam.

Carrying a fur-wrapped "coup stick," he demonstrated in pantomime how he had saved his platoon from annihilation after it had stumbled upon a large, well-concealed Viet Cong encampment. Women of the tribe in feathered war bonnets danced the part of the enemy. In an exploit reminiscent of Sergeant Alvin York in World War I, Carson Walks-Over-Ice shot and killed more than two dozen Viet Cong soldiers and captured two machine guns, yet escaped without a scratch, even though bullets had ripped his clothing, buzzed his

Andrew Bird-In-Ground, pictured in uniform at Landing, Florida, during training in 1941, gained a reputation as a fearless soldier in Europe. Modest about his exploits, he explained why he had fought so hard. "Because my address at the time I enlisted was in Oregon, I was afraid that if I were killed in combat they would not bury me on the [Montana tribal] reservation. I was not trying to be a hero." So extraordinary were his exploits that his Crow people believe special powers protected him.

Chief Medicine Crow of Montana posed in Washington, D.C., during the 1880 visit of a Crow tribal delegation to meet the President and serve as Indian diplomats in buckskin. Medicine Crow's Plains-style war shirt bears mementos of battle against Teton Sioux and Blackfeet in a long war for territory. A talented artist as well as a warrior, during his trip East he drew pictures of zoo animals as well as of the Capitol and warships on the Potomac.

ears, torn his watch from his wrist, and plucked his St. Christopher's medal from the chain around his neck. A staff sergeant in the paratroops and the survivor of a dozen firefights, Carson never feared for his life because, as he says, "I had a special feeling that I would make it." Besides, two relatives had dreams predicting his return.

One of these prophetic visions had been chillingly specific. While undergoing the Sun Dance, an uncle had seen a soldier leaning on a cane and standing in the entrance to the lodge. It was Carson. Several weeks later the family learned that Carson had been severely wounded in the leg while participating in a combat patrol.

Carson knew he would survive the war and he did. A friend and brother-in-arms knew he would be killed, and he was—on the same day that Carson was wounded. This soldier was Richard Spider, a Crow Creek Sioux whom he met in Vietnam. Carson said, "We did everything together. We were in the same company, and fought in the same battles." On his return home, he visited Fort Thompson in South Dakota. Here Richard's family

Members of the Crow tribal community, left, assemble for a 1989 sunrise service at an open-air Sun Dance lodge in Wyola, Montana. About 1900, above, three Piegans blow eagle-bone whistles to assure good weather for their own ceremonial observance. Opposite, Takes Paint, a Blood, undergoes a Sun Dance ordeal in 1892 by pulling against a cord tied to a pole. The line has been fastened to the dancer by a skewer driven through his chest muscles. Though such piercing is rare today, the Sun Dance still represents the ultimate sacrifice to the Sacred Powers and demonstrates the dancer's unquestioning faith in his traditional religion.

"adopted" Carson, a traditional means of replacing a loved one who has died. In turn, Carson named his second son Richard.

Religion has always been intrinsic to the Native American lifeway. The spirit world is very important and it is hard to find anyone in the community who does not believe in a Supreme Being. Rituals and sacred objects are closely held, with few non-Indians allowed access to the secrets of the kiva, the Sweat Lodge, or the Sun Dance.

Many Indians practice both their traditional religion and some form of Christianity. When a close friend was asked whether it was inconsistent to be both a staunch Baptist and a devout traditionalist, he laughed and said, "Not at all! When I am in the Baptist church I pray to God through an intermediary, the minister. When I pray to God the Indian way, I go outside and use my direct line."

A tribesman closely associated with the Native American Church of North America explains it this way: "Our respect for The Maker is really the same as that of our non-Indian brothers. For instance, while we pray to He-Who-Made-Everything on one side of the mountain in the tipi, our non-Indian brother may be praying to God in his church on the other side of the same mountain. We are both praying to the same Supreme Being."

One of the more visible manifestations of Indian religion is the Sun Dance, the highest religious expression of the Plains Indians. Despite strenuous efforts on the part of Christian missionaries and government officials to eradicate the Sun Dance, it has not merely survived, it flourishes. Piercing—the practice of inserting rawhide thongs under the flesh of the chest and back and then tearing them through the skin—is once again becoming common in some groups.

The Sun Dance is often a four-day ceremony in which the participant must abstain from food and water while dancing and blowing a whistle made from a hollow bone of an eagle's wing. Thongs, used by those who pierce themselves, attach the dancer to the central post of an open-air lodge. With only a star blanket (light cotton coverlet with patchwork stars) for protection, those who attempt the Sun Dance often suffer from extremes of weather.

Some participants collapse from pain, hunger, and exhaustion, especially if the skin is broken.

Many men undergo the Sun Dance more than once. Bobby Talks Different, a Vietnam veteran of the Gros Ventre tribe, has participated eight times. "I did this," he said, "to keep my promise to the One Above. Eight of us from the Fort Belknap Reservation went to Nam together, and I promised the One Above that I would do a Sun Dance for each life that returned. All eight of us came back, and I thanked the One Above by undergoing eight Sun Dances. The others never knew of my vow."

George Horse Capture has undergone four Sun Dances, all of them with the Arapaho tribe on the Wind River Reservation in Wyoming. In his forties and beset by diabetes, high blood pressure, and heart trouble, Horse Capture ignored the risks because "four" is a sacred number and by completing that many he could fulfill his original vow.

The author was honored to assist as a reed cutter at George Horse Capture's fourth Sun Dance. Fresh stalks to rest upon are the only luxury dancers are allowed once they have entered the lodge and, with 90 men undergoing the ceremony, it became increasingly difficult each day to obtain a sufficient number. Moreover, the appropriate reeds could only be obtained from waist-deep wetlands infested by snakes, leeches, and mosquitoes.

Joseph Horse Capture, George's son and a college student in his early twenties, also accompanied the reed cutters. When asked if he ever planned to undertake the Sun Dance, Joseph grinned and replied, "No, I don't think so, but if I do, one reason will be to have the satisfaction of knowing that my dad is out here cutting these darn reeds for me."

Although much of the beauty, strength, and vitality of Indian culture has survived, much has been lost or is endangered. Indians increasingly turn to museum curators and archivists for help in preserving and sometimes in reintroducing elements of their culture that have been taken from them. In one instance, an Ojibwa family had been unable to recollect the burial prayers and ceremonies requested by an elderly relative; they were able to obtain this information from the Minnesota Historical Society. Also, several museums have rescued and preserved very sacred objects and provided private settings for Indian visitors to pray in the presence of these treasured relics.

How unfortunate that almost five centuries had to pass before the rich and diverse cultures of the peoples of North and South America could be accepted and appreciated. As we shall see, it is already too late for some tribes. In all corners of the New World, entire peoples have simply ceased to exist, victims of disease, dislocation, and exploitation.

Accurate population figures in 1492 are difficult to ascertain. Although modern scholars agree that cycles of disease, warfare, and cultural collapse played crucial roles in the conquest and colonization of the New World, their estimates of population vary greatly. Generally accepted totals for central Mexico, which had the densest population in 1492, range from 10 to 12 million. Peru, home of the Incas, may have held nine million. For the entire Western Hemisphere, the total perhaps approached 40 million. For territories now part of Canada and the United States, a total of two mil-

In 1924, John Peabody Harrington of the Smithsonian's Bureau of American Ethnology, wearing earphones at left, monitors a recording made by Margarita Campos, a Panama Indian. Frances Densmore, also of the BAE, appears opposite with Mountain Chief, a Blackfoot, who is translating a song by means of sign language.

lion is suggested by Smithsonian physical anthropologist Douglas Ubelaker. He recently completed the first tribe-by-tribe analysis of North American native population since the initial systematic survey completed in 1910 by James T. Mooney of the Bureau of American Ethnology.

New World population figures have become an increasingly popular topic among scholars, but little new information is available to justify high estimates. Europeans made some early census counts but these came after the initial and often greatest loss of life. Nonetheless, the "depopulation" figures most often cited are so vast, much like the numbers of lives lost during the Holocaust of World War II, that a meaningful perspective is difficult to achieve. The most optimistic scholars, however, admit that the arrival of the Europeans had a serious effect on New World populations; just how detrimental is open to question.

An important part of the debate over population levels involves the island of Hispaniola, where Columbus established the first permanent colony in the New World. In neither Haiti nor the Dominican Republic, which share this island today, are there any descendants of the original inhabitants. No one knows what their numbers were in 1492, although current estimates range from 60,000 to as many as eight million, but by 1600 they were extinct.

Bartolomé de Las Casas, the Dominican friar and

polemicist whose father and uncle had come with Columbus to Hispaniola in 1493, believed that three million natives had perished after little more than a decade of Spanish occupation, the result of disease, warfare, forced labor, and enslavement. He wrote, "Who of those born in future centuries will believe this? I myself who am writing this and saw it and know the most about it can hardly believe that such was possible."

Explorers recorded a few specific impressions of the tribes they encountered. Columbus described the Taino Indians he met in the Bahamas as "a loving people, without covetousness," and called their speech "the sweetest and gentlest in the world." Henry Hawkes, an English visitor to New Spain in 1572, spoke of the natives as a people "of much simplicity, and great cowards, voide of all valor, and are great witches." On the other hand, William Bradford, who would become governor of the Plymouth Colony, told of "savage people" to be found in Massachusetts, describing them as "cruell, barbarous, and most treacherous, being most furious in their rage, and merciles wher they overcome." Yet Francis Pastorius, writing in 1700 of the Indians in Pennsylvania, said they "strive after a sincere honesty, hold strictly to their promises, cheat and injure no one."

Even today, native peoples of North America are as dissimilar culturally, linguistically, and physically as the peoples of Europe. So diverse, in fact, are the Indians of the hemisphere that they are probably descended from several different Asiatic groups that migrated in fits and starts into the New World from 20,000 to 5,000 years ago.

Despite the diversity, research suggests some broad foundation traits present at the time of the Columbian encounter, especially in the North. The list includes animism, totemism, and mysticism reminiscent of Siberian shaman practices; a unity of community and religious life; broad-based tribal authority shared among chiefs and elders; an emphasis on handicrafts; a strong interest in trade; and economies based on hunting-and-gathering and horticulture. Certain generalizations based on regional subsistence patterns and cultural factors are also possible. In lands now American and Canadian, more Indians lived along coastal waters than

A Mexican tribe of remote areas in Sinaloa and Durango states, the Huichols practice a complex religion that cherishes hallucinogenic visions induced by eating cactus buttons known as peyote. Images for face painting, at left, and the colorful yarn panel, top, reflect psychedelic sun patterns seen during ritual trances. The sun itself assists in the woolen artwork, softening adhesive wax on a wooden panel. The artist presses the yarn into the wax.

in the interior of the continent; more lived on the Pacific Coast than on the Atlantic Coast; more lived in the South than in the North.

An important determinant of population density was farming. Where Indians practiced farming—less than half the total land area—the population was generally much larger than in non-farming regions. The only exception in North America was the Pacific Northwest with its rich marine resources.

Contrary to popular misconceptions, plants were a major source of Indian sustenance. According to anthropologist Harold Driver, in terms of total population and total diet, "horticultural products furnished about 75 percent of all the food consumed by North American aborigines." A recent Smithsonian study by anthropologist Bruce Smith claims the discovery of a center of plant domestication by Indians in the vicinity of the ancient Tennessee River Valley.

Although the Indians shared many characteristics, both racial and cultural, language was not one of them. So many distinct languages and dialects were spoken in North and South America—more

than 2,000—that one anthropologist calls the situation an "American Babel." This linguistic diversity contributed to the development of the famed Indian sign languages. The exception to the rule of diversity are the Inuit people (as Eskimos prefer to call themselves), whose language, with only two dialects, can be understood over a span of 3,500 miles from Siberia to eastern Greenland. Even in the old dogsled days, a good joke could cover the distance in a matter of months. This language has maintained its integrity for as long as 5,000 years, perhaps entering North America with the first Inuit at about the time Abraham led the ancestors of the Jews out of Mesopotamia.

Frequently a tribal name designates the tribal language: the Blackfeet speak Blackfeet, the Cherokees speak Cherokee. Generally the tribal languages are part of a larger relationship. Scholars have sorted these languages into families, groups of languages with a common ancestor. The Crow, who speak a Siouan language, are linguistically related to the Hidatsas. They probably spoke a common language no more than 1,000 years ago. Other

Siouan speakers are the Winnebagos, Mandans, Iowas, Otos, Omahas, Osages, Poncas, Quapaws, Kansas, and, of course, the Dakotas or Sioux. The total number of languages spoken in North America was about 550, with at least 200 used today by tribes of Canada and the United States.

The term "tribe" is somewhat misleading because relatively few New World peoples had the true political organization usually associated with the word. It is most often used to describe native groups that spoke the same language, shared a culture, occupied a common territory, and lived communally.

Whatever their labels, the groups native to North America present a kaleidoscope of lifestyles, which are presented in more detail after this initial chapter. From the Arctic to the Gulf of Mexico, from the Atlantic to the Pacific, the differences were—and remain—many and extreme. Some peoples used dogs as beasts of burden and means of transport, others carried their goods by bark or dugout canoe. Some relished cooked puppy while others resorted to it only in times of famine. Some delighted in

Tireless runners, Mexico's Tara-humara can carry heavy burdens up and down the rock-strewn slopes of gorges as deep as the Grand Canyon. To live, they grow corn along the continental divide of the Sierra Madre, Mexico's "Mother Range." The group at left performs during Easter Holy Week, while a dancer, above, coats his body with an earth pigment. Though Christian, these people observe ancient nature rites.

war and torture while others considered violence as insanity.

The reasons for diversity were in part environmental, in part cultural, arising from collective endeavor and shaped by conscious choice. "Environment limits, but it does not determine," note anthropologists Robert Spencer and Jesse Jennings. Differing combinations of land, climate, and resources, for example, fail to explain why certain tribes on the Great Plains became nomadic hunters while others developed agriculture, or why Inuit people primarily eat meat and fat and avoid the abundant edible seaweeds of their region.

At least a dozen primary culture areas can be identified in North America, beginning with the Arctic, home of the Inuit people. These hardy folks, last of the native groups to arrive on the North American continent, were few in number, yet they occupied an enormous and inhospitable landmass, some of it permanently ice-covered. So isolated were those who lived farthest north, the Polar Eskimos, that they met their first Europeans in 1818. Only

then did they discover that other people occupied the earth.

Genetically, the Inuit people have been called a single family, sharing the same gene pool and, until recently, having little chance to marry outsiders. Socially, they lived in small family groups, placing a great premium on self-reliance and hunting skills. The Inuit people conceived of a spiritual relationship between the hunter and the hunted. Therefore, care was taken not to offend an animal's soul, and all aspects of hunting were ritualized. Even the simplest of Inuit tools and gear received intense artistic attention as a mark of respect to the spirits around them.

A remarkably cooperative, cheerful people, they shared freely with others. A Greenlandic hunter of the High Arctic put the matter of wife-lending into some perspective with the simple statement, "The hunter who must travel in winter cannot survive without a woman's help." Companionship was probably less vital to survival than sewing skills for the repair of warm but delicate fur clothes and boots, the nursing of a sick or injured visitor, and the care of his dogs.

Although the people of the Arctic have attracted a great deal of scholarly attention, virtually the opposite is true of their Athapascan neighbors just to the south. The reason is the reader's fascination with the ability of the Inuit people not only to survive but to thrive in their universe of ice, the "Friendly Arctic," as explorer Vilhjalmur Stefansson called it.

The Athapascans are more typical of those native peoples usually termed Indians. It is useful to recognize that all American Indians started out as Subarctic hunting people who either crossed over from Asia to Alaska on dry land that once occupied the site of today's Bering Strait, came by boat, or crossed on ice, the Arctic or near-Arctic being point of entry to North America for Indian as well as

Inuit. As people moved farther and farther south they adjusted to new ecological conditions, and hundreds of new cultures developed.

Hunting-and-raiding tribes of the Plains have provided an archetype of the North American Indian for people the world over. Completely compelling is the image of these fiercely independent wanderers: tipi camps, flashing eagle-feather war bonnets, painted ponies—all part of a tradition of militancy that enabled peoples of the prairies to hold the white man at bay until well into the 19th century. Splendid warriors and their superb leaders—Quanah Parker of the Comanches, Dull Knife of the Cheyennes, Crazy Horse and Sitting Bull of the Sioux—still live in the imagination. The stern reality of that lifeway flourished for less than a century, however, though elements of the magnificent horse culture that spawned it have endured for 200 years and still exert a force.

Eastern tribes were first to lose their grip on the lands of their ancestors due to pressures from the whites. Perhaps the most important Algonquian confederacy at the time of European contact was

An Inuit mother carries her child beneath a fur parka (1915). The beaded talisman has been magically endowed. Left, human skulls rest atop a timber platform in the treeless Arctic, where logs from Siberian forests wash across the top of the world.

Samuel Curo of Mesa Grande, California, holds a golden eagle that will be ceremonially smothered as part of a Hopi religious ritual so that its spirit can rise to its ancestors to appeal for rain.

the Delaware, once occupying a vast seaboard area that included parts of present-day Delaware, New Jersey, New York, and Pennsylvania. These proud people are remembered primarily for the state that bears their name and for the name they called themselves, the Lenni Lenape, the "real men." Forced to leave their homelands, moving at least eight times between 1742 and 1867, bands claiming Delaware descent can be found today in Oklahoma, Kansas, Wisconsin, and even Canada, but not in Delaware. Little wonder, then, that the Walum Olum, a long, traditional history of the Delawares painted on bark and found in an Indiana village in the 1820s, begins: "Halas, halas! we know now who they are; these Wapsinis [white men] who then came out of the Sea to rob us of our land; starving wretches! with smiles they came, but soon became Snakes . . . ."

Terror and tragedy also haunt lands near the Pacific, where a charge of genocide has been leveled at the American pioneers who moved into the densely populated Californian culture area. Although most of the tribes occupied only about two-thirds of the present state, they used about one-third of all aboriginal languages spoken north of Mexico. Indians of California included the tallest (Mojave) and shortest (Yuki) peoples. Tribes were typically small, often no more than large bands. They usually foraged for food—acorns were a mainstay of

During a pilgrimage to the Grand Canyon, Hopi priests pause at a sacred site to offer prayers of thanks for a nearby salt deposit. The location of this and other pilgrim sites, known only to the most faithful, are periodically disclosed to younger devotees.

their diet—and they wove splendid baskets.

The southernmost culture area, Mesoamerica, encompassed present-day Guatemala, Belize, El Salvador, parts of Honduras and Nicaragua, and Mexico south of the 21st parallel. Sovereign here in their respective heydays were the Aztecs and Mayas, empire builders sometimes called the Greeks and Romans of the New World. Recent and very important archeological discoveries indicate that traits prefiguring Maya and Aztec civilizations began first in Peru about the time the Old Kingdom pharaohs of Egypt were building the great pyramids after 2800 B.C. Mesoamericans, however, probably originated their civilizations independently.

At its zenith, Mesoamerica contained a population of 25 million, greater than that of all the other culture areas combined. Intensive farming made

this possible, a capability supported by large irrigation systems and a totalitarian government that efficiently regimented all available labor.

Spanish conquistadors may have sent the Aztec civilization crashing down, but they did appreciate and readily adopt one feature of Aztec administrative practice, a system for collecting revenues from conquered peoples. Historians have capitalized on good colonial paperwork—tribute lists prepared by Spanish clerks—thereby obtaining some of their most reliable data on the population, settlement patterns, and political organization of the native peoples here.

This world of the North American Indians as encountered by the Europeans, a world now broken and swept away, is known only from ruins, artifacts, explorers' notes, and the correspondence of colonial clergy and bureaucrats. Yet the dominant European and Europeanized society continues to conjure up romantic images that bear little resemblance to the lifeways of the Indians of today or yesterday.

One cliché that can be put to rest is that of the "vanishing red man." Indeed, two million Indians live in the United States today, possibly a greater population than in 1492. In one sense, however, Indians did vanish: once settled on reservations in

Animal symbolism suggests the involvement of Native American peoples with a world of nature spirits: Inuit bag, below, and Indian bear-paw pot, opposite, evoke this magical realm.

the late 19th century, they were out of sight and out of mind. Some tribal cultures weakened during these times of pressure, if not of persecution, when the federal government outlawed even the practice of Indian religion. Most tribes have survived the difficulties and have rekindled their traditional life in recent years. Tribal languages have become the medium of cultural resurgence. Prominent and vigorous in Indian country today, bilingual programs are often motivated by a concern that children will gain English and rely on it before they learn their own tribal tongue.

The importance of language in preserving culture becomes obvious when one realizes that the religion, traditions, and history of the Indians were not written but recorded in the memories of tribal members. In many instances, the stories were passed down through a succession of specially trained individuals who were selected in youth and given the responsibility of retaining their people's oral history. When such links with the past were disrupted, a tribe faced the threat of losing its history.

Joseph Medicine Crow, one of the best-known storytellers of the Crow people, was born before 1920. He was the first of his tribe to graduate from college and to obtain a master's degree; he would have been the first to obtain a Ph.D. (in anthropology from the University of Southern California) had not World War II intervened. Today he is widely respected as a tribal historian, having gathered stories from the elders since his own youth.

Medicine Crow's understanding of the strengths and weaknesses of both oral and recorded history makes his work especially valuable, particularly in the compilation of an accurate history of the Crow people. "Unfortunately," he says, "the traditional historians and storytellers are all gone now and I must work with their children and grandchildren who have been exposed to their views and recitals of the old stories."

One of Joseph Medicine Crow's grandfathers was White Man Runs Him, the favorite scout of Colonel George Armstrong Custer during the army's Sioux campaign of 1876; another grandfather, for whom he was named, was Medicine Crow, one of the tribe's last war chiefs. Both of these old warriors lived well into the 20th century, and instilled in

their grandson an appreciation for the history and culture of their people. Joseph Medicine Crow in turn took it upon himself to record and save not only their stories but also the recollections of other elderly tribal members. He has deposited these memoirs in the archives at Little Big Horn College, located at the Crow Agency on the reservation near Hardin, Montana, and sponsored and staffed by the Crow tribe.

Elsewhere, tribal historical and ethnological materials have been saved by numerous concerned and interested individuals, both Indian and white. Perhaps the most comprehensive effort to conserve such materials was the program funded by Doris Duke of New York. For this program, seven state universities—those of Arizona, Florida, Illinois, New Mexico, Oklahoma, South Dakota, and Utah— cooperated in a massive project to record on tape Indians' memories of their own past, their version

of Indian-white relations, and their views of American history in general.

A similar collection of ethnographic material consists of songs and music collected by ethnologist Frances Densmore between 1907 and 1940, the single most important body of traditional American Indian music. Affiliated for more than 50 years with the Bureau of American Ethnology (BAE), Densmore seemed almost the classic model of a Victorian woman except for her cigarette smoking, which endeared her all the more to her Indian informants. "My work," she wrote in 1942, "is to preserve the past, record observations in the present, and open the work of others in the future."

A similar philosophy motivated her eccentric BAE colleague, linguist John Peabody Harrington. Rude, fanatic, and compulsive, Harrington was obsessed with the belief that the Indians were disappearing, and devoted his life to recording their

languages and lifeways. A driven man, he eventually surrendered all social life to his genius and his obsession: tons of field notes, manuscripts, and sound recordings resulted. These he secreted in various nooks and crannies around the country, lest colleagues steal his data, and scholars today at the Smithsonian Institution still do not know if they have it all.

It was my privilege to assist when, as director of the National Anthropological Archives at the Smithsonian Institution, I developed an Indian intern program with the assistance of Dr. Dave Warren. Now also a member of the Smithsonian staff, he served then as director of the American Indian Cultural Program at the Institute of American Art, located in Santa Fe, New Mexico. A member of the Santa Clara Pueblo and a speaker of Tewa, he was also the leading force behind the American Indian cultural renaissance that swept the United States in the turbulent '60s and '70s.

It was in 1973 that Dave Warren came to me with an interesting proposal for a program at the Smithsonian Institution that would encourage young American Indian men and women to pursue careers as librarians, archivists, historians, and anthropologists. How far such efforts throughout the continent have come in recent years! Today several hundred individuals study Indian culture, and we look forward to two new National Museums of the American Indian—one as part of the Smithsonian family of museums on the Mall in Washington, D.C., and the other for New York City. Canada's magnificent Museum of Civilization in Hull, Quebec, has set a splendid example for the interpretation of the cultural life of native peoples. Mexico's museums and monuments are legendary, as are those of other Latin-American countries.

As part of the effort to convince Smithsonian officials to expand our modest documentation program, Dave Warren arranged a whirlwind tour of Indian country. He knew that tribal leaders could demonstrate firsthand the sincerity and depth of their desire for access to the cultural materials held by the Smithsonian Institution. Our two-day blitz began with a morning meeting at Ignacio, Colorado, with the Southern Ute tribal council, and ended the following evening at a supper furnished by the tribal council of San Ildefonso Pueblo in New Mexico—with intermediary stops at the Navajo and Zuni reservations, and at Warren's home pueblo.

For me, the most poignant and most meaningful moment during the trip occurred at the meal with

Dramatically bedecked Tewas, at left and opposite, dress up like Apaches to play the part of ritual hunters in their tribe's Deer Dance. Other Tewas put on antlers and emulate the quarry while the hunters harmlessly shoot sunflower stalks over the heads of the "deer." The dance itself seeks an atonement with the spirits of animals taken in the chase. Such sympathetic magic, part of rituals as old as time, is intended to guarantee the well-being of the game animal and to assure an ongoing supply of food from the land.

the San Ildefonso tribal council. As I sat down, our host, Ramos Sanchez, escorted an elderly woman to the seat next to me. "Dr. Viola," he said, "I would like you to meet María, the potter. She is our living treasure. When I was at the Smithsonian, I saw some of her pottery on display, so I thought you would like to meet her. We normally shield her from Anglos, who always want to meet her, but this is a special occasion." It was very special indeed.

Another surprise awaited as the evening drew to a close. An elderly gentleman rose from his chair and, making a statement in the Tewa language, instantly cast a chill over what had thus far been a cordial affair. His remarks, which were not translated, sparked a debate among several of the Indians in the room. After about half an hour of this discourse, the same man stood up and declared in English. "You people from the Smithsonian. We want you to know you will always be welcome at San Ildefonso. When you leave, we will go to the church and pray for your safe return to Washington."

On that pleasant note the evening ended. Warren and I went to a nearby motel and the Indians proceeded to their church and homes. What had caused the trouble? I asked Dave Warren the following day. "This," he replied, "is what was said: 'What do these people from the Smithsonian want of us? They already have everything. There is nothing left to take.'"

The discussion that had ensued after dinner had been an effort by Ramos Sanchez to explain that we from the Smithsonian were not there to collect artifacts. "You don't understand," he had told the elder. "The Smithsonian has been saving many things for the Indian people and now wishes to let them have some of them back." He told the council about the intern program and the opportunity it would provide for Indians to get copies of sound recordings, photographs, and documents for use in their home communities.

Ramos Sanchez saved his most telling argument for last. While in Washington on a trip he had identified for the National Archives an old wax cylinder of flute music cut years ago by Frances Densmore. The flute player on the recording was the very man who had started the debate.

A usable legacy remains, thanks in great part to people such as the old man at San Ildefonso who had recorded with Frances Densmore, to the potter María, and to all the collectors and contributors and many others who cared and provided support at all levels. Today the tribes possess an important remnant of the rich culture and history of the continent's native peoples, a treasured legacy almost miraculously saved from 500 years of the corrosive change that was set in motion by the Columbian voyages of first encounter.

A ceramic storyteller, by Nora Naranjo-Morse of New Mexico's Santa Clara Pueblo, appears at left. Called Pearlene, *she represents the potter's alter ego, just as the tiny children stand for her own twins. Opposite,* Acorn, *the youngest dancer at a Montana pow wow in 1989, reflects the dauntless spirit shown by so many Indian and Inuit people.*

A 1519 map offers a rare glimpse of Spain's initial stronghold in the Caribbean islands, centering on what is now Haiti. The banner refers to the Antilles and the decorative figures may be Africans, brought as slaves to replace lost Indian manpower. Right, a male effigy from Canada was wrought by Beothuks, native New-

Landfalls

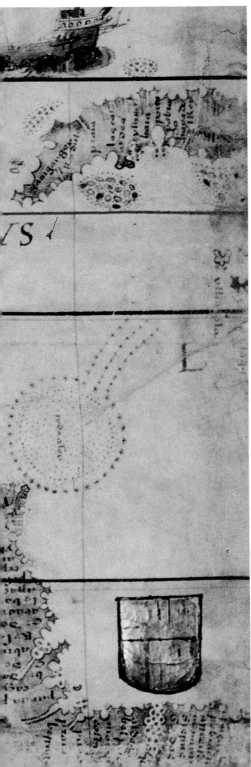

*foundlanders who painted them-
selves with red iron oxide,
prompting Europeans to call them
the "Red Indians."*

A Viking settlement site in Newfoundland after A.D. 1000 provides the only direct evidence of actual contact between foreigners and native North Americans before the arrival of Columbus. With thousands of years of shipping in the Old World, however, it seems likely that other "discoveries" of the New World might have been made, either by accident or by design. No matter whether Viking, African, Asian, Irish, Roman, Phoenician, or any other plausible or implausible pre-Columbian contacts took place, such encounters had little demonstrable impact on the destinies of either the Eastern or Western Hemisphere. Yet the Columbus voyages of discovery transformed both forever.

When Columbus and his men first stepped ashore on October 12, 1492, claiming for the Spanish Crown that little atoll in the Bahamas (today called Watling Island and also known as San Salvador), awe and wonder filled the Taino Indians. As Columbus himself reported, "they believed very firmly that I, with these ships and crews, came from the sky . . . . and in such opinion, they received me at every place where I landed, after they lost their terror." This scene of astonishment occurred whenever native peoples of the New World met Old World visitors for the first time—and it kept happening all over the Americas for more than a century, continuing well into the era of permanent European settlement.

"They are affectionate people and without covetousness and apt for anything, which I certify," Columbus continued. "I believe there is no better people or land in the world. They love their neighbors as themselves and have the sweetest speech in the world and gentle, and are always smiling." Columbus penned this tribute after nearby villagers helped him salvage stores and equipment from the *Santa Maria*, which had foundered on a shoal. He thought they were Hindus, Spice Islanders, or at least Chinese.

Like the *Santa Maria*, the dreams of Christopher Columbus also ran aground, and upon a very hard reality indeed. The New World simply was not the East Indies or Cathay, the source of sudden, vast wealth that the "Admiral of the Ocean Seas" had envisioned for himself. And yet the West Indies were potentially rich beyond reckoning, although

their resources first needed to be organized and knocked into shape before they could be harvested by the native peoples for the benefit primarily of foreigners.

Wealth was to pour out of the Americas, but not for Columbus. Others reaped the first, ephemeral harvest of gold and silver, but a far more enduring legacy emerged. As historian Alfred W. Crosby declares, "The Columbian exchange of peoples, plants, products, and diseases, and ideas, [was] the most important event in human history since the end of the Ice Age and in natural history since the end of the Pleistocene era."

This unstoppable process of interchange fed first on the claims of Columbus, and later upon the wealth of the New World itself. The conquest of the Aztec empire by Hernán Cortés in 1521 provided the initial major impetus to this juggernaut of empire. This was "the real discovery of America," according to geographer D.W. Meinig. A dozen years later Francisco Pizarro invaded Peru and took the treasure of the Inca. These two expeditions and the gold, silver, and jewels sent back to Spain

ensured that the Europeans would never relinquish their hold on the New World. Such riches also stimulated European colonialism as it expanded into Africa, Asia, and the wider Pacific realm. Thus we perceive the crucial difference between any earlier contacts and the Columbus voyages: Spain's support of Columbus's quest paid off handsomely enough to help restructure the economy of Europe and establish an era of overseas empires.

Columbus himself embodied late-medieval Europe's obsession with both religion and worldly gain and the power that goes with them. A driven man, devoted to certain narrowly focused goals, he was obsessed with the desire to find a short route to the fabled Orient—and then with the belief that he had. That the first natives he encountered wore a few simple ornaments of precious metal only served to confirm his fixed idea that his fortune lay just ahead. Soon ships bearing the flags of half a dozen other nations followed in Columbus's wake.

Although Spain's Italian navigator may have gone to his grave still believing he had reached Asia, his competitors knew otherwise. Within a

Spain's discovery of gold in the West Indies brought slavery, torment, and death to island peoples. Above, colonists on Hispaniola maim Indians who produced too little of the precious metal. Opposite, Timucuas of Florida dredge a river bottom for gold nuggets. Beginning in the early 16th century, as Indians perished, early Europeans imported African slaves, top.

decade of Columbus's discovery, the notion of a New World was being discussed, even if not fully understood. In 1507, only 15 years after Columbus's first crossing of the Atlantic, German cartographer Martin Waldseemüller set speculation to rest by boldly publishing a map that featured two new continents. The southern one he called America, a name that other cartographers soon applied to the northern one as well.

The failure to call the New World "Columbia" may be an injustice that will never be corrected, but Columbus bestowed a similarly unfair misnomer on the peoples he found in the New World: "Indians," the name they have been saddled with ever since. It could have been worse, Indians joke: what if Columbus had been seeking the Virgin Islands or Turkey!

Whatever their rightful name, the people of the Caribbean welcomed Columbus, whose conduct towards them set the pattern for centuries to come: unfortunately, Columbus viewed the Indians as a commodity to be harvested. He left behind 39 men, most of them from the *Santa Maria*, to begin the acquisition of riches pending his return the following year. No more overseers seemed to be needed, even though the population of the island rivaled that of Portugal, because, according to him, the natives "[were] naked and without arms and [were] incurable cowards." Accordingly, he informed their royal highnesses that he could provide them with as many slaves as they wanted, promising to send only idolaters.

Columbus classified the aboriginals as either "good" Indians or "bad" Indians, labels the white man used to usurp human rights well into the 19th century. The good Indians were the peaceful, sweet, and loving Arawaks who had proved so helpful to him in his time of need. Bad ones were the "Caribs," a supposedly warlike tribe of cannibals who preyed upon their helpless neighbors. Scholars now believe that the Arawaks and Caribs were one and the same, though it soon made no difference. Arawak or Carib, whoever was caught was enslaved, a fate many avoided only by dying first. It was just a matter of time, a short time, until they were all dead, the first of many peoples to become prematurely extinct during the Columbian era.

The New World provided a botanical treasure trove of foods unknown in the Old World, including tomatoes, potatoes, chocolate, squash, many kinds of beans, and pineapples. Hot peppers, such as those appropriately called ring-of-fire, left, originated in central Mexico. First cultivated in Mexico was Zea mays, or Indian corn, as displayed by Navajo Ella Deal, right. A taste for tobacco spread from the New World, where Brazilians are shown smoking the plant, below, in 1557.

The great changes in the world of the American Indians began when Columbus returned from Europe in 1493. He now commanded 1,500 men on 17 ships, whose decks were laden with supplies and livestock: cows, calves, pigs, sheep, goats, and, especially, horses—the animals that were to revolutionize life for many tribes. This animate cargo from Columbus's ark was unloaded onto the island of Hispaniola (today occupied by Haiti and the Dominican Republic), or La Isla Española, as it was originally named, which soon became the nucleus of Spain's New World empire. From this vantage point, the initial exploring expeditions, or *entradas*, were launched into North and South America, mounted on and fed from the large herds of horses and cattle that thrived on the lush grass of this island staging ground. The horses were issued to the thousands of adventurers, soldiers, and clergy-

men who arrived to make their fortunes or to carry God's word to the idolaters.

With the establishment of Mexico City and the settlement of Puerto Rico and Cuba, Hispaniola lost its early importance as the center of Spanish exploration and exploitation of the New World. Yet it was on Hispaniola that the future was revealed in the form of the hemisphere's earliest "boom towns," the first of a myriad that were to spring up on the widening American frontier. Such highly unstable communities attracted restless and foot-loose seekers of fortune, individuals who were eager to escape boredom—if not the authorities back home.

In just over a century, Spain carved out a New World empire that extended from the Rio Grande in the north to the Río de la Plata in the south and from La Florida in the east to California in the

Indian slaves in the Yucatán, opposite, haul supplies for the army of Spanish conqueror Hernán Cortés, pictured at left beneath the number 18. Tales of great cities and gold artifacts, such as the Mixtec effigy bell, below, spurred Cortés to meet Aztec Emperor Montezuma II at Tenochtitlán, site of modern Mexico City, during the autumn of 1519.

west—a domain 8,000 miles in length and 5,000 in breadth. The heartland of the empire lay in the green and golden tropics—source of that first flush of wealth in precious metals and emeralds. Lands now part of the United States were situated far to the north, where Spain's impression was slighter, though still distinct.

Within a decade of the establishment of Hispaniola, the Spaniards had discovered the peninsula of Florida. No serious colonizing occurred here for another half-century, and then only in response to threats against that frontier by the French and the English. Within 40 years, however, the Indian population of Hispaniola had virtually imploded; nearly 90 percent had died, primarily from European diseases. African slaves, arriving in 1510, brought additional diseases, and few of the original people of this part of the Caribbean survived the New World pandemic of 1519.

Though the pace of change was far slower in Florida, the result was similar, with the region's original tribes all but extinct by 1729. Sandy Florida had little gold or silver, so the Spanish came primarily for strategic reasons, and a military outpost helped to protect their New World empire from French and English freebooters. Operating from St. Augustine, which was established in 1565,

Jesuit and Franciscan missionaries gained both temporal and ecclesiastical control of the original people. Whatever their motives, these clerics undermined the basic cultural structure and the Indian society collapsed. A mestizo class (part Indian and part Spanish) emerged as the Indian population gradually dwindled and finally disappeared.

Neglect helped to save the Indians of the Southwest. The entradas of Francisco Coronado and Hernando de Soto had not encouraged an investment of manpower and money for expansion into that sprawling and inhospitable region. Only the knowledge that thousands of heathen souls remained unconverted gave Spanish authorities reason to consider colonization, a decision that was deferred until the administration of Juan de Oñate, appointed in September 1595 as Governor and Captain General of New Mexico. Three years later he led a force of 400—numbering 129 men, their wives, children, and servants—into the Rio Grande country. Since conversion of the Pueblo Indians was one of his highest priorities, eight Franciscan friars accompanied the expedition.

Expansion into the Rio Grande Valley now seemed feasible and logical. Here, 50,000 people inhabited 60 communities scattered along 200 miles

Nicknamed "White Dove of the Desert," Mission San Xavier del Bac, opposite, near Tucson, Arizona, was constructed by Franciscans around 1797 to "attract by its loveliness the unconverted [Indians] beyond the frontier." It may be the United States' finest example of Spanish baroque architecture. Below, Tohono O'odam Indian girl lights candles at the mission during All Souls' Day in 1988. The sculpture of Our Lady of Mount Carmel, left, by Rafael Aragon (c. 1838), blends Spanish and Indian elements.

of the Rio Grande from Senecú in the south to Taos in the north. Each community, or pueblo, consisted of a compact group of multitiered structures surrounded by irrigated gardens; each was self-contained and independent, aside from certain broad tribal loyalties. Although totally lacking any overriding political structure, the Indian towns gained some unity from the fact that they were isolated islands in a wider sea of roving Apache and Navajo raiders, who not only plundered the pueblos but traded with the very people they robbed. The settled groups were noted for their tranquil nature, which seemed to make them ideal prospects for religious conversion.

At first, Oñate had no problem whatsoever with the Pueblo peoples. Each community welcomed him and willingly offered food. They even vacated two pueblos, renamed San Juan de los Caballeros and San Gabriel, to shelter the Spaniards. The friars, meanwhile, dispersed throughout the Pueblo world and began harvesting souls for Christ.

The situation rapidly deteriorated as the Spaniards found life less than ideal in their empire's far northern reaches, known as La Frontera del Norte. Here, as elsewhere in the New World, benevolence and brutality often went hand in hand. The hitherto peaceful Indians became restive under the demands of the Spaniards, whose failure to find gold and silver made them increasingly surly and belligerent. Violence ensued in 1598, when the residents of Acoma Pueblo assaulted some of Oñate's soldiers, killing at least a dozen and driving the rest from their village.

With brutal and swift force and with the aid of several cannons, Oñate's force of 70 soldiers destroyed the pueblo, killing scores of people and taking 600 captives. The men were mutilated and the women and children enslaved. Oñate had made his point. Cowed by this barbarity, the majority of the Pueblo Indians offered no more outward resistance to Spanish domination until the great uprising of 1680.

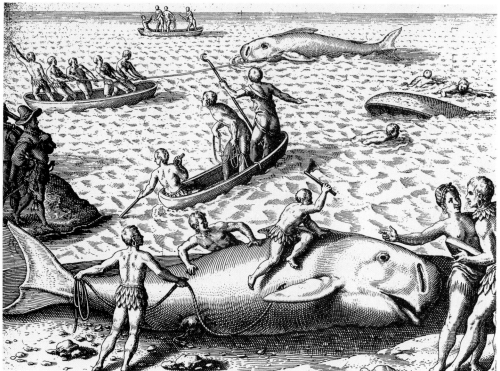

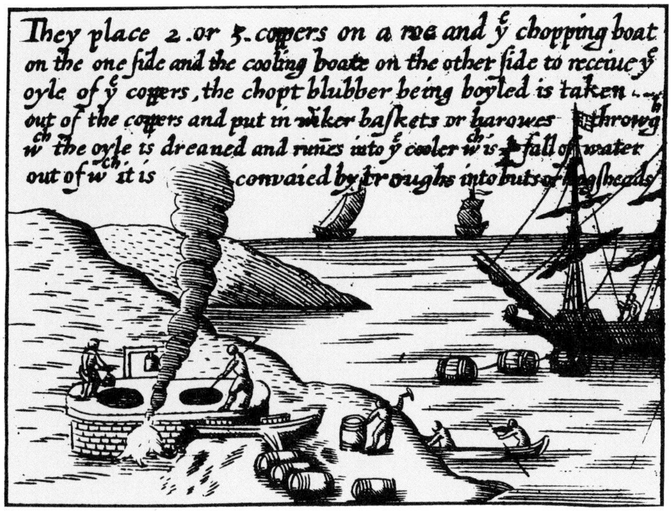
They place 2.or 3.copers on a roe and ye chopping boat
on the one side and the cooling boate on the other side to receive ye
oyle of ye copers, the chopt blubber being boyled is taken
out of the copers and put in wiker baskets or barowes throwgh
wch the oyle is dreaned and runes into ye cooler wch is full of water
out of wch it is convaied by troughs into buts or hogsheads

A detail from Pierre Descaliers' map of 1546, opposite, depicts Europeans whaling off the Strait of Belle Isle, Canada. The three-masted vessel anchored near La Terra Dv Labovrevr, *or Labrador, was probably manned by Basques. Opposite below, coastal natives assist Europeans in bringing harpooned whales to shore. Above, an old English cartoon shows the tryworks where whale blubber is rendered for its oil.*

Although New Mexico was to endure, this Spanish sally into North America achieved no economic or military importance. Santa Fe of 1610, like St. Augustine of 1565, was simply one more frontier outpost out of the hundreds serving some small purpose in the overall imperial structure. It was never more than a provincial administrative center.

In 1610 Spain was virtually at the peak of her power in the New World; her colonial system was already well in place by the time England and France were beginning to appreciate the importance of established colonies. They had been content to pillage, plunder, and harass Spain; now they were to become players in the game of empire, a far-from-trivial pursuit with long-term consequences for peoples of North America who had hitherto escaped the Spanish.

From New Spain, the focus shifts to Newfoundland where, following the voyages of John Cabot at the close of the 15th century, an active maritime industry flourished under Basque whalers in the north; French fishermen caught cod farther south. As many as 30 Basque whaling ships operated along the Newfoundland coast during a six-month season beginning each June. Ashore, fires burned under iron cauldrons at the tryworks, where blubber was rendered for its oil; barreled, the product was transported abroad to light lamps and for other purposes. Basque whale hunters prospered until the late 1580s when war broke out between England and Spain, and thereafter the English and the Dutch took over the business.

Whaling stations acted as magnets for the natives of Labrador, attracting Indians and Inuits alike, and fishermen made an additional catch by trading in furs and game. Archeological excavations of Eskimo dwellings in Labrador's Hamilton Inlet have uncovered caches of European goods. One site in particular contained trade beads by the thousands and other glass goods, nails, spikes, ceramics, including pipe fragments, buttons, spoons, knives, and the all-important shooting supplies—lead shot, gunflints, and spare parts. According to archeologist Susan Kaplan of Bowdoin College, the Inuit occupants of this house "were amassing European-made materials for trade to their northern neighbors as well as for their own use."

A cadre of native entrepreneurs had emerged by the end of the 18th century. One man who traded along the north Labrador coast reputedly owned two boats and supported a household of 37 people. Another, Tuglavina by name, ran a two-masted sloop along the southern Labrador coast from Nain to Belle Isle. By stimulating trade, the whaling stations, unlike earlier Viking communities, significantly changed the life of the region's Indians and Inuits. For a long time England and France seemed content with fishing and casual trade with coastal peoples. Eventually they tried to establish permanent colonies, only to have their initial efforts thwarted by harsh winters. The Cartier-Roberval attempt at settlement of 1541, at the future site of Quebec, ended after only a year. Marquis de La Roche, Lieutenant General of New France, landed 50 convicts on Newfoundland's Sable Island in 1598; five years later he rescued 11 survivors. At this time, New France was no more than a place where Frenchmen fished in the summers and occasionally bartered with the natives for furs.

Samuel de Champlain made New France a reality. For the site of his colony he, too, selected Quebec, for whoever possessed it also controlled access to the St. Lawrence Valley. The ground was easy to defend and fertile land for crops lay close at hand, beside open meadows for cattle. That first winter of 1608-09 cost Champlain dearly, though; more than 20 of his 32 companions died.

England fared little better with its North American colonies. As on the Newfoundland coast, contact between fishermen and Indians was maintained for a century or more before permanent settlements arose. Early encounters were sporadic, significant only after England developed a serious interest in her claims to North America. In *A Briefe and True Relation* of 1602, John Brereton described his experiences on board the *Concord*, which had been sent to New England to investigate the natural riches of the New World. He found the natives keenly interested in trade, offering vast quantities of valuable furs for the most trivial English products. "They misliked nothing," he recalled, "but our mustard, whereat they made many a soure face."

Aboard the *Archangel*, Captain George Waymouth spent a month during the summer of 1605 sailing Maine coastal waters in search of a likely site for permanent habitation. He enjoyed friendly

Above right, Capt. John Smith, founder of Jamestown, threatens Pamunkey Chief Opechancanough, who refused to supply the colonists with corn in 1608. Ancestors of the unidentified Wampanoag man, right, helped the Pilgrims survive the winter of 1620-21. By 1675, whites had made deadly enemies of the Wampanoags.

C. Smith taketh the King of Pamavnkee prisoner -1608.

relations with the Indians until, as he claimed, he suspected them of plotting against him, whereupon he plotted against them. He took three ships' visitors into custody, captured two more Indians from shore, and transported the five to England. By way of justification, he claimed to promote the "true zeale of promulgating Gods holy Church," and declared that the Indians would be sources of information for later visitors to New England, a belief that his superiors in Plymouth shared.

Sir Ferdinando Gorges, Waymouth's contemporary, wrote, "Captain Weymouth [*sic*] . . . brought five of the natives, three of whose names were Manida, Skettawarroes, and Tasquantum, whom I seized upon. They were all of one nation, but of several parts and several families. This accident must be acknowledged the means under God of putting on foot and giving life to all our plantations."

Waymouth and his backers immediately put their captives to good use. They taught them English and used them to propagandize the virtues of life in New England. One person envious of this tactic was the Spanish ambassador, who reported that the Indians were being trained to say "how good that country is for people to go there and inhabit it."

The plan to use these captives as interpreters and guides, however, went awry: a Spanish man-of-war intercepted two who had been shipped out to help establish a colony back in New England. One, Tahanedo, eventually joined a vessel bound for Maine but jumped ship and was later found enjoying life as a local chieftain, and quite disinterested in assisting his former captors.

English explorers continued to kidnap Indians. Captain Edward Harlow brought back five captives from Martha's Vineyard in 1608; six years later, Thomas Hunt seized 27 and then sold them in Málaga, Spain, where Spanish friars eventually rescued the majority. One of those seized by Hunt was the famous Squanto, the Wampanoag who was to contribute so much to the success of Plymouth Colony. After being sold in Spain in 1614, Squanto had escaped to England, where he joined up with the Newfoundland Company and once again crossed the Atlantic. Unhappy back on home ground, he

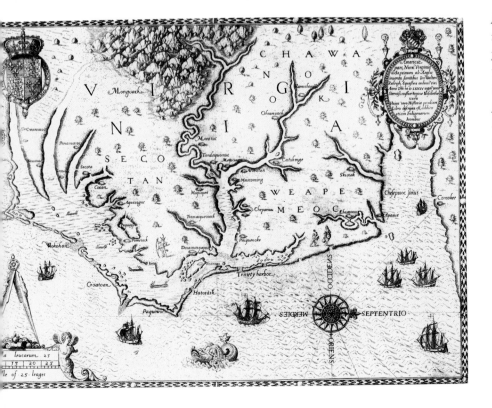

Map of mystery purports to show the site of Sir Walter Raleigh's famous Lost Colony of "Roanoac," which was established on a North Carolina island in 1587 and whose population vanished. Drawn by Englishman John White in the mid-1580s, it also includes the names of several coastal villages where colonists may have taken refuge with local Indians after the settlement failed.

Siberia, rugged Asian homeland of the ancestors of ancient Americans, appears on an old Russian map, below. Yakut, Evenk, Chukchi, Koryak, and Itelmen peoples, depicted on the map from left to right, may have migrated to North America between 3000 B.C. and 1000 B.C., perhaps settling the Aleutian chain. Right, Aleut girls from the Valdez-Copper River region display traditional nose-ring jewelry in a 1903 photo. Opposite below, Aleut girls appear in a 1984 photograph.

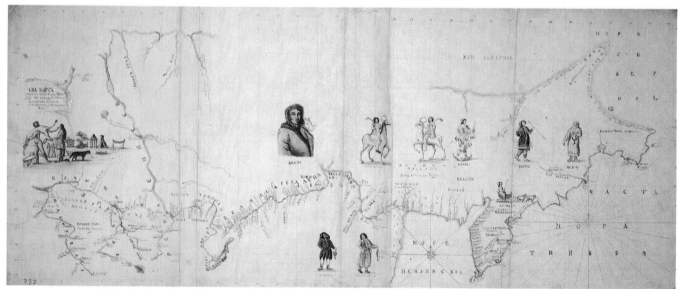

obtained passage to England with Captain Thomas Dermer and then accompanied him to Cape Cod in 1619, only to discover that plague had wiped out his tribal village.

Not only did Squanto live with the Pilgrims for two years and teach them about farming and frontier survival (many were former city dwellers ill-prepared for country life) but he secured the cooperation of neighboring tribes. Thus, writes historian Alden Vaugan, "Squanto survived to greet the Pilgrims and form a living link between the early years, with their scattered contacts between Indians and Englishmen, and the era of permanent colonization that began in 1620."

Englishmen who had settled farther south before Plymouth had no Squanto to ease their transition and no plague to eliminate the original inhabitants. Jamestown Colony was established in 1607 in the midst of a powerful Indian confederacy controlled by the great chief Powhatan and his elder brother Opechancanough. Had these brothers so willed, the Virginia colony would have perished in its first year.

The two Indians had cause, since their initial contacts with Europeans ended tragically. Opechancanough, in fact, captured Captain John Smith a few months after the colony was founded and took him to a village at the mouth of the Rappahannock River to see if he could be identified as the Euro-

pean who, a few years before, had killed and kidnapped some of their people. Earlier yet, the brothers may have attacked Englishmen near the site of a colony that failed.

Historian David Quinn suggests that survivors of Sir Walter Raleigh's famed Lost Colony of 1587 were massacred on Powhatan's orders and that revenge for various kidnappings by the English might be implicated. When the Carolina colony on Roanoke Island broke up before 1590, whites may have taken refuge with friendly Indians, living with them for as long as 17 years before both the foreigners and the local people felt Powhatan's wrath. His warriors may have killed the whites and their Indian benefactors as late as May 1607 — less than a month after the Jamestown settlers on the *Susan Constant*, *Godspeed*, and *Discovery* sailed into Chesapeake Bay.

Forty years later, Russia also sought influence in America, but far away in the North Pacific, and the first exploring voyages came to naught. A century and a quarter after the settlement of Jamestown, Czar Peter the Great made Russia's first serious bid for North American sovereignty and sponsored two star-crossed voyages under the command of Vitus Bering. This Danish-born navigator lost his life during the second expedition but gained the credit for an Alaskan landfall in 1741. As at Jamestown and the Lost Colony, conflict eventually emerged — to the detriment of native peoples.

When Czar Peter failed to gain international acceptance of Russian dominion, aggressive Siberian fur hunters moved in. Within three years they had created a base of operations and begun to exercise de facto control over trade and territory. These hardy frontiersmen first acquired the Commander Islands off Asia's Kamchatka Peninsula and, by working their way eastward along the Aleutian chain, reached Kodiak Island in 1762.

Here they encountered the aboriginal occupants of the Aleutian Islands, a mild, Stone-Age people related by race and language to the Inuit, or Eskimos. The Aleuts, who lacked tribal organization, formed dispersed family groups and inhabited half-buried houses. Rugged and resourceful, they harvested marine fauna of the frigid Arctic waters and were willing to fight for their independence.

A law unto themselves, the Russian fur hunters nearly annihilated the defiant Aleuts. They robbed, enslaved, and murdered them by the hundreds, sometimes destroying or transplanting entire communities. In time, Aleuts were scattered throughout Russian America, from the Pribilof Islands in the Bering Sea to Fort Ross in California. The Siberians' search for furs ruined Aleut hunting grounds; wildlife disappeared and Aleuts starved, adding one more grievance to a long list of abuses. When the Siberian fur hunters first forced their way into the Aleutians, the native people numbered perhaps 20,000; after a century only 2,500 remained, many of them mixed-bloods.

Russian-Indian relations changed dramatically after 1781, when Grigory Shelikov and his Siberian fur merchants organized a company. Russia eventually included native peoples in the enterprise and gave them status within the empire.

By 1800, European influence had touched virtually every native group on the North American continent, except perhaps the Polar Eskimos, the Inuits of northern Greenland. The interior tribes, of course, felt the impact of the European presence in the form of trade goods long before they ever saw a white man. The remarkable speed with which inland tribes obtained cloth, beads, metal tools, and even horses and guns bears witness to the active and extensive Indian trading networks.

Francisco Coronado, the first European to visit the Great Plains, observed tribal life there during the 1540s. He reported that the nomadic buffalo-hunting Indians regularly visited the settlements of their sedentary neighbors. Here they traded tanned hides for corn, with each group "going to those which are nearest, some to the settlement of Cicuye, others toward Quivira [Kansas], and others to the settlements situated in the direction of Florida."

The effectiveness of these trade networks is documented by archeological evidence as well as by early observations. Catlinite, the stone preferred by Indians for their tobacco pipes, is found most often in one quarry in Minnesota, yet it was used by Indians from Texas to Canada, and from California to Maine. Similarly, copper from the upper Great

George Catlin's 1848 painting of the sacred source of the red pipestone mineral catlinite—named for him—in Minnesota, left, portrays tribesmen quarrying the soft substance, which they will later carve into such items as the Santee Sioux effigy pipe of a buffalo facing a tree stump, below.

Lakes reached archeological sites as far south as Mexico.

Unfortunately, diseases of European origin seem also to have traveled along the trade routes. In some instances, goods may have been contaminated; in others, the traders themselves may have been infected. Authorities now believe that disease killed between 50 and 90 percent of America's Indian population, primarily during the 1500s, with later outbreaks in New England and nearby areas. Plagues, of course, were not new to Europeans: the onslaught of the Black Death had occurred from 1347-51. While many whites also died of disease in America, they succumbed to different illnesses, and not to the common afflictions and childhood maladies of Europe. Of course, the outsiders enjoyed reinforcement of populations from densely populated homelands, which the indigenous peoples did not.

Disease virtually cleared New England of its aboriginal population. A third of the region's 25,000 native people fell victim to a mysterious plague in 1616-17, only the first of a series of epidemics that swept that area in the 17th century. Landing at Plymouth three years later, the Pilgrims lost half their company to illness, malnutrition, and other causes during the first three months ashore.

Although the righteous Puritans regarded the plague on the Indians as a sign of God's favor to his "Elect," the incredible death toll appalled them. One witness reported, "the bones and skulls . . . made such a spectacle . . . that, as I travailed in that Forrest nere the Massachusetts, it seemed to me a new found Golgotha."

Although it is not always possible to identify the disease or diseases involved in a specific plague, most of the early epidemics are attributed to eruptive fevers, and smallpox was most often implicated. Smallpox, chickenpox, measles, typhus, and perhaps others probably struck simultaneously as conditions favoring the spread of one disease often facilitated the spread of all.

How differently history might have turned out had the European explorers and early colonists dealt with Indian tribes at full strength, rather than with native populations that were decimated

and demoralized by diseases they could neither resist nor understand. How long, for example, would Mexico's millions have tolerated the 600 conquistadors of Cortés? According to Friar Toribio de Benevente, author of *History of the Indians of New Spain* (1541), "when the smallpox began to infect the Indians, there was so much sickness and pestilence among them in all the land that in most provinces more than half the people died . . . ."

It was the same story throughout the Americas, from New Spain to New France. No matter how unsophisticated the natives, they quickly realized the source of their troubles. As reported in a 1616 issue of *Jesuit Relations*, "[The Indians] are astonished and often complain that, since the French mingle with them and carry on trade with them, they are dying fast and the population is thinning out. For they assert that, before this association and intercourse, all their countries were very populous and they tell how one by one the different coasts, according as they have begun to traffic with us, have been reduced by disease."

Even on the northern Plains, one of the last regions penetrated by Europeans, smallpox appeared early; the silent killer spread from tribe to tribe much as had the horse and gun—by physical contact, often through trade and intertribal warfare.

An incident of the time illustrates this terrible mode of transmission. In 1781, Blackfeet scouts chanced upon a Shoshone village on the south bank of the Bow River and, as it was strangely silent, watched for some time. No people were visible, although horses grazed among the tipis. At first, the scouts suspected a trap, but curiosity finally overcame caution: venturing into camp, they discovered that all the people in the tipis were dead. Overjoyed at their luck, the scouts looted the camp and returned home heavily laden. Unfortunately for the Blackfeet, the Shoshones had died of smallpox, and the easily acquired prizes were contaminated. As many as two-thirds of the Blackfeet tribe died within weeks.

Little wonder, then, that the Native Americans had no love for the European intruders. From North to South, East to West, the Indians shared the same tragedy, the same heartaches, the same feelings as the unknown Maya who lamented, "There was then no sickness; they had no aching bones; they had then no high fever; they had then no burning chest; they had then no abdominal pain; they had then no consumption; they had then no headache. At that time the course of humanity was orderly. The foreigners made it otherwise when they arrived here."

Doleful masks for devilish dancers—Fariseos, or "enemies of Christ"—were donned by Opata tribesmen of northern Mexico during Holy Week observances. At right, native peoples suffer from smallpox, one of numerous devastating diseases brought by Europeans.

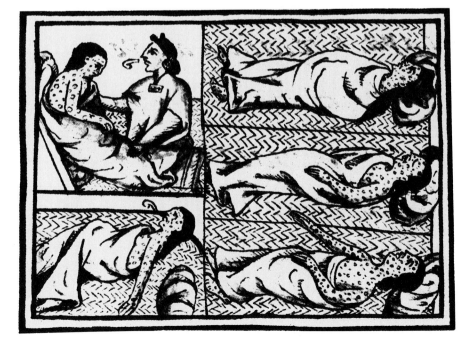

The Horse Culture

The horse originated in what are now the Americas more than 40 million years ago. It became extinct in its homeland, but, unlike most species, it was able to make a comeback: dispersing from the New World to the Old via the then exposed land bridge to Siberia, it eventually reached Europe and, at the end of this roundabout route, the Spanish re-introduced the horse to America. In 1493, on his second voyage, Columbus brought horses back to the Western Hemisphere after an absence of 10,000 years.

Spain's *conquistadores* rode horses and used them effectively against the Indians they encountered, who were frightened of the "sky dogs," believing they were monsters or messengers of the gods. When the Hopis saw their first horses they paved their way with ceremonial blankets.

The Native Americans' awe of horses quickly gave way to a powerful urge to obtain these wonder-ful creatures, but the Spanish were equally desirous to keep them out of Indian hands. Nonetheless, by the late 1700s virtually every tribe in the Far West was mounted or at least had access to horses (some of the mountain tribes ate rather than rode theirs). Recent scholar-ship has revealed the probable routes and methods by which Indians of the Plains and the American Southwest obtained their mounts. This remarkable story highlights the trading acumen and adaptability of the American tribes. Also, inevitably, the acqui-sition and use of firearms soon accompanied the possession of horses by Indians. Indeed, the widespread distribution of guns and horses worked to create the militant horse tribes of the prairies and the Far West.

Historians once attributed the actual re-introduction of the horse to the Great Plains to 16th-century explorers Francisco Coronado and Hernando de Soto. It was thought that runaway mounts stocked the

A Navajo petroglyph, left, on the wall of Massacre Cave in Can-yon del Muerto, Arizona, records the 1804-1805 Spanish expedition of mounted soldiers led by Lt. Antonio Narbona. Above, a soli-tary horse appears in the Navajo Tribal Park, also in Arizona.

Plains with the great wild herds so familiar in the lore of the West. Subsequent research, however, has discredited this theory. Although both expeditions were well mounted—Coronado's, for instance, had 558 horses—these animals simply could not have been producing offspring, for Spanish law required soldiers to ride stallions. Only two of Coronado's horses were mares, and both returned to New Spain with him. It is now generally accepted that the Indians acquired their horses a century later from Spanish herds in New Mexico. Some they stole, but most they obtained as a result of the Pueblo Indian uprising of 1680. From New Mexico, horses moved rapidly north and east along established trading networks, although some were captured during intertribal raiding. However obtained, mounts represented wealth, status, power, and the ability to move people and goods with efficiency and speed.

The Lakota are typical of the tribes whose cultures were transformed by the horse. In the 1760s some Lakota were canoeing people of what is today Minnesota;

within 30 years the western Lakota had become part of the greatest light cavalry history has ever known. The horse drew them toward the prairie, the gun drove them from canoe country.

The spread of horses from the West was nearly simultaneous with the introduction of firearms from the East, the latter allowing

A Wahpeton Sioux cotton tipi liner, below, depicts a fight between Indians on horseback and Indians on foot. Some of the horses are Appaloosas, bred by the Nez Percé people of Idaho and Washington State. Woman's saddle pouch, left, was made by Yakimas who lived in Washington State.

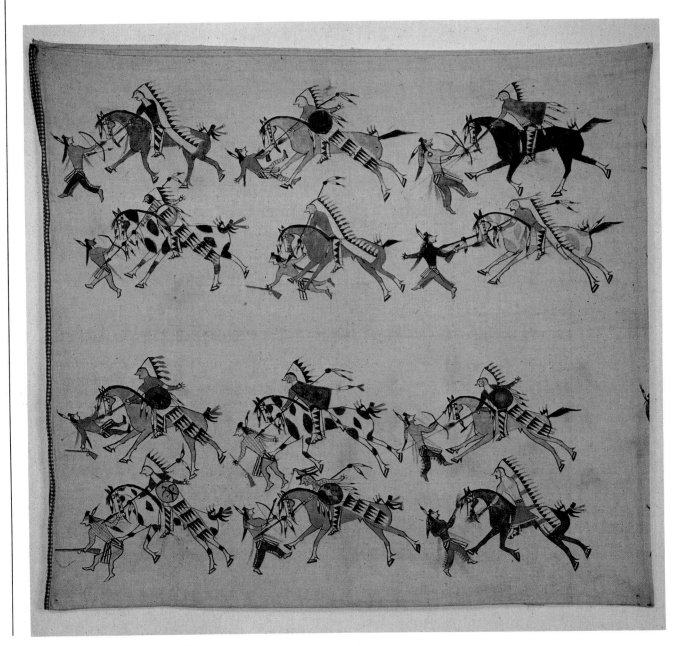

John Inness's "The Buffalo Hunt," above, brings to life one of the most dramatic—and vital—activities of the Plains Indian. Typical tack for horses included a rawhide thong or hackamore noosed around the horse's lower jaw and sometimes a blanket or small hide cushion, such as the Sioux pad saddle at left. Generally, Indian men rode bareback, like the hunter, above center, mounted on a pinto.

easterly tribes to push westerly people out onto the Plains. The guns arrived despite initial trade embargoes. As early as 1622, within two years of the arrival of the Mayflower, the Puritans petitioned the British Crown to pass the first law against supplying weapons to Indians, "upon Paine of our high Indignation," but such regulations proved almost impossible to enforce. By 1628, according to Plymouth Colony Governor William Bradford's reckoning, the

Indians of New England owned more than 60 guns, with the number increasing every year. The situation so perplexed him that he later composed a poem, entitled "A most desperate mischief."

For these fierce natives, they are now so fill'd
With guns and muskets, and in them so skilled,
As that they may keep the English in awe
And when they please give to them the law;
Thus like madmen we put them in a way,
With our own weapons us to kill and slay:

As the wars of empire intensified, suppliers profited mightily from the gun traffic. Colonies vied in this commerce, relaxing their laws so as not to be undercut in trade. Later, certain tribes located along strategic waterways, such as the Arikara, Hidatsa, and Mandan Indians, who lived in villages along the Missouri River, for a time enjoyed a thriving business as the middlemen of the complex trade network that moved horses east and guns west. The Crow Indians of the Yellowstone country were another such intermediary. They obtained horses and mules from their Flathead, Shoshone, and Nez Percé suppliers, and then exchanged the animals at the Hidatsa and Mandan villages for muskets, gunpowder, and lead.

So impersonal an economic force as trade can prove dramatic as its impact becomes evident at the human level. Imagine, for example, an Indian's shock at first confronting an enemy on a horse, or first fighting a warrior armed with a gun. Similarly, the confluence on the northern Plains of the two opposing streams of trade—where eastern and western routes met—provided a crucial impetus to American Indian history.

One witness to this fateful encounter was a Cree Indian named Saukamaupee, who during the winter of 1787-88 related his account to Hudson's Bay fur trader David Thompson. As a young man, Saukamaupee had lived with the Piegan Indians, who are Canadian relatives of the Blackfeet. The Piegans were continually

In C.M. Russell's painting, opposite, horses drag tipi poles and camp gear by means of a frame called a travois. Dogs originally served as beasts-of-burden, both pulling and carrying packs. Frederic Remington's "Ghost Riders" evokes the sense of unity between the Indian and his horse.

at war with their Shoshone neighbors, and Saukamaupee participated in several conflicts. In a battle that took place about 1730, several Shoshones rode horses, which he and his Piegan friends had never seen before. Swinging their stone war clubs, the mounted Shoshones charged and quickly routed the Piegans. To help fight their new overpowering enemy,

the frightened Piegans sought assistance from their Assiniboine and Cree neighbors to the east, who did not have horses but who had obtained a revolutionary new weapon of their own, the "fire stick." The next time the two foes met, ten Cree and Assiniboine musketeers assisted the Piegans, and it was the surprised and terrified Shoshones who fled.

The Piegans soon got their first close look at a Shoshone horse, which had died from an arrow wound in its belly. "Numbers of us went to see him," Saukamaupee recalled, "and we all admired him; he put us in mind of a stag that had lost his horns, and we did not know what name to give him. But as he was a slave to Man, like the

dog, which carried our things, he was named the Big Dog." Later, because horses were the size of elk, the Piegans began calling them *ponokomita*, or "elk dog," which remains their word for horse.

Such encounters were experienced over and over again, in tribe after tribe, offering us insight into a crucible of change for which the horse and the gun provided the spark. The new, highly effective combination of mobility and firepower fueled a startling social and technological revolution among Indian peoples, one that predestined the violent encounter that would erupt between whites and Indians as American settlers began to stream west to claim Indian lands.

In a painting by Edward Hicks, below, Quaker William Penn concludes a treaty—never broken—with Delaware leaders in 1682. Opposite, a 1630 sketch for a coat of arms for the Netherlands' New Amsterdam colony features beavers, chief objects of the Dutch fur trade.

Cultures in Collision

Scholars, philosophers, lawmakers, and many others have, over the centuries, tried—and mainly failed—in their efforts to generalize about what happens when people of different cultures meet and mingle. A prime example is the melting-pot concept from the United States. While the present work reveals broad patterns of cultural interaction, this and other chapters let the facts speak for themselves. A few guidelines, however, are provided for the reader who attempts to thread the complex cultural maze. The most basic rule: the exceptions far outnumber the rules.

A phenomenon called ethnocentrism was hard at work from the very beginning of European involvement in America. To the newcomers from abroad, Indians were nearly always considered outsiders and certainly not equals. Distrust and conflict were common. While Europeans of different classes and vested interests might bicker among themselves, they often united in their dislike, if not abhorrence, of beliefs, values, and customs that Indians held dear. Since the foreigners dominated most relationships, they worked to impress their culture on the Indians, and Christianity figured prominently. Also, as George Horse Capture noted in the introduction, many of the common people who came from Europe had few if any cultural legacies other than raw greed and cunning sharpened by centuries of feudal domination, rigid class structures,

famine, and plague. As a professor of sociology remarked to his class, "If you don't know who brought your family name to America, don't try to find out. You'll probably be in for a shock." Bandits, pirates, and brigands of all sorts had a field day in the New World.

In the case of Spanish colonization, hundreds of humble Indian cultures and two high civilizations—Mexican and Incan—were bound to collide with the acquisitive conquistadors and colonists. Agents of the Crown and the Church were pledged to higher callings and aims. Interactions along similar lines also occurred when the Northern Europeans arrived, but on a much smaller scale, as lands north of the Hispanic domain were often sparsely populated. A century after Columbus's arrival in the New World, England and France joined Spain in the quest for American empire, and the Netherlands was also preparing for an entrance; Russia would arrive only during the third full century (1741) of the great Columbian drama.

Leader of the first permanent English settlement in North America, Capt. John Smith prepared this map of Virginia in 1607. The map is oriented with north at the right. Captured by men of the Powhatan Confederacy in late 1607, Smith's life was spared at the request of Pocahontas, opposite, daughter of the tribe's leader, Powhatan, and later John Rolfe's wife.

Within two centuries of Columbus, most Indian tribes throughout the continent had been able to make official and personal adjustments with the various representatives of the European powers in their vicinity. The catastrophic disruptions typical of the era of first encounter lay in the past. Some fortunate tribes, particularly those of the Far West, enjoyed freedom and even a cultural renaissance thanks to the horse and the gun. Everywhere, marvelous European manufactured items attracted Indians to the colonials, and it seemed that comparatively good times might last forever.

Whatever deals the Europeans and Indians were able to make at official and informal levels, the colonials approached Indians with an undisguised sense of superiority. Whether of high or low degree, the typical European expected and demanded Indian acquiescence and accommodation and regarded Indians who resisted or objected as enemies. Though each European power fulfilled its own ambitions and dealt with the Indians in its own style, the theme of colonial superiority always dominated. Citizens of the new United States—although they rejected control by the Crown—retained the deeply ingrained British lust for land. Indians occupied the land, however, and the States were hell-bent to possess it.

Frenchmen and Russians, primarily concerned with the fur trade, cared more for Indian hunting skills than for Indian real estate; thus trading posts were the hallmarks of their presence. Spaniards sought precious metals, salvation for heathen souls, and protection from their Old World neighbors, and so mines, missions, and presidios (fortified garrisons) marked the northern progress of New Spain. While the English Crown favored policies similar to those of the French, English colonists wanted land, and the stone walls of their farms and the palisades of their forts symbolized their desire for land and the lengths they would go to get it and keep it.

Racial and cultural attitudes and relations also differed. As a 1514 roster of Spanish landholders on Hispaniola indicates, racial blending began almost immediately. Of the 349 landholders listed, 146 were married and living with their wives, of whom 92 were Spanish and 54 Indian. Today, many Hispanic Americans have several Indian ancestors. Most Americans of English, German, Dutch or other Northern European heritage do not, while many Indians north of Mexico claim one or more European forebears and some Indians possess African ancestors. Whatever the peopling process, based on inclusion or exclusion of native peoples, demographics changed radically during the course of 500 years. Non-Indians in North America progressed from an absolute minority to an overwhelming majority and, at each stage in the process, the tenor of relationships between Indians and colonials changed substantially.

Russia may well have been the least damaging of the major colonial powers in its treatment of New World natives. This record is somewhat misleading, of course, because the Russians were the last to arrive and the first to leave, and at no time did their investment in North America of material, money, and manpower approach that of their English, French, and Spanish rivals. Moreover, as we have learned, the early Russian fur traders at times behaved as insensitively and destructively as their Western European counterparts.

Ætatis suæ 21. A°. 1616.

Aleksandr Baranov, czar of the Russian-American Company, certainly put profits above native rights. On Kodiak Island, he forced native men, women, and children into his employ and reduced them to the status of indentured servants. So extreme were his tactics that the clergy pleaded for his recall, but his worldly success placed him beyond rebuke.

An uneasy peace prevailed until a quiet Sunday morning during June 1802, when Tlingit warriors attacked Sitka without warning and obtained an easy victory because most of the hunters were away. Encouraged by American sailors, the Tlingits killed a dozen or more men, confiscated many sea otter skins, and captured three Russians, five Aleut

Listen to the Land

by Russell Bourne

After founding New Hampshire's Dartmouth College in 1769, Eleazar Wheelock raised the nearby edifice of Moor's Indian Charity School to train tribal missionaries.

When I came back to tornado-blasted Connecticut from Maine's serene Penobscot Bay in the summer of 1989, I found a scene of horror. And change. The formerly beautiful "Cathedral Pines" of Cornwall—so movingly described as a primeval woodland by William Cronon in his *Changes in the Land*—were no more. Jaggedly ripped-apart trunks and a madman's tangle of contorted limbs were all that could be seen of a once majestic forest built upon ancient rocks. How ironic, I thought, that Cronon had given his book that change-oriented title while rhapsodizing about the permanence of these woods, now shattered beyond recall.

Some months later I attended a meeting in Rhode Island at which a Narragansett Indian spokesman retold the story of the permanence of his people in the southeastern corner of New England. "We've always been here," he narrated. The eternal presence to which he referred is not, of course, as long-ago as the era after the glaciers' disappearance (roughly 10,000 years ago), when paleo-people roamed here hunting mastodons. Sacred stories and myths of the Narragansett people recount the subsequent shiftings and invasions that finally resulted in their settlement of the region along with other competitive Algonquian peoples some 1,700 years ago (by which time the climate had become much like today's).

The first contact of these far-traveled Americans with Europeans—the Vikings—seems to have occurred only 700 years later,

if evidence in archeology and sagas is to be credited. Additional finds demonstrate that sporadic contact with fishermen, castaways, explorers, and other unwitting disease-carriers went on until the colonizations by New England's Pilgrims and Puritans in the second and third decades of the 17th century. The Pilgrims, seeking a secure site for their "plantation," happened upon an off-Cape Cod haven already cleared but strangely empty. A European-induced plague had swept away the native farmers just three years before the *Mayflower* arrived in 1620. Thus had God not forgotten "His owne," but had opened "up a way for them," the Pilgrims wrote.

Wampanoag sachem Massasoit (real name: Ousamequin, "Yellow Feather") immediately saw that a

treaty with the Pilgrims would strengthen his hand against neighboring Narragansetts. Remarkably, the document that he and Governor John Carver signed formed the basis for a creative peace that would last for 50 years—not permanent, but impressive. Indeed, it looked for a time as if the English settlers and the shrewd diplomats from various Algonquian peoples might succeed in working out a harmonious, biracial society sustained by trade and hunting partnerships.

The islands south of Cape Cod

offer yet another example of this cooperative, productive mode. When a Nantucket lookout spotted a whale off the beach, waiting crewmen of both races would hurl their light but lethal craft out through surf to slay the leviathan. The team of seaborne hunters communicated among themselves in Nattick, the native tongue, for the island's original occupants had been a-whaling for centuries; Europeans had to learn the tongue's tricks to succeed. Fortunate indeed were these natives of the coastal islands, it appeared, to have developed such a harmonious relationship with the English settlers. And handsome, too. In the words of explorer Giovanni de Verazanno: *This is the goodliest people and of the fairest condition that we have found in this our voyage; they exceed us in bigness, they are the color brass, some of them incline more to whiteness, others are of a yellow color, with long and black hair which they are careful to turn and deck up: they are of a sweet and pleasant countenance.*

Yet today the Gay Head Indians of Martha's Vineyard manifest a deep and credible bitterness at how they have fared in the shadow of the white-dominated society that developed on the island. Recently, after intense and effective agitation, the Gay Heads won a substantial settlement in resolution of land claims. They continue to demand redress for historic privileges and territorial rights taken away.

Observers may wonder at how these native-settler associations, which began so fraternally in New England, could have turned into

Bowl, c. 1650, by a sculptor from the Nipmuc tribe of Massachusetts, is one of the oldest surviving wooden artifacts crafted by New England Indians.

such a tragedy—a tragedy marked not by total annihilation (as in some other parts of the country) but by remorseless incompatibility. For some answers, the curious might look back to causes and effects of the cruel Pequot War and the all-enveloping King Philip's War that blasted the region in 1637 and 1675. Though some Christianized Indians were spared and a number of native peoples survived these wars by their own wiles, Algonquians lost prominence and power. Worse, all chances of red and white societies working together toward a mutually acceptable destiny were terminated . . . a grim model for America-to-be.

In this quest for what may prove permanent—or enduring—historians of former times relied exclusively on the Puritans' propagandistic accounts of 17th-century events. Scientists in the 1980s and 1990s, on the other hand, have embarked on a new approach to what makes for an enduring society. They are probing the land for fundamental

clues to the nature of the people whom the land has brought forth. This is archeology of the most sensitive, cultural sort. Perhaps by studying old layers continually buried under new, they may conclude that the deaths and rebirths are concomitants of our cataclysmic, creative earth. Forests are blasted; people erupt in battle. Yet land and people endure.

Dr. Paul A. Robinson of the Rhode Island Preservation Commission—to name one of these analytical scientists—has discovered that while many Narragansetts were welcoming and profiting from trader contact, their teeth and physical strengths were being corrupted by sugars and starches (not to mention liquor) obtained at the trading post. His collected artifacts indicate, however, that even as this perhaps unintentional corruption was taking place, the religious strengths of some Narragansetts were being bolstered. The people, it seems, were calling more desperately upon the spirits of the land for sustenance; traditions vitally important for survival were being put in place.

In this process of listening to and being guided by the land, native voices are also (finally) being heard: ethno-historians, folklorists, and even politicians are paying attention as Algonquians vigorously project their own past and future. Though that long-ago time of biracial harmony may never be re-lived, it's no longer impossible to believe that one day the mutual heritage may be fairly claimed by both people. To scientist and poet alike, the time has come to listen to the land.

A girl of mixed Spanish-Native American heritage stands before ruins of Tumacacori Mission, built in 1822 in southern Arizona. Jesuit and later Franciscan missionaries maintained outposts among several Indian tribes in this region beginning in the late 17th century.

hunters, and 18 women and children. Only one person profited from this affair, an opportunistic British sea captain who forced the Tlingits to surrender their booty. He not only kept the skins but extorted 10,000 rubles from Baranov for the return of the captives.

Baranov took the setback in stride and, with the aid of a Russian warship, recaptured Sitka and eventually reestablished harmony with the Tlingits, who learned vegetable gardening from the Russians and kept them supplied with produce and game. Soon, 1,500 Indians or more were living on the site of their old village, abandoned when the Russians returned. Relations between the cultures improved.

Baranov continued his southward course down the Pacific Coast of North America and in 1812 established Fort Ross, the only permanent non-Hispanic settlement in early California. Situated 90 miles north of San Francisco Bay, it soon became an agricultural and fur trading center. In keeping with the Russians' official Indian policy, Baranov contracted with the Pomo Indians for up to four square miles of land on the Pacific Coast and hired tribesmen as agricultural laborers. A tri-cultural community evolved, with Russian administrators, Aleut hunters, and Pomo farmers. Some of the Pomos learned to speak Russian, adopted aspects of the Russian Orthodox rite, and intermarried with Fort Ross residents.

Since settlement was not a major objective, the Russians displaced relatively few inhabitants and then only locally. Furthermore, Russia recognized quite early that amicable relations with the natives were essential for a profitable trade. Keeping their hands out of tribal affairs, the Czar and his colonial agents promoted cooperation with native peoples and considered them citizens of the Russian empire. No wonder, writes historian Lydia Black, that among the native peoples of Alaska the Russians are remembered as models "of intercultural communication and integration."

Conversely, from the 1500s on, the average Indian learned to view the English seasonal traders and explorers as threats as well as sources of manufactured goods. The colonists, who came after 1600, viewed the Indian as either a menace or a hindrance, or both. Such opinions can be examined in light of England's previous experiences in Ireland, where never-ending conflict had already fixed the notion that expulsion or extermination was a practicable means of dealing with people attached to their ancestral lands. The fact that Indian methods of warfare sometimes included torture, scalping, and other "uncivilized" forms of behavior only served to harden English attitudes against them. Even the highly religious Puritans saw nothing wrong with sending a few heathen souls to hell in exchange for property.

Interracial tension continually marred relations between Englishmen and Indians, establishing a legacy of bitterness and brutality that the United States inevitably inherited: the spirit of that first Thanksgiving at Plymouth did not persist. The cruel reality, the fundamental conflict between the English colonists and the Indians, concerned land title. Although some Spanish experts of the times, such as Francisco de Vitoria, argued that Indians held legal title to their land, English colonists favored the opinion of Swiss jurist Emmerich von Vattel, one of the first writers on international law. He ruled that title depended on the use made of land and that civilized people possessed a higher claim to the land than "savages."

In the Puritan view, as expressed by John Winthrop of Massachusetts Bay Colony, "that w[hi]ch lies common & hath never been replenished or subdued is free to any that will possess and improve it, for God hath given to the sonnes of man a double

Father Narciso Durán offers an Indian child an apple in an 1841 drawing of life at Mission San José de Guadalupe, at what is today San José, California. Southwestern and Californian missions defined the limits of Spanish colonial and later Mexican influence in the north.

right to the earth, there is a naturall right & a Civill right." Ignoring the fact that agriculture supplied the aboriginal New Englanders with most of their food, and that many Indians there lived in permanent villages, Winthrop felt comfortable in allowing them "noe other but a naturall right to those countries . . . [for] they inclose noe Land, neither have any setled habitation nor any tame Cattle to improve the Land by . . . ."

Others, notably Rhode Island's Roger Williams, disassociated themselves from nearly all positions held by Winthrop and the Puritans, including opinions on Indian land rights. Such differences between those who would grant Indians the rights held by those of their own group and those who viewed the Indians as a problem to be removed would persist throughout the history of Indian-white relationships.

Because the colonists themselves, the individual colonies, and the Crown had different policies regarding Indian affairs, no unified approach emerged until it was too late to do much good.

English Indian policy and practice remained divided, confused, and even contradictory throughout the colonial period. Puzzled, frustrated and eventually bullied, the Indians hardly knew what to think or do.

Missionaries often attempted to deal with the problems, with varying degrees of success. Not only did the English lack the religious ardor of their European neighbors, but the Indians had little enthusiasm for their stark and dour devotions. "Heathen they are & heathen they will remain," grumbled one English clergyman after three fruitless years in the American mission field. In contrast, the legacy of the Russian Orthodox Church still abides among Alaska's native peoples.

Faced with the history of upheaval between settlers and Indians in territories that became the United States, we easily forget that some decent and dignified relationships were forged on all fronts, even in the earliest days. Squanto, of course, initiated one of the most famous partnerships, befriending the Pilgrims at Plymouth. Here, out of sheer desperation, more than 100 English people made common cause with local Indians, on whom their survival depended.

With proper encouragement, Indians not only allowed the vulnerable and inexperienced newcomers to live, but the Indian sachems—leaders who served as the area's "senior service"—showed the Pilgrims the ropes. Whites who know today's Indians well are not in the least surprised: there was a real basis for the old stereotype of the noble red man and woman. We learn of shared feasts, Indian midwives assisting pioneer women in childbirth, business partnerships, honorable marriages between Indians and whites, and various other ties

and loyalties among individuals and families of the different races. These people, whether white or red, appear to have been the true frontier nobility: many of them will appear in these pages.

The experiences of Jamestown Colony, rather than those of the Pilgrims at Plymouth, established the broad pattern of English-Indian relations along the Atlantic Seaboard. Situated on swampy ground in the heart of the powerful Powhatan Confederacy, Jamestown colonists lived through first years that were precarious at best: of 7,000 colonists sent there by the Virginia Company after 1607, only 1,200 remained in 1624. Yet thanks to the efforts of several capable governors and the arranged marriage between planter John Rolfe and Pocahontas, the comely daughter of Chief Powhatan, relations remained fairly amicable for several years despite rising Indian discontent.

Peaceful coexistence between colonists and the established population seemed possible until March 23, 1622, when Powhatan's warriors struck without warning. Within hours, 347 Englishmen had died. It was a grievous but not fatal blow for the colonists, who retaliated with such devastating force that they shattered the confederation and broke the power of the Virginia tribes. The Indians may have continued to annoy Jamestown colonists, but no longer were they a threat.

Scenes from the mid-18th-century Cronica de Mechoacan *of Fr. Pablo Beaumont depict Indians seeking conversion to Christianity as they undergo instruction against temptations, learn of dire punishments for transgressions, and, finally, are baptized into the faith. Right, "I am Catarina Ort[e]ga's," say the Spanish words woven into the lip and center of this basket made by a Chumash woman of California.*

Colonist Robert Bennett, who participated in a peace conference with the "great Kinge Apochanzion" and his leading chiefs and warriors, reported an example of Jamestown's revenge. "After a manye fayned speches," Bennett boasted in a letter to his brother, the colonists concluded the proceedings with an old English custom, a toast to each other's health and good fortune. Bennett did not know the exact death toll, but believed 200 Indians died because the wine they drank "was sente of porpose in the butte . . . to poyson them."

The English were not alone in their potential severity to nearby tribesmen. When challenged, the Spanish could act ruthlessly. Part of the reason was human nature, especially as expressed by armies of freebooters. Policy may have been dictated by councils at court, and administered from imposing colonial headquarters and cathedrals, but venal and sometimes desperate persons carried out what passed for policy in native villages, in the rain forests, and even in the golden cities of Mexico and Peru. Far from the official eyes of bishop and king, greedy men might exercise power over life and death, taking whom and what they wanted and exploiting land and people to gain all the wealth they could, as quickly as possible. Hernán Cortés, conqueror of Mexico, succinctly explained his avarice to Montezuma, reportedly advising him, "I have a fever that only gold can cure." That malady was highly contagious.

Yet policies, institutions, and customs arose which worked to soften the impact of the abominations of the early decades of the 1500s. Over time, the record reveals a core of positive accomplishment in Spain's relations with American peoples. She was the first nation to recognize formally the rights of occupancy of the Indians and to defer to tribal self-government. The New Laws of the Indies, proclaimed in 1542, stipulated that the Indians were "free persons and vassals of the Crown," that lawsuits among Indians were to be decided "according to their usage and custom," and that nothing was to be taken from them "except in fair trade."

In a sense, the New Laws of the Indies anticipated the concept of trusteeship later adopted by the United States and provided for centuries later by the United Nations with respect to dependent

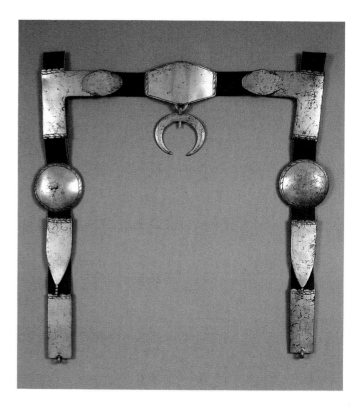

peoples. Under Spanish guidance the Indians enjoyed protection before the law virtually equal to that of a native of Spain, and yet they were considered special wards of the Crown.

Even the notorious *encomienda* system was intended by the Crown as a means to protect the Indians of New Spain from the evils experienced by their Caribbean brethren, who were enslaved and destroyed by the early conquistadors. Essentially, the encomienda was a program designed to reward faithful soldiers by "entrusting" Indian laborers to their care, while it also sought to fulfill the Crown's promise to the Pope that the Indians of New Spain would be converted to the Catholic faith and protected from harm. This relationship was carefully spelled out, with designated Spaniards entitled to labor from Indians according to formulas and schedules and territorial boundaries. Cortés, for example, received 70,000 Indians in a tract of roughly 2,000 square miles.

In return for Indian support, the *encomendero* or Spanish overlord was obligated to attend to the physical and spiritual well-being of his charges. The potential for abuse in such a system is obvious.

Silver bridle decorations, left, by Atsidi Chon, one of the first Navajo master silversmiths, exemplify motifs and workmanship that characterize this traditional craft. Made of wool from Spanish-introduced sheep, Navajo rugs and blankets, below, are among the finest examples of the weaver's art.

Despite safeguards, Indians suffered the loss of lands even though their property was not considered part of an encomienda. Since the grants were inherited from generation to generation, the Indians were often reduced to a state of slavery. This flawed system was outlawed during the final days of the 18th century.

The other institution in New Spain that was intimately associated with Indian policy was the *reduccione*, or mission. Spanish friars gathered Indians into villages to protect them from slave hunters and to teach them Christianity, gardening,

and simple crafts. Thrusting onto the native peoples a blend of paternalism and theocracy, these settlements flourished under Franciscans and Jesuits, who organized great numbers of missions from Argentina to California.

Whatever their good works, the famous California missions served primarily as military outposts charged with protecting the Pacific gateway to Mexico. In the 18th century, the march of the Russian fur hunters stirred Spain to establish the chain of 21 missions and four presidios that eventually linked San Diego and San Francisco across 600 miles.

"The idea of the missions was as artificial as it was noble," writes scholar Fernando de los Rios; "it was impossible to maintain them in isolation nor was it possible to suppress every sort of human impulse . . . it was a city-convent without place for the initiative of the individual man, without place for adventure."

Although Spain did not negotiate treaties with Indians, it did issue grants to particular tribes, thus recognizing and confirming tribal occupation of these territories. Boundaries were delineated and tribal rights upheld by an establishment that also allowed Indian communities to maintain their own forms of government. The strengths and weaknesses of Spain's policy are demonstrated by the Pueblo peoples of what is today the state of New Mexico, and whose lands and system of government have survived 400 years of political and social change.

Following the arrival of Governor Juan de Oñate in 1598, and his brutal suppression of Acoma Pueblo, several tribes of Pueblo Indians endured

Bark from the paper birch gave dwellers of the northeastern woods a material of many uses. Artist Paul Kane painted bark lodges, left, of an unidentified tribe on the banks of Lake Huron, 1845. Best known of all birch-bark products are canoes, such as that shown above in a painting by Frederic Remington, "Evening on a Canadian Lake," 1905. Birch-bark canoes were made in many types, reflecting different uses and styles among tribes. A Huron tray of birch bark, right, is trimmed with moose hair and decorated with a deer-hunting scene.

Spanish ecclesiastical and political domination for the better part of a century. Not until 1680 did the excessive demands of the encomienda system and Jesuit interference in cultural life finally provoke these patient, peace-loving people into armed rebellion. They rallied under Popé, a Tewa religious leader from San Juan Pueblo. For the first time in their history, several Pueblo peoples organized themselves politically, their sole purpose being to expel the Spanish from their country. They succeeded with remarkable ease as Popé assaulted

Beadwork on a vest from Canada, above, illustrates Indian craftsmanship using foreign materials. Métis of Alberta combine European clothing with fur hats, sashes, and moccasins of Indian design. A mixture of French or Scots with Cree or Assiniboine, the Métis ("mixed-blood" in French) evolved a unique culture.

Santa Fe, killing as many as 500 Spaniards and forcing 1,000 more to flee southward to El Paso del Norte. There the Spaniards regrouped, delaying some 15 years before attempting a return.

Having accomplished their goal, the Pueblo peoples resumed their former way of life. Their political unity was relatively short-lived, however, and completely fell apart after Popé was deposed for behaving too much like a dictator, having ordered the assassination of dissidents and having appropriated beautiful women for himself and his commanders. Little organized resistance, then, met the returning Spaniards in 1695, and all the pueblos except those of the Hopi in northern Arizona were once again under Spanish control by 1696; the Hopi people remained independent until they were swallowed up by the United States after the Civil War.

Both the Spaniards and the Pueblo tribes learned from their conflicts, eventually adjusting their behavior to allow mutually satisfactory relationships to develop. Spanish missionaries appeared more tolerant than before and no longer attempted to control every detail of Pueblo cultural life. The tribes, in turn, treated the good fathers with respect and observed some of the external rituals of the Church, but continued to practice and believe as before. In recent years, when asked the number of true believers among his Indian parishioners, a Franciscan priest at Acoma Pueblo replied, "I don't think I have any."

Except for a few Frenchmen along the Mississippi River and French-Canadian border, the Indians living west of the Mississippi needed to contend only with the Spanish who, unlike the English along the Atlantic Coast, were represented by very small populations at remote outposts along the *Frontera*, the northern frontier of New Spain. Following the "reconquest" of New Mexico, the Spanish and the more sedentary tribes of the Southwest evolved a comfortable relationship that was, however, destined to be disturbed by the "apaches," a generic term used to describe their enemies—primarily the Indians we know today as Apaches and their equally aggressive kinsmen, the Navajos. These tribes, of different linguistic origin than others of the area, harassed the settled communities of the Frontera for generations.

Samuel de Champlain, explorer and founder of the French colony in Canada, brought down the wrath of the Iroquois on the French when he sided with the Iroquois' traditional enemies, the Hurons, in a battle in 1609, below. In 1632, Franciscan lay brother Gabriel Sagard published a personal account of travels and observations among the Hurons with a dictionary of their language, opposite. Jesuits baptized Catherine Tekakwitha, right, a Mohawk girl who was shunned by her people when she became the first Indian nun. Called the "Lily of the Mohawks," and pictured here in 1680 by Father Claude Chaucetiére, she was recently beatified.

Though peaceful by preference, Spanish settlers and their Pueblo allies engaged in a deadly contest with Apache and Navajo raiders, who regarded small farmers and ranchers as a source of animals, European goods, and captives. From around 1700 to the late 19th century, raids and wars against Spanish, Mexicans, and Americans flared periodically. Occasionally, areas of the Southwest became depopulated as a result of these raids and reprisals. Both sides aimed to take women and children captive. The Spaniards and their Mexican successors sold Indian prisoners to recoup the enormous costs associated with such conflict, and the Apaches replaced losses from violence, disease, and low birth rates with prisoners they took during raids.

Running Indian slaves was risky business. A royal edict issued by Spain in 1800 stated that Havana, a prime outlet for captives until the Mexican Revolution of 1821, would accept no more Apache males. They were simply too violent, and Apache women were almost equally so. Records document one episode in which 51 female captives assaulted their dragoon guards and escaped.

Neither the Spanish nor the Mexicans were ever able to cope adequately with the raids. Writing in 1796, a colonial official admitted that the fault did not lie entirely with the Apaches, and suggested that the Spanish had themselves partly to blame for the wars, the inevitable legacy of "trespasses, excesses, and avarice."

The Spanish fared a little better in California, mainly because no tribes either as large or as belligerent as the Apaches inhabited this heavily populated corner of Indian America. Furthermore, the Spanish in California were never numerous, and missionary zeal took the place of military aggression.

Benevolent or not, the Catholic padres had to work long and hard for the few converts they won. The first mission founded in Alta California—San Diego de Alcalá—recorded no baptisms during its initial five months and only 83 after four years (1769-73). Nonetheless, many Indians eventually overcame their initial fears and joined mission communities, though less for the Christian faith than for food.

"Indians are usually caught by the mouth," admitted one Franciscan in a moment of candor. A favorite dish of the converts at Mission San Gabriel, located near what was to become the Pueblo de Los Angeles, was *pozole*, a thick soup made of pork or other meat, corn, and chile.

In California as elsewhere, the Indians soon tired of the strangers in their midst and, particularly, of the religious interference in their way of life. Probably reflective of widespread resentment are the comments recorded at the trial of Toypurina, a woman shaman arrested for plotting an assault on one of the missions: "I hate the padres and all of you for living here on my native soil . . . for trespassing upon the land of my forefathers and despoiling our

tribal domains." Her punishment was banishment to another mission.

As with New Spain, New France built a reputation for comparative tolerance of Indian lifeways. There is, however, little evidence to support the existence of any deliberate, pro-Indian policy on the part of the Bourbon rulers. Scholars disagree as to the reasons for the cordiality between the French and the Indians. Certainly, fur traders and their parent companies in eastern Canada possessed several advantages over English colonists in Massa-

chusetts and Virginia. First of all, the French did not begin life in the New World by dispossessing a native population: the site chosen for Quebec was uninhabited. Jacques Cartier described parts of Maritime Canada as ". . . the land God gave to Cain." It did not attract hordes of would-be settlers. More important, France directed its colonial economic strategy towards furs and fish, not farms, and French colonists generally went along with these aims. The Indians did not have to fear for their lands as did those who lived near English

Enduring legacies of the Russian colonial period in North America, double-barred crosses and an onion-domed church mark an Orthodox mission, founded in 1825 on Atka Island in the Aleutians. Although Czarist administrators such as Aleksandr Baranov, left, could be brutal with Aleuts, Eskimos, Tlingits, and other native peoples, the Russians sought furs rather than land and settlements. Below, an Aleut woven-grass purse bears the imperial Russian double-headed eagle and the inscription "His Imperial Highness."

colonists, who largely ignored their home country's colonial policy toward the Indians.

To make the fur trade profitable, the French needed Indian assistance, and they became both business and marriage partners. The magnificent *coureurs de bois* and *voyageurs*, woodsmen and masters of the canoe who kept trade and communication in motion, learned Indian tongues, married into tribes, and helped establish a far-flung trading network. The French eventually had so many personal and family ties to native groups that violence seldom seemed to be a solution to interracial problems. Furthermore, the Indians and their offspring appreciated French egalitarianism and camaraderie.

The French had their troubles, of course. The worst stemmed from perfectly good intentions and a solid relationship with the Hurons, a confederation of four highly organized woodland tribes living in Ontario near Lake Simcoe in a region known as Huronia. An Iroquoian-speaking people numbering about 20,000, they were recognized as great traders as early as 1600. Hurons and the other dominant tribe in the region, the Algonquins, welcomed the French and soon emerged as middlemen in the vast fur trading network of New France. Relations began well.

France was welcomed all the more warmly because the Hurons and Algonquins needed help against an old foe that threatened their very existence. So, unknowingly, France irritated the Iroquois. This rival alliance, a powerful and militant confederacy of five Iroquoian-speaking peoples, consisted of the Cayugas, Mohawks, Oneidas, Onondagas, and Senecas—joined in 1722 by the Tuscaroras. Obviously, the Iroquois were a force to be reckoned with, and it was the misfortune, albeit unintentionally, of the French to incur their wrath.

Samuel de Champlain is usually blamed for this antagonism, because it was he who assisted his Huron allies in two battles against the Iroquois, but he could hardly have done otherwise. Friendship with the Hurons was essential to the success of the French fur trade. Moreover, the friendly rela-

tions among the French and the Hurons and Algonquins had previously alarmed the Iroquois. As Canadian historian W. J. Eccles points out, "Champlain was merely an agent of existing forces; he did not create them."

The underlying problem was the insatiable Indian appetite for European trade goods. Just as French middlemen along the St. Lawrence River supplied the Hurons and Algonquins with guns and trade goods, Dutch and English merchants operating from stations in the Hudson River Valley served the Iroquois. Payment for goods received was in furs, and, when the desirable animals were depleted in one area, hunters sought out new hunting grounds, invariably infringing on another tribe's territory. Thus, the competition for European products served to increase and intensify existing intertribal rivalries and animosities.

An already unstable situation further deteriorated when Jesuit missionaries arrived in 1634. Competent, dedicated, and zealous, the French

priests fanned out across Huronia and became a potent force for change in the Northeast. At first, the Hurons tolerated the missionaries because they did not want to jeopardize their access to French trade goods, but, like their brethren throughout the New World, they became increasingly impatient with interference in their cultural life and demands to change their customs.

Had the plague not arrived simultaneously with the French priests, the Hurons might well have taken some action against the Iroquois during the 1630s. But disease carried away fully half of the Hurons, including many of their tribal elders and religious leaders. The Jesuits seemed impervious to the disease, and some of the Hurons blamed the missionaries for their problems and embraced their former religions even more fervently. Others saw a failure of the old gods and turned to Catholicism for protection. Ideological conflict rent Huronia as the confused and frightened Indians sought to restore order to their chaotic world.

Sensing vulnerability, the Iroquois embarked on a campaign of conquest during the late 1640s, seeking to expand their hunting grounds and also perhaps to replace their Huron enemies as middlemen in the lucrative fur trade. The final blow came in the spring of 1649 when Iroquois war parties, hundreds strong, surged into New France. Demoralized and desperate, the Hurons abandoned their villages and fled to the French for protection. To cope with the flood of refugees, the Jesuits resettled many of them on Christian Island in Georgian Bay. This proved to be a tragic mistake, for the French lacked the resources needed to support the refugees and, of 6,000 Hurons, fewer than 300 survived the winter.

Historian James P. Ronda blames well-intentioned but blindly ethnocentric Jesuits for the Huron disaster. In his words, "The mission dream was to produce a Huron society purified of its cultural sins and united by Christianity . . . . The dream became . . . a nightmarishly divided society, half Christians and half traditionalists, and fully at war with itself." Sadly, the Jesuits promoted the very conflicts and divisions they had hoped to prevent.

The collapse of Huronia also threatened the existence of New France as the Iroquois gained a strangle hold on lower Canada. The need to break this stalemate, to find and enlist other Indian allies, and to extend the fur trade led in later years to the explorations of René-Robert Chevelier de La Salle, Father Jacques Marquette, and Louis Joliet.

Backed by their Dutch and English patrons, the

An Aleut hunter prepares to harpoon a whale in an 1817 painting by Russian artist Mikhail Tikhanov. An Aleut man, right, portrayed by artist Louis Choris around 1816, wears a traditional hunting hat and waterproof parka, while the woman displays European clothing and an Orthodox cross.

Iroquois were not about to let the French expand into the lucrative Mississippi River Valley. Beginning in 1680, the Iroquois embarked upon a series of campaigns designed to destroy New France, and they nearly succeeded. By the end of the decade, Iroquois war parties were roaming the outskirts of Montreal.

Intermittent warfare continued for another ten years until both sides agreed to halt hostilities. French officials and Iroquois diplomats met in August 1701 at Montreal to work out a truce. The Iroquois had realized that they were exhausting their manpower for no useful purpose, while the French had seen that their real enemy was England and not the Iroquois. The negotiated peace ended a century of conflict between French and Indians, but set the stage for the wars of empire among England, France, and Spain that dominated the 18th century.

The Dutch had been eliminated as contenders for American empire before these other colonial power struggles engulfed the continent. Yet ironically it was the Dutch who had managed to upset the balance of power in these parts. Thanks to the efforts of English-born Henry Hudson in 1609, the Low Countries laid claim to an extensive area between the Hudson River and the Delaware, calling it New Netherland. Dutch interest in North America, however, remained largely commercial until the 1620s, when the first colonists arrived. Their most important community, New Amsterdam, started out as a fort on Manhattan Island.

Dutch relations with the Iroquois in New Netherland, where the Iroquois were the dominant group, were fairly harmonious, with the Dutch following a pragmatic policy, generally giving the Indians whatever they wanted. However, in wars of the 1640s, the Dutch drove the Algonquian-speaking Wappinger Indians from their traditional lands along the east bank of the Hudson and forced them to disperse among other tribes of the region.

Since the Iroquois wanted guns, the Dutch provided them, and the Iroquois became the scourge of New France, using firearms before other Indians could obtain them. The Dutch may have put business above common sense, but they did have the wisdom to keep guns out of the hands of their most immediate neighbors along the coast and to cultivate the trust of the Iroquois who operated in the interior. Indeed, so highly valued was this friendship that the Netherlands and the Iroquois established a formal alliance in 1618. Thus, when the English conquered New Netherland in 1664, they were heir to Dutch-Iroquois goodwill as well as to some remarkably strategic real estate.

From the early 1600s, growing international rivalries proved a mixed blessing for the tribes and their confederations. Competition between nations sometimes brought higher prices for skins and furs, but also opened the way for unsavory aspects of the fur trade, especially the introduction of alcohol, which Indians came to cherish but which soon debauched and demoralized entire peoples. In the long run, the international rivalries led to international warfare, yet another curse for the Indians.

An unidentified native of the Northwest Coast, left, adorns himself with a Chilkat blanket woven of cedar-bark fiber and dyed mountain-goat wool. Fighting knives, below, used by warlike peoples of the Northwest Coast, were often made of metal taken from shipwrecks.

Advancing to the tune of "The Grenadier's March," Gen. Edward Braddock and 1,300 British regulars fell into an ambush on July 9, 1755. Shown in the background, the English lost half of their number to 850 Frenchmen and Indians, allies in a series of wars for control of North America. Braddock might have avoided the trap had he used Indian scouts. Assigned to Braddock, young George Washington survived the disaster.

End of the Beginning

Eastern Indians were already beleaguered by the beginning of the 18th century. Pawns in the wars of empire, they found themselves increasingly entrapped by forces they neither understood nor welcomed. "We don't know what you Christians, English and French together, intend," lamented one Iroquois spokesman, "we are so hemmed in by both, that we have hardly a hunting place left. . . . We are so perplexed . . . that we hardly know what to say or think."

Despite their malaise, the Iroquois remained strong during the years leading to the colonial rebellion. They controlled parts of New York, Pennsylvania, and the Upper Ohio River Valley. Their power had long flourished in the complex colonial structure, drawing strength from the conflict of French and English ambitions. The Iroquoian alliance readily dispatched war parties 1,000 miles to punish enemies who had attacked their allies and they even crossed the Mississippi River to strike the Pawnees for such temerity. The Iroquois political system was so sophisticated that some scholars believe it influenced the framing of the United States Constitution.

Benjamin Franklin paid the Iroquois Confederacy a backhanded compliment when speaking at the Albany Congress in 1754. He said he found it hard to believe that the 13 American colonies could not agree to a political union when "Six Nations of ignorant savages" had formed one. Ironically, Franklin's proposed union would seal the fate of the Iroquois and others.

So long as several European powers contested control of North America and sought tribal partnerships, the larger Indian alliances could play one outsider against another. Thus the Iroquois, Hurons, and others were able to enjoy a modicum of prosperity and independence. However, the balance of power would not last. Between 1689 and 1763, four great wars of empire—King William's, Queen Anne's, King George's, and the French and Indian War—would leave the English colonists as the primary force, to the disadvantage of the Indians living in what would become the United States of America. Eastern tribes indirectly contributed to their own destruction by serving in the armed forces of all the contending countries. England, France,

PRÆVALEBIT ÆQUIOR.

A woodcut from 1758, above, depicts a symbolic struggle between the English, at left, and the French for the loyalty of the Indians.

Spain, and the American colonies all came to appreciate Indian military support and allegiance as much as Indian furs and land.

To attract and retain tribal loyalty, the colonial powers developed a whole panoply of gifts and ceremonies built around the concept of the "delegation." The need for delegations is explained by the fact that leadership within tribes was a shared responsibility. Nowhere in aboriginal North America, except perhaps in the empires of the Southeast and Mexico, could single Indian leaders speak for an entire tribe and expect their decisions to be followed. Nations conducting business needed to deal with a group of leading elders and warriors; hence the emergence of delegations as a component of Indian-white relations.

The French evidently conceived the idea of nurturing tribal military support by transporting

delegations to the royal court. According to John Nelson of Boston, a former captive of the French, the Bourbon rulers frequently invited "a few of their most eminent and enterprising Indians" to Versailles. Writing in 1696, Nelson urged the British Board of Trade to counteract French influence among the Indians by inviting prominent chiefs to England. A few such visits would "give counterpoise to the French reputation and greatness," he predicted.

The first formal Indian delegation visited England in 1710. Consisting of three Mohawks and one Mahican known as the "Four Kings," they had been assembled by New England officials who wished to persuade Queen Anne to support colonial plans for an invasion of New France. The delegates included Hendrick, one of the most influential leaders of the Iroquois Confederacy, and Brant, grandfather of the celebrated Joseph Brant, who was such a valuable ally of the British during the American Revolution.

Before their trip to London, the delegates first visited Boston, where they received a "correct impression" of British military strength. A martial display of spectacular proportions provided the highlight of their visit as the chiefs sat in a dinghy surrounded by five British ships-of-the-line. On signal, the gunners touched off their cannons, "first from their topps & decks in platoons, and then with their great guns upon one an other until we were all lost in Smoak," marveled one witness. The Iroquois were impressed. They urged the British to begin the invasion at once, saying "we have already too manie Men to take All Canada."

The delegates reached London in April 1710, where they enjoyed a round of social and diplomatic festivities normally bestowed on foreign potentates. They reviewed four troops of the Life Guard at Hyde Park, they appeared before the Commissioners for Trade and Plantations, they rode the queen's barge to Greenwich, they visited a hospital and a workhouse. The Bishop of Norwich received them and the Lord Bishop of London preached a sermon to them at St. James' Chapel. William Penn took them to dinner at the Devil's Tavern in Charing Cross.

The audience with Queen Anne was, of course, their most important appointment of all. Obviously well coached by their colonial patrons, the Iroquois urged the queen to capture Canada. Great economic benefits would accrue both to England and her Iroquois allies should this happy event occur. If Her Majesty did not see the wisdom of this action, the delegates suggested, then they must either forsake their homeland or remain neutral in the current struggle with France, neither of which they wanted to do. By all accounts the fruits of the visit exceeded all expectations. Queen Anne heeded their plea for assistance by paying more attention to England's Indian allies as she intensified the colonial struggle with France. At the very least, the visit cemented the already strong friendship between England and the Iroquois Confederacy.

According to one British historian, "the link formed by this long and strange journey of these foreign envoys became one, and not the weakest one, in the chain of loyalty of Indian to England."

Many courtesies and gifts helped win over the Indians and such favors became an important aspect of the delegation experience. The people of London lionized the sachems, showering them with attention and souvenirs. To aboriginal eyes the conferring of gifts held special significance, and a failure to provide a generous supply of presents foredoomed diplomatic missions. An American Indian agent probably expressed it best when he declared, "Without presents, an Indian has no ears."

The chiefs most valued those gifts that denoted authority, such as medals, flags, canes, commissions, and uniforms. Of these, medals ranked highest in the eyes of the Indians and all the colonial powers, including Russia, gave them to leaders. Made of solid silver and bearing the likeness of the reigning monarch, these decorations often came in two sizes, with the larger ones going to the principal chiefs of a tribe or band. Customarily suspended from a wide, colorful ribbon, the medals were bestowed with great pomp and ceremony. Indians so valued these impressive tokens that they often took them to the grave. One recently unearthed near California's Fort Ross bears an imperial crest on the obverse and, in Cyrillic letters, the message "Friend of Russia" on the reverse.

Although less durable than medals, flags were also treasured. All European nations are known to have presented them to Indians, yet few flags survived because the chiefs kept them on display in their villages until they disintegrated. A Spanish official, writing in 1779, claimed that most of the Indian villages around St. Louis could boast only a flagpole adorned with "some rags full of holes and patches."

The Spanish also presented their loyal Indian vassals with the cane, or *baston* (staff of office). A uniquely Spanish symbol of authority, it reached Indians of New Spain as early as 1690. So essential were such gifts to Indian friendship that the United States, upon gaining its independence from England, had no choice but to continue the tradition. For instance, the symbolic value of the

Mohawk Chief Tiyanoga, or Hendrick, below, sailed to England with two other Iroquois leaders in 1710 to meet with Queen Anne. He died fighting for England 45 years later at the Battle for Lake George, right. This major British victory helped ignite the worldwide Seven Years' War.

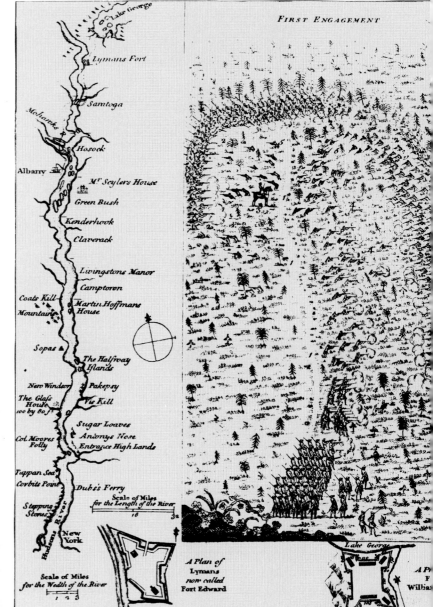

Spanish cane was acknowledged by the United States in 1863 when President Abraham Lincoln gave one to each Pueblo tribe of the Southwest in recognition of friendship.

These diplomatic gifts were more than mere secular symbols of allegiance and authority. Among some tribes they took on religious qualities. Jean-Baptiste Truteau, a St. Louis fur trader who visited an Arikara village in 1795, noticed that the head chief displayed a Spanish flag at the entrance to his earth lodge and wore a medal around his neck. Inside, the chief had arranged a sort of altar for his Spanish commission and burned incense before it. "They hold such things as medals, flags, and letters in such deep veneration," Truteau explained, "that whenever these are taken from their wrappings,

they are smoked and hold the most important place at their feasts." This smoking, or ceremonial puffing of tobacco smoke on objects of merit, was apparently designed to propitiate the spirit residing in the piece.

As the outbreak of the wars of empire grew ever closer, many Indian leaders embraced the French. This seemed the wisest course to them as Frenchmen acted both reasonably and sympathetically. The French made no demands on their land and spoke with one voice, whereas the different English voices represented conflicting interests—the Crown, individual colonies, and various land speculators, traders, and other opportunists.

Aware of the problem, the British Board of Trade decided to organize and centralize Indian affairs in

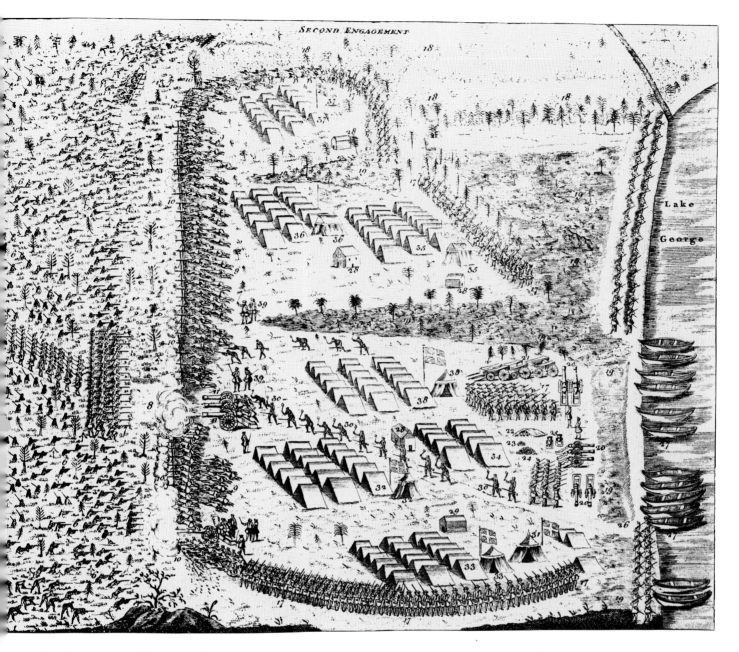

Lake George

the American colonies under a superintendent. This decision was important because it prefigured the Indian administration later adopted by the United States. In the end, the board appointed two superintendents: William Johnson in the North and Edmund Atkin in the South.

Though timely, coinciding as it did with an outbreak of hostilities in the French and Indian War (1754), the appointments added little to military effectiveness. Once again Indians played a significant role, but most of their efforts were on the side of the French. The greater problem of trust, and the English lack thereof toward Indian auxiliaries, is illuminated by the crushing defeat of the British General Edward Braddock.

Fewer than ten miles from his objective at the site of modern-day Pittsburgh, and with young George Washington in attendance, Braddock was maneuvering as part of a grand plan to end the war handily. Disdaining to fight Indian-style (in irregular lines, from concealment, and with the help of Indian scouts), the general and his force of 1,300 regulars were ambushed. Of the 850 men fighting for France that July day in 1755, two out of three were Indians. With 50 Indian scouts, one British official declared, Braddock and his troops would never have been trapped.

After Braddock's decisive defeat most of the Indian nations on the American frontier threw their support to the French cause, with only the Iroquois remaining uncommitted. Although they tried to remain neutral, several hundred Iroquois warriors

finally consented to aid the English, thanks to William Johnson, superintendent of Indian affairs. Formerly an English fur trader living in the Mohawk Valley, he had become such a fast friend of the Iroquois that the English commissioned him "Colonel of the Six Nations."

"Father of Six Nations" might have been an equally appropriate title. In addition to boasting several Indian wives, he sired perhaps 100 children during his long and productive career. Due to the generosity of his Iroquois friends he emerged as one of the largest landowners in colonial America. His last wife was Molly Brant, a Mohawk, whose younger brother, Joseph, became Johnson's protégé and a mainstay of the British during the Revolution.

Hendrick, one of the Four Kings who had visited England in 1710, responded to Johnson's plea for volunteers to help the British. Now 70 years old and extremely corpulent, he answered the call to arms along with 200 Mohawk warriors. Prior to the Battle of Lake George (1755), Hendrick reportedly said: "If . . . [my warriors] are to fight they are too

Trusted by the Iroquois, Irish fur trader William Johnson, below, succeeded in gaining them as allies for the British. Appointed Superintendent of Indian Affairs for the Northern Colonies in 1755, he established "Johnson Hall," left, near modern-day Johnstown, New York, as his home and diplomatic headquarters, where council meetings, like that in the foreground, were commonplace.

few; if they are to die, they are too many." His Mohawk warriors fought and many of them died, including the old sachem.

Unfortunately for France, Indian allies and a handful of victories were not enough to defeat England. The British simply put more soldiers on the land and more ships in the sea. So effectively did their fleet blockade New France that neither reinforcements nor supplies could reach the French army or their Indian supporters. One tribal auxiliary of the French grumbled that he and his com-

panions received "hardly a loaf of bread."

The war ended three years before it was officially concluded in 1763. A French defeat in Canada prefigured British victories in the South, where Spain's Creek and Cherokee allies entered the fight only to be soundly defeated, the Cherokees losing perhaps half their warriors. While a weakened Spain clung to Louisiana, the English managed to oust the French from North America. This last turn of events stunned the Indians of the Midwest. Tribes allied to the French for a century or more feared the

Above, in 1760, Ottawa Chief Pontiac offers the pipe of peace to Maj. Robert Rogers, who has conveyed friendly intentions from the British. His mission, he assured Pontiac, was to remove the French from Fort Detroit.

future as it quickly became apparent that the English victory had destroyed their bargaining power. Gloated one British officer, "We can now talk to our new Allies in a proper stile, as their services are not Necessary."

Indian apprehension and discontent only deepened when their experiences showed the English to be stingy, greedy, and vindictive. The French had given many presents and often allowed them to buy trade goods on credit. Not so the English, whose Indian policy was now being determined by harsh and arrogant officials such as Lord Jeffrey Amherst, head of the British military forces in North America. "When men of whatsoever race behave ill, they must be punished but not bribed," he ruled.

Amherst refused powder and shot to France's former allies, which angered them even more since they were now dependent on guns for hunting. If they died of starvation all the better, Amherst

believed. In fact, to hasten their demise, he suggested sending "the Small Pox among those dissatisfied tribes."

The fear and frustration of the Great Lakes groups finally erupted during 1763 in what is often called Pontiac's Conspiracy. Pontiac was a remarkable Ottawa chief whose village lay only a few miles from the site of Detroit. He listened to the message of an Indian messiah called the Delaware Prophet, who promised that the white men could be defeated if the tribesmen returned to their native ways.

Pontiac persuaded many of his neighboring tribes to join in a coordinated attack on a dozen British outposts in what was then considered the Northwest. Although his surprise attack on Detroit failed, most of the others succeeded as one by one the western posts fell to poorly armed but resourceful attackers. In one instance, Chippewa lacrosse players on Mackinac Island chased a loose ball into the fort and suddenly turned on the garrison. Only Detroit, Fort Pitt, and Fort Niagara remained in British hands by the end of July 1763.

The uprising eventually lost its momentum, and by summer's end militancy had given way to complacency as the warriors went home to resume

Foiled and furious, still clutching sawed-off muskets beneath their blankets, Chief Pontiac of the Ottawas and his party of chiefs and warriors leave Fort Detroit, above. They were ejected under guard after the discovery of their plot to seize the post from inside. Nine other forts fell to Pontiac and his allies during the rebellion of 1763. Right, threatened with the destruction of their villages, Indians return white prisoners taken during Pontiac's rebellion.

normal activities. Even Pontiac, who had been led to believe that the French would help him, returned to his village, but not before he had conducted one of the longest sieges in American history. He had remained outside Detroit from May 1763 until the end of October and left only when he realized that his Indian allies had long since abandoned the war.

Charismatic though he was, even Pontiac could not overcome the innate individualistic personality of the Indian, probably the most telling reason why coordinated resistance to the white man was so often doomed to failure. Nonetheless, Pontiac's patriots made Lord Amherst pay dearly for his arrogance. As many as 2,000 Englishmen were captured

The first frontiersmen to find a good wagon route through the Appalachians, Daniel Boone and his trail-blazing companions gaze at the woodlands of Kentucky in a Henry Beville painting, below. This party opened up the Cumberland Gap in 1769 and settlers swarmed into the Ohio Valley in violation of Crown regulations, further displacing many hunting-and-farming tribes of the East.

or killed before the end of hostilities. Pontiac himself made peace with the British, but by doing so he lost the support of his followers. He was murdered by a Peoria Indian in 1769.

The uprising brought some benefit to the Indians, however. The king's ministers immediately tried to address native concerns and did enact some worthwhile legislation. Most significantly, they produced the Proclamation of 1763, which prohibited settlement beyond a line drawn along the crest of the Appalachian Mountains. The British also tried to implement an equitable program to control the evils rampant in the Indian trade by issuing licenses and appointing Indian agents, but these high-minded efforts fell afoul of the colonists who were already resentful of British controls on American activities.

As a result, the regulations had little impact on Indian affairs. Without a qualm, squatters settled on Indian lands while traders reaped a swindler's harvest. Lord Dunmore's War of 1774 inevitably followed Pontiac's rebellion.

Shawnees and a handful of Mingo allies attempted to defend their rights against the onrushing whites, only to be swept aside by the Virginia militia. By this late date, whatever thoughts the British Crown might have entertained about native rights had become secondary to a more immediate imperial concern of enforcing royal rule over rebellious colonists.

For much of North America, Lord Dunmore's War closed the colonial drama, which had opened more than 280 years earlier with Columbus admiring "a loving people, without covetousness." From this "idyllic scene," wrote the late Indian historian D'Arcy McNickle, the Europeans "moved on to a definition of the rights of these loving people in the lands comprising their native world; then foundered on the problem of creating a defence of those rights."

The European system, which controlled much of the planet until the end of World War II, was challenged quite early and with success in the Americas. And though the United States turned the old colonial "way of the world" upside down, Indian peoples in the new land of liberty would swiftly lose what little freedom they had retained up to 1776.

Inheritance Lost

Overleaf: From before the Revolutionary War until the late 1800s, tipi encampments characterized Indian life on the Plains.

Ben Franklin, right, defended Indian rights during his term in the Pennsylvania legislature and wrote on tribal affairs.

A New Nation

Masquerading as self-reliant warriors, disgruntled Americans hurl English tea into Boston Harbor to protest taxes in 1773.

Among the Patriots, the break from the home-land was accompanied by a surge of discontent and resentment. This was aimed not only at the British but at any Indian ally of England, or merely any Indian. Revolutionary fervor instantly affected the lives and destinies of all the eastern tribes, though half a century elapsed before the shot fired in Massachusetts was "heard round the world" by the Indians in California.

From the Atlantic to the Pacific, for most Indians in the path of United States expansion, the Revolution opened the way for change unlike any seen in North America since Columbus. Colonialism's nearly three-century sway throughout North America was transformed dramatically because of this new republic. Not even the most visionary European statesman could have imagined such a nation when Spain initiated the struggle for New World land, riches, and political domination in 1492.

The bitter legacy of the War of Independence for the organized eastern tribes was their universal loss of both freedom and bargaining power. Whether friends or foes, combatants or allies, they all received much the same treatment after the Revolution. At best, all the tribes east or west were considered irrelevant to the future of the nation.

The Indians had little effect on the military outcome. Yet their participation produced two far-reaching emotional and psychological consequences that shaped white attitudes and government policies for decades. One was a reputation for brutality inspired by the atrocities that are inevitably alleged in every war. The other was the notion that the Indians deserved punishment for joining forces with the British.

At first, neither the Patriots nor the British planned to involve Indians in their conflict. It was not humanitarianism that prompted this attitude, however, but the knowledge that Indians did not follow the rules of "civilized" warfare. Neither combatant wished to tarnish its image in the parlors of Europe by being the first to enlist "savages."

Such scruples were soon discarded and the colonists made propaganda from the Indian style of warfare. According to the authors of the Declaration of Independence, King George had "endeavoured to bring on the inhabitants of our frontiers,

Connecticut missionary Samuel Kirkland, right, won the Oneidas and Tuscaroras to the Patriot cause at the outbreak of the Revolution. A carved hand decorates the end of a Seneca ball club, below, a weapon from the westernmost of the Iroquois tribes of New York. Most Iroquois warriors sided with the British. Col. Guy Johnson, opposite, portrayed with an Indian believed to be the Mohawk Chief Joseph Brant, took over as England's Superintendent of Indian Affairs for the Northern Colonies after the death of his father-in-law, William Johnson, in 1774. Speaking to the Iroquois about the rebellious colonists in 1775, he hoped British troops would "bring the people to their sences, . . . to shew them their great mistake, I expect it will soon be over."

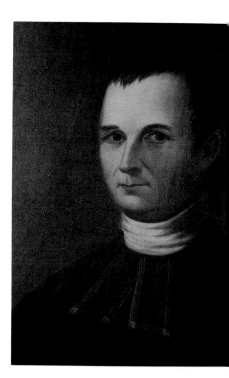

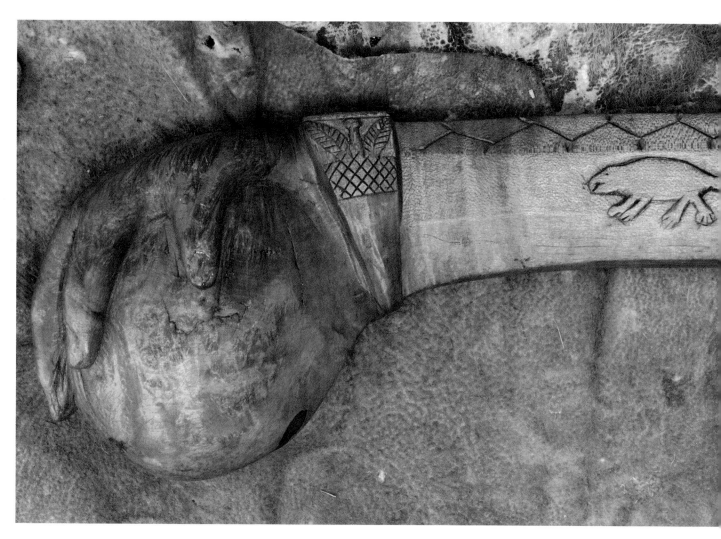

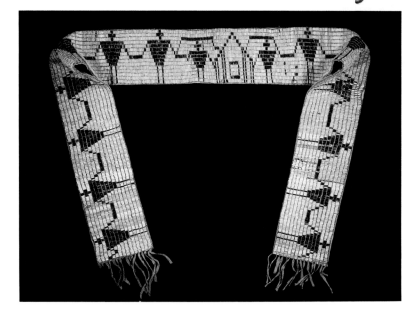

Well-armed, early-18th-century
Iroquois war chief, right, wears a
mix of traditional and European
clothes. Six-foot-long Washington
Covenant wampum belt, above, is
an Iroquois version of the 1794
Treaty of Canadaigua, intended to
protect their land claims in central and western New York. Map,
opposite, sketched by Guy Johnson
in 1771, shows the territories of
four of the six tribes of Iroquois.
The Tuscaroras and Oneidas lived
together, while most of the
Mohawks moved to Canada prior
to 1776.

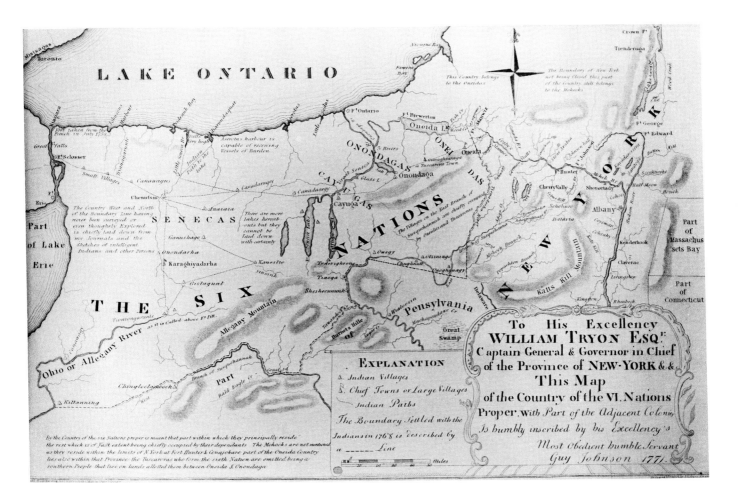

the merciless Indian savages, whose known rule of warfare, is an undistinguished destruction of all ages, sexes, and conditions."

Most Indians now were loyal to England because the better part of their trade goods came from there. The colonists could hope only for Indian neutrality since few tribes saw any reason to support the Patriot cause: most trespassers on their hunting grounds were colonists.

The fact that the Continental Congress offered the Delaware Indians their own state after the Revolution in return for their support indicates the desperation of the situation. This tender, which the Delawares rejected, resembled the clause in a 1785 treaty with the Cherokees allowing them to send a representative to Congress. Neither was likely to be accepted by the American public.

The Indians most directly involved in the Amer-

ican Revolution were the six member tribes of the powerful and primarily pro-British Iroquois Confederacy. By occupying a strategic location along the Hudson River, they were well situated to drive a wedge between the New England and Middle Colonies while forming a barrier between those colonies and the frontier.

Moreover, the seemingly insatiable land-hunger of the American colonists had already alarmed members of the confederation. At Fort Stanwix in 1768, the Iroquois—at the urging of their benefactor and superintendent, William Johnson, who profited handsomely from the transaction—established a line that was to fix the border between white and Indian settlements and prevent unlawful encroachments. In return for lavish gifts, the Iroquois ceded to the British Crown a large tract of land in central New York and Pennsylvania.

The Mohawks agreed to the pact even though they lived east of the line. Only after white settlers began to occupy their rich and fertile country did the Mohawks realize the blunder they had made. By then it was too late, and their only recourse was to move. In April 1773, they appealed to the Oneidas for a place of refuge: "Our lands are all claimed by the white people, even the village where we reside; the very ground under our feet."

Despite ample provocation, the Iroquois attempted to remain clear of the troubles between Great Britain and her rebellious subjects. Unfortunately, political factions within the tribes began to shred the spirit of unity that had sustained the confederacy for more than two centuries.

The factionalism was most severe among the Oneidas. Occupying four large villages in the vicinity of Oneida and Oriskany Creek in present-day New York, the Oneidas and their Tuscarora kinsmen were an acculturated people. They tended

thriving fields of corn and lived in substantial wooden dwellings with glass windows.

The Oneidas and Tuscaroras were also Christians, espousing the Presbyterian tenets of their beloved missionary, Samuel Kirkland, a New England Puritan and ardent Patriot. Kirkland, who claimed "a peculiar affection for Indians" since his youth, had a profound influence on his Christian converts despite subjecting them to church services of such length that even his own superiors censured him for being overzealous. Kirkland certainly exceeded the bounds of human tolerance, if this journal entry is a fair indication of a typical Sabbath: "I have had but half an hour retreat from eight in the morning to ten in the Evening—yet I feel as if I had done nothing for God—[and] am not only an unprofitable but an unskillful servant."

We have no way of knowing what God thought of His humble servant, but the colonists had reason for gratitude because Kirkland almost single-

An idyllic painting, opposite, by Thomas Davies, depicts Native Americans at the foot of Niagara Falls. By the mid-1700s, many Iroquois villages contained houses with glass windows, top. Elaborate diplomacy, including the giving of wampum, above, and ritual speeches marked Iroquois political life. The city of Salamanca, above right, lies at the center of the Senecas' Allegany Reservation in New York at the Pennsylvania border. Seneca veterans, right, (left to right) Stan Fox, Larry Pierce, and Raymond Jimerson attend a ceremony on the Cattaraugus Reservation. They are modern Iroquois warriors.

handedly kept most Oneidas and Tuscaroras from siding with the British during the Revolution.

As early as 1775, the Oneidas organized their own militia company under Captain Thawengarakwen (alias Honyery Doxtator). According to pension files in the National Archives, he "collected a company of Oneida Indians who were friendly to the Americans in their struggle for liberty, and entered into the military service of the Revolutionary War." He even recruited his wife, Dolly, who, at the Battle of Oriskany Creek, not only handled her own musket but loaded her husband's gun after a ball broke his right wrist. The Oneida militiamen performed admirably. Recalled one white comrade, they "fought Like Bull dogs." Their loyalty to the Patriot cause brought further personal sacrifice when their Iroquois kinsmen turned against them.

For Iroquois as well as for colonial families, the American Revolution was a civil war. One Oneida fighting with the Americans was captured by his own brother, a supporter of the British, who then handed him over to the Senecas for execution. Also loyal to the British side was Joseph Brant, a commander of the Mohawks commissioned as a captain. During July 1780 he stormed through the homelands of the Oneidas and Tuscaroras, burning their settlements and corn fields. Fleeing Brant's wrath, they appealed to the Continental Congress and spent the remainder of the war in army barracks in Schenectady, suffering grievously from cold, hunger, and smallpox.

Although the American Revolution exacted its heaviest toll among the Indians living on the northern frontier, it affected the southern tribes as well. Here the primary protagonists were the Cherokees under Chief Dragging Canoe. Angered and dismayed by continued encroachments upon their lands, the Cherokees ignored the advice of their British advisors and, in the spring of 1776, struck at outlying American settlements in Georgia, Tennessee, Virginia, and the Carolinas.

Within two weeks of the first attack, however, the colonial militia had begun to rally. The Cherokees soon found themselves confronting an enormous army of 5,000 to 6,000 frontiersmen converging on their villages from several directions. So swift and decisive was the retaliation that the Cherokees

Onondaga Chief Captain Cold, above, kept the Iroquois council fire burning on the Buffalo Creek Reservation until his death in 1847. Oren Lyons, above right, Onondaga chief and spiritual guardian, holds a passport issued by the Iroquois, who consider themselves a sovereign nation. Frontispiece from a 1786 spelling primer written in Mohawk and English, far right top, shows Mohawk children at school in Grand River, Ontario. Ninety-nine years later, kindergartners line up for class at the Akwesasne Mohawk Indian School on Cornwall Island, Ontario.

could do little but flee, leaving their own homes and fields to be laid waste by ax and torch. Instead of regaining ground already lost to the Americans, the Cherokees were forced to make still further concessions in a series of treaties inflicted upon them as the price of peace.

For the most part, the other southern tribes played a minor role in the Revolution. Realizing an American victory was not in their best interests, the Creeks, Choctaws, and Chickasaws wished to see the rebellion crushed. However, the British did not use their support wisely or well. An assault on the Spanish garrison in Mobile in 1780, for example, failed largely because of the cowardice of the Loyalists fighting alongside their Choctaw allies. A few months later, the valiant Choctaws were again embarrassed by their friends when British regulars failed to support them after they had fought their way through Spanish lines encircling Pensacola.

Although ill-served, England's allies among the

Chief Joseph Brant, above left, was a well-educated and charismatic Mohawk who led his people against the

Colonists during and after the Revolutionary War. A victim of American propaganda, he was depicted, above, as the murderer of prisoners in the Wyoming Valley of Pennsylvania during 1778. He was never there.

southern tribes remained loyal to the end. Sadly, they even sought to be evacuated from St. Augustine with the British populace in the waning days of the Revolution. "We cannot take a Virginian or Spaniard by the hand—We cannot look them in the face," declared one Indian leader upon learning that the British were leaving them behind. "If the English mean to abandon the Land, we will accompany them."

The St. Augustine commandant described the unhappy situation of his Indian allies: "The minds of these people appear as much agitated as those of the unhappy Loyalists on the eve of the third evacuation; and however chimerical it may appear to us, they have very seriously proposed to abandon their country and accompany us, having made all the world their enemies by their attachment to us."

As to the persistent, damning charge of Indian atrocities, the record indicates that both whites and Indians committed depredations. History books gloss over the fact that George Rogers Clark once ordered four Indian captives tomahawked within sight of Fort Vincennes in order to intimidate the British garrison into surrendering. Nor is the fact advertised that many frontier soldiers took Indian scalps as souvenirs and committed other acts considered beyond the pale of civilized behavior.

Until recently, historians chose to focus on Indian atrocities such as the brutal death of Jane McCrea, who fell victim to a quarrel among warriors fighting for General Burgoyne. Later immortalized by John Vanderlyn's dramatic painting, the highly publicized incident was used to great advantage against the British by Patriots even though the unfortunate victim was a Loyalist engaged to a soldier in Burgoyne's army.

White charges of Indian brutality, justified or not, had a positive effect on the course of the con-

Seneca Chief Red Jacket, below left, resisted white inroads on his land and people after the Revolution. His medal, in detail below, was presented to him by President George Washington in 1792. In a French map cartouche from 1776, opposite, Patriot and Tory fight over flags while a troubled Indian watches.

flict and, where survival was at stake, desperate Patriots were not above employing psychological warfare. One person who contributed more than his share to the Indian atrocity legend, apparently for propaganda purposes, was Benjamin Franklin.

Hoping to weaken British resolve at home, Franklin printed a page from an imaginary Patriot newspaper, titled "Supplement to the *Boston Independent Chronicle.*" It featured the report of a New England militiaman who had just captured a store of plunder from a Seneca war party. Supposedly included were eight large bundles of scalps the Senecas had taken from the heads of American colonists and were shipping to King George as evidence of Indian loyalty to the Crown.

A detailed inventory supposedly accompanied the scalps, certainly a literary device that does credit to Franklin's imagination and ingenuity. Bundle number one, for example, contained "forty-three scalps of Congress soldiers . . . stretched on black hoops, four inches diameter; the inside of the skin painted red, with a small black spot to note their being killed with bullets. Also sixty-two of farmers

killed in their homes; the hoops red; the skin painted brown, and marked with a hoe; a black circle all round to denote their being surprised in the night; and a black hatchet in the middle, signifying their being killed with that weapon."

Each bundle was described in similarly fanciful but believable detail. "A little red foot," painted on 98 scalps, indicated the victims had been farmers killed in their homes, having "stood upon their defense, and died fighting for their lives and families." Eighteen scalps marked with "a little yellow flame" were of prisoners who had been "burnt alive, after being scalped, their nails pulled out by the roots, and other torments." One bundle contained the scalps of 88 women; three others consisted of the scalps "of some hundreds of boys and girls." The inventive Franklin saved the worst for last—"a box of birch bark, containing twenty-nine little infants' scalps of various sizes; small white hoops; white ground; no tears; and a small black knife in the middle, to show they had been ripped out of their mothers' bellies."

A postscript by the "editor" describes the horror and indignation of the thousands of Bostonians who had seen the scalps. "It is now proposed," the editor noted, "to make them up in decent little packets, seal and direct them; one to the king, obtaining a sample of every sort for his museum; one to the queen, with some of the women and little children; the rest to be distributed among both Houses of Parliament; a double quantity to the bishops."

Foremost among Indian villains in the popular literature is the same Joseph Brant of the Mohawks, described by one 19th-century writer "as the most ferocious being ever produced by human nature." The Mohawk leader is often characterized as an evil monster who forsook his education and gentlemanly upbringing to unleash his bloodthirsty warriors on helpless settlements, most notably in the terrible raids in the Mohawk and Wyoming valleys where scores of civilians were murdered, including a number of prisoners.

As a matter of record, Brant was not even present in the Mohawk Valley during the raid, and he never condoned the brutality spawned by the Revolution. But it was hard to restrain his own warriors when frontiersmen slaughtered Indian women and children or dug up Indian graves to steal the burial gifts and scalp the corpses.

Brant, in fact, once returned a captive child with this note: "Sir, I send you by one of our runners the child which we will deliver, that you may know whatever others do, I do not make war on women and children." In a postscript evidently referring to the Tory rangers who usually accompanied his warriors on their raids, Brant added: "I am sorry to say that I have those engaged with me in the service, who are more savage than the savages themselves."

The Indians' post-Revolutionary troubles only began with the Treaty of Paris, by which the British surrendered all claim to their lands as far west as the Mississippi River, making no mention of Indian rights to this vast country. The Loyalist Indians were understandably outraged, as were the British officials most closely associated with them. At the very least, one official reasoned, England should have held fast to the line drawn at Fort Stanwix in 1768. "It might have been easily reserved and inserted . . . which would have saved the Honor of Government with respect to that Treaty."

Quite simply, the American treaty negotiators believed the Indians no longer had rights to the western lands. As negotiator John Jay expressed it, "With respect to the Indians we claim the right of preemption; with respect to all other nations, we claim the sovereignty over the territory."

The outcome was particularly cruel for those Indians who had remained neutral during the Revolution or, ironically, those who had assisted the colonies. The Oneidas, for example, mark the end of the war as the beginning of their "time of troubles," a period of continued decline that did not end until well into the 20th century. Even though the Continental Congress guaranteed the Oneidas their New York lands, even though Oneidas fought and died with Patriot armies, even though Oneida corn sustained Washington's troops in their darkest hour that terrible winter in Valley Forge, the tribe received evil for good from the American colonies.

Between 1785 and 1842, the Oneidas negotiated with the state of New York more than 30 treaties by which they saw their land base reduced from some five or six million acres to little more than 1,000.

By then only a handful of Oneidas still lived in the state. The others were dispersed, some to Canada, others to Wisconsin. Overall, the covenant chain of the Iroquois Confederacy had been irreparably broken by the American Revolution.

Would the fate of the Iroquois Confederacy have been any different had all the members sided with the colonies? Barbara Graymont, an authority on the Iroquois, thinks not. "The Americans," she writes, "would never have permitted them after the war to maintain their community and their lands intact. The subsequent fate of the Oneidas and their Tuscarora dependents shows this truth only too clearly."

The immediate legacy of the Treaty of Paris was continued warfare on the frontier. Having obtained the western country from England as a result of the treaty, the new republic proceeded to incorporate it into the United States. The fact that several militant and angry tribes still occupied the land seems to have had little impact on the Founding Fathers.

In the Ordinance of 1787, the document which provided for the administration of the Old Northwest (today's Midwest east of the Mississippi River), the government notes that "the utmost good faith shall always be observed towards the Indians; their lands and their property shall never be taken from them without their consent; and in their property, rights and liberty, they shall never be invaded or disturbed, unless in just and lawful wars authorized by Congress. . . ."

Several "just and lawful wars" were not long in coming. The Indians of the Old Northwest, having witnessed the fate of their eastern brethren, were determined to prevent a similar takeover of their own country. These tribes, primarily the Delawares, Miamis, Wyandots, Ottawas, and Potawatomis, formed a loose confederacy and declared the Ohio River the boundary between whites and Indians. The United States, however, recognized neither the confederacy nor the boundary, making conflict inescapable.

Indian resolve in the Old Northwest drew strength partly from the continued presence of British traders and officials, who viewed the results of the Colonial rebellion as a temporary setback, not a defeat. At issue was a string of military posts

The U.S. Army's Fort Harmar, above, shown here in an 1842 lithograph, was built on the Muskingum River in the 1780s in a vain attempt to prevent white settlers from invading Indian lands of the Ohio country.

controlling the waterways along the Canadian-American border, with England very reluctant to surrender them as required by the Treaty of Paris. The posts, in fact, remained a source of tension between England and the United States until Jay's Treaty resolved the matter in 1794.

Great Britain's desire to hold the posts was motivated in part by concern for the welfare of her former allies, in part by the economic benefits that accrued from the thriving Great Lakes fur trade. British advisors, who certainly helped the Indians form their confederacy, were hoping to establish a buffer state between the Ohio River and Canada that would both protect the region from American encroachment and allow Great Britain to continue its control of the fur trade.

Two obstacles prevented this imaginative solution from being implemented. One was the inability to get the various tribes to work in concert. In January 1789, for instance, a handful of tribal leaders decided to break faith with the British. They met at Fort Harmar on the Ohio River and signed a treaty with the United States by which they accepted the terms of previously contested agreements in exchange for $9,000. Incidentally, this was the first time the United States acquired land from Indians by purchase instead of conquest.

The other obstacle to the Indian state was the fact that white people living on the frontier, many of them Scotch-Irish, were exceedingly clannish and determined to support each other in their westward career. A law unto themselves, they had no intention of honoring boundary lines, regardless of the consequences.

Those who settled beyond the boundaries soon ran into trouble that they could not handle by themselves. Indians may have killed as many as 1,500 Kentucky settlers between 1783 and 1790. The continued influx of settlers into the Ohio country outraged the Indians and, as a result, the United States found itself at war with the northwestern tribes before the year 1789 was out.

The Indian wars of the Old Northwest are a monument to frontier greed and arrogance. Rather than trying to work out an equitable solution to Indian grievances, which would have meant bridling frontier aggression, federal officials chose instead to send two punitive expeditions against the Ohio tribes. Both expeditions were soundly thrashed. The first, under the command of General Josiah Harmar, walked into an ambush along the Maumee River that cost 183 American lives. Not deterred by that encounter, federal officials launched an

even more ambitious assault on the Ohio tribes the following year.

This time the Indians won a stunning victory. At dawn the morning of November 3, 1791, warriors led by Little Turtle of the Miamis and Blue Jacket of the Shawnees surprised the encampment of Arthur St. Clair, governor of the newly created Northwest Territory. St. Clair and a handful of soldiers eventually stumbled to safety, having left behind 630 dead and 283 wounded comrades. The defeat was the worst ever suffered by American forces against Indians. It destroyed the army—and the governor's career.

Little Turtle and his allies now considered themselves invincible, a belief reinforced by British assurances of support. This time the Indians had reason to believe the promises because the British built a new post, Fort Miami, below Detroit on the Maumee River in violation of the Treaty of Paris.

120

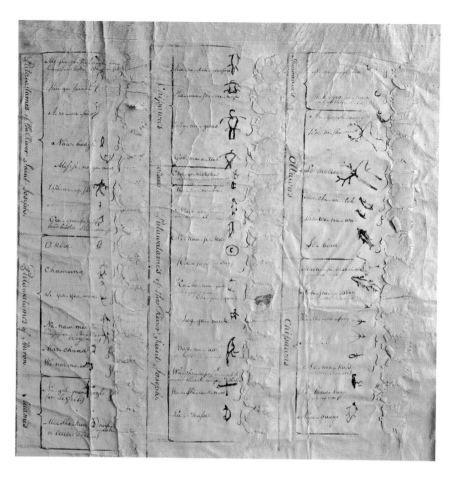

In a representation of the turning point at the Battle of Fallen Timbers of 1794, left, Gen. Anthony Wayne's dragoons crush the last organized Indian resistance in the Ohio country. The peace treaty dictated by Wayne at Fort Greenville in 1795, right, forced the Miami Confederacy, Shawnees, Wyandots, and others to give up most of the present-day state of Ohio and part of Indiana. Signatures of some of the 1,100 chiefs and warriors who signed the Treaty of Greenville appear right, top.

I Alexander McGillivray, Agent to the Creek nation of Indians, and Brigadier-General in the service of the United States, do solemnly swear to bear true allegiance to the said United States of America, And to serve them honestly and faithfully against all their enemies or opposers whomsoever, and to observe and obey the orders of the President of the United States of America, And the Orders of the Officers appointed over me, According to the articles of war, and the true intent and meaning of the secret articles of the treaty of peace, made and concluded between the united States of America, and the Creek nation of Indians, On the seventh day of the Present month of August

Alex: McGillivray

Sworn before me in the City of New York
This Fourteenth day of August in the year
of our Lord One thousand Seven hundred and
ninety.

John Blair   an associate judge of the supreme
Court of the United States —

In the presence of
HKnox Secy of War

The secret oath of allegiance to the United States, above, signed in 1790 by Creek Chief Alexander McGillivray, suggests this leader's diplomatic skills. Of Scottish, French, and Indian ancestry, McGillivray played Spanish Florida off against the United States.

President Washington responded by giving "Mad Anthony" Wayne command of the western army. A seasoned veteran of the American Revolution, Wayne prepared carefully and systematically for his eventual showdown with Little Turtle. Instead of rushing into combat, he spent the better part of two years drilling and disciplining his troops and building a series of forts along his line of march.

Little Turtle and a small contingent of his Miami followers were with the force of 2,000 warriors that took up a position in a tangle of brush and storm-tossed trees known as Fallen Timbers, near present-day Toledo. The methodical Wayne took so long to get there, however, that many of the restless Indians simply became tired of waiting. Some returned to their villages; others were lounging about Fort Miami, four miles away, when the American attack finally came.

The Battle of Fallen Timbers was brief and there were few casualties. Although only 50 Indians died in the fighting, it was a psychological disaster for the Ohio tribes, who discovered at the last moment that the British had no intention of coming to their aid. In fact, the garrison at Fort Miami shut the gates against the retreating warriors. "This," Joseph Brant later muttered in disgust, "is the second time the poor Indians have been left in the lurch."

Broken in spirit, the Indians watched meekly as Wayne razed their villages, burned their crops, and built Fort Wayne at the head of the Maumee. The final insult inflicted upon the disheartened tribes was the Treaty of Greenville, which Wayne dictated and Little Turtle and others signed in August 1795. In return for minor financial concessions, the midwestern Indians surrendered most of Ohio and part of Indiana and then, embittered and demoralized, retreated once again into the American wilderness.

Of the southern tribes, the Cherokees were still smarting from their defeat during the Revolution, while the Chickasaws and Choctaws, who lived far from the settlements, remained peaceful but cautious. Not so the Creeks, whose country was being overrun by speculators and settlers from Georgia, dubbed "People-greedily-grasping-after-land." Armed and encouraged by the Spanish, who still occupied east and west Florida, the Creeks were at war with the Georgians in a conflict that threat-ened to engulf the entire southern frontier.

Leader of the Creeks was the frail but gifted mixed-blood Alexander McGillivray, an astute and canny diplomat who managed to act as a middle-man between both nations. McGillivray had visions of a southern tribal confederacy similar to the one north of the Ohio but under the influence of Spain, because he realized the Creeks alone could not long withstand the pressure on their lands from the citizens of Georgia.

Hoping to win McGillivray's friendship, President Washington invited him and other Creek leaders in 1790 to New York City, where they signed a treaty of friendship. Although secret clauses made McGillivray a general in the U.S. Army and awarded him an annuity of $1,200, the treaty did little more than anger the people of Georgia, who saw it as an impediment to evicting the Creeks from their state.

When McGillivray died in early 1793 the Creeks were thrown into turmoil, and no other states-man rose up to take his place. The factionalism that emerged eventually erupted into a civil war that was played out upon the broader stage of the War of 1812.

In fairness to federal officials, the alienation of tribal peoples was not entirely willful. The Founding Fathers were preoccupied with persuading a doubtful international community to take the United States seriously and with convincing their own countrymen that an independent union of the colonies was viable. They simply overlooked the original owners when the time came to form a working government.

One needs no better evidence of this than an examination of the United States Constitution. Only once does this venerable and time-tested charter of American democracy even mention Indians—in the simple five-word phrase "and with the Indian tribes" apparently added as an after-thought to the commerce clause. Upon this slender hook was eventually hung an enormous structure of federal legislation, Supreme Court decisions, Indian agencies, superintendencies, and the Bureau of Indian Affairs.

Although almost all components of what was to form the "Indian policy" of the United States were borrowed wholesale from British practices, the new nation inaugurated one unique program, the "factory system." Humanitarian in concept and mercantile in nature, the plan provided for a network of government-operated trading houses. These outposts were to stock quality merchandise and offer it at little more than cost to their Indian patrons in exchange for their furs. Factors were to be literate, trustworthy, and interested in the welfare of the Indians.

The system opened in 1795 with two stations, one for the Cherokees and one for the Creeks, but others were intended for all tribes. In time, the factories would make the Indians completely dependent on American trade goods, thereby winning them away from Spanish and English influence. Once that was achieved, commerce rather than costly military garrisons could be used to control the Indians on the frontier: the threat of deprivation would supposedly keep them peaceful.

Trading posts such as the one depicted at left gave many western tribes access to manufactured goods in exchange for pelts. European demand for furs drove white trappers ever westward into Indian country. Above, beaver on the Missouri River are pictured by artist Karl Bodmer.

Too many countervailing forces doomed the factory system. Not only did private American fur traders resent the government competition and the United States Congress give only token support to what could have been a significant humanitarian program, but also the Indians preferred British and Spanish trade goods and friendship. In fact, Indians looted and burned several trading posts during the War of 1812. These losses, along with the effective opposition of fur magnate John Jacob Astor and others, persuaded Congress to abolish the system a few years later.

If given half a chance, however, the factories might have succeeded in winning Indian friendship to the United States. Wrote one Canadian observer in 1812, "Of all the projects of Genl Washington, after effecting the separation of those Colonies from the mother country; I apprehend this of the Trading houses best calculated to undermine the influence of Great Britain, with the Indians."

Banner and eagle over New Orleans, below, and Napoleonic emblem, opposite, confirm the Louisiana Purchase of 1803. The ornate "skippet" with its wax impression and case came with the deed. This vast land deal sealed the fate of tribes caught in the path of Manifest Destiny's westward expansion.

Indian Destiny Sealed

The election of Thomas Jefferson as President in 1800 heralded both the beginning of a new century and dramatic changes for Indians on both sides of the Mississippi. All the scattered actions and events were part of a vast process of migration and settlement called Manifest Destiny, whose outriders, Lewis and Clark, would soon trek to the Pacific and blaze a trail for others.

Now managing its own affairs, the United States turned its attention away from Europe and toward an unspoiled continent ready for the taking. Yet barriers appeared, often the work of the British, who still hoped to reclaim the 13 breakaway colonies. England was anxious to preserve its empire and to regain its rights over and dues from both white men and red.

Patriots, who had hung together so as not to hang separately, knew that Great Britain had nooses to spare. They expected a British attempt to strangle this newborn nation in its cradle and they did not have long to wait. The War of 1812, called by some America's Second War of Independence, saw the forces of Manifest Destiny gain strength, however.

Mandan Indians near the Missouri River touch York, slave of Capt. William Clark, during Lewis and Clark's transcontinental trek of 1804 to 1806. Indians often attributed great powers to York's black skin color and tried to rub it off.

Great Britain, France, and Spain—all three still players in the game of North American empire at the turn of the century—lost power and influence, but Manifest Destiny brought manifest disaster to the Indians. Their time of desperation was at hand.

Taking advantage of France's need for capital during the Napoleonic Wars, America made the Louisiana Purchase of 1803 and consolidated her claim to lands west of the Mississippi River as France retired from contention. With Americans in ever greater numbers crossing the Appalachians to settle Kentucky and the lands beyond, Old Dixie emerged overnight as the far western frontier. Landless and dispossessed people around the globe looked to the United States for the good soil and fresh opportunities which this new country provided, though all comers would take land and livelihood from the Native Americans. In the meantime, Britain's noose tightened around the collective neck of the young United States and all the rancor and spleen of revolutionary days returned.

Perhaps no program could have prevented the violence that engulfed the American frontier during the War of 1812. In addition to briefly sustaining European colonial ambitions, this inglorious conflict also provided the last hope of Indians in the path of Manifest Destiny. They fought to maintain some semblance of freedom and to contain the young republic that threatened to overwhelm them. British and Spanish intrigue found a receptive audience among disaffected and embittered tribes.

Indians readily seized opportunities to redress grievances that had simmered for decades. Their catalyst was the message preached by two Shawnee nationalists: one the famous warrior Tecumseh, often described as the greatest Indian who ever lived; the other his brother Tenskwatawa. As a teenager, Tecumseh fought with the British in the Revolution and stood in the forefront of the action on the Ohio frontier, losing a brother at Fallen Timbers.

By 1805, at age 37, he had become an ardent nationalist, advocating united Indian resistance to all whites. Eloquent and visionary, Tecumseh exhorted the midwestern tribes to form a great confederacy in order to halt the tide of American expansion. He declared, "Where today are the Pequots? Where the Narragansetts, the Mohawks, the Pocanets and many other once powerful tribes of our people? They have vanished before the avarice and oppression of the white man, as snow before a summer sun. . . ."

Vital to Tecumseh's success was his younger brother Tenskwatawa, "the Open Door," also known as "the Prophet," a holy man and mystic. Some historians, most notably R. David Edmunds, believe that much of Tecumseh's success was due to his brother's influence: "Throughout American history, during periods of significant stress, Indian people traditionally have turned to religious leaders or revitalization movements for their deliverance."

The Shawnee Prophet may have been hailed in his day, but it is Tecumseh, owing in part to his hero's death on the battlefield, whom history remembers. Yet regardless of who deserves the credit, the brothers managed to attract followers from many midwestern tribes. Tecumseh and the Prophet urged the various peoples to surrender no more land, return to traditional lifeways, and forsake all alcoholic beverages and other corrupting influences of the white man. Within a few years, the brothers had assembled a sizeable community of believers at Prophetstown, a thriving village at the junction of the Wabash River and Tippecanoe Creek.

Although the presence of Prophetstown alarmed nearby white communities, the Indiana frontier remained calm until Governor of the Indiana Territory William Henry Harrison induced some Potawatomi and Delaware chiefs to sell additional tribal lands. According to the Treaty of Fort Wayne, signed in September 1809, the government obtained three million acres for an initial $7,000 in cash and

$1,750 a year thereafter. This brought the total to 110 million acres of Indian land the government had obtained since 1800. Another Indian war became inevitable when Harrison ignored Tecumseh's plea to rescind the treaty.

Leaving Tenskwatawa in charge of Prophetstown, and with strict orders to maintain the peace, Tecumseh (whose mother was Creek) carried his message to the southern tribes. The white man must be destroyed, he exhorted his Creek kinsmen: "Burn their dwellings. Destroy their stock. The red people own the country. . . . War now. War forever. War upon the living. War upon the dead; dig up their corpses from the grave; our country must give no rest to a white man's bones."

Tecumseh's message found a receptive audience among a faction of militant Creeks known as Red Sticks (after the painted charms they carried into battle), but the wily Harrison struck first. His force marched upon Prophetstown and provoked an attack by Tecumseh's outnumbered followers.

Silver medallions, such as the Jefferson Peace Medal of 1801, above, were prized by Indian leaders. It bears the image of Thomas Jefferson on one side, clasped hands and crossed pipes on the other. European nations presented flags, medals, ceremonial staffs, and other official items to the Indians, and the United States continued the tradition.

The Battle of Tippecanoe boosted Harrison into the Presidency, but it could have cast him into oblivion. The Indians surprised his camp at night and fought him to a standstill. When they failed to gain the easy win predicted by The Prophet, however, they lost heart. Thus Harrison received an unearned and undeserved victory. The general could hardly believe that the Indians, whose losses were probably fewer than his own, broke off the attack and abandoned Prophetstown.

The defeat of the Indians at Tippecanoe did not prevent an Indian war, which ignited along the frontier and added its flames to those of the War of 1812. This latter, greater conflict eclipsed the lesser, and today few people realize that two wars of independence were being fought on North American soil in the second decade of the 19th century: one by the heirs of Adams, Jefferson, and Washington; the other by the heirs of Powhatan, Philip, and Pontiac.

Certainly no one fought harder than Tecumseh, who was the backbone of the British forces on the western front as they opposed America's westward advances. He directed as many as 15,000 warriors and was instrumental in the surrender of Detroit. Unfortunately, his ally lacked his courage and tenacity, and allowed the Americans to carry the fight into Canada. When the British retreated to Fort Malden on the Canadian side of the Detroit

Tecumseh, the Shawnee statesman from the Ohio country whose portrait appears at near right, saves a white captive from torture, below. After fighting for the British, Tecumseh turned to Indian nationalism after 1795 as the only way to retain Indian lands east of the Mississippi.

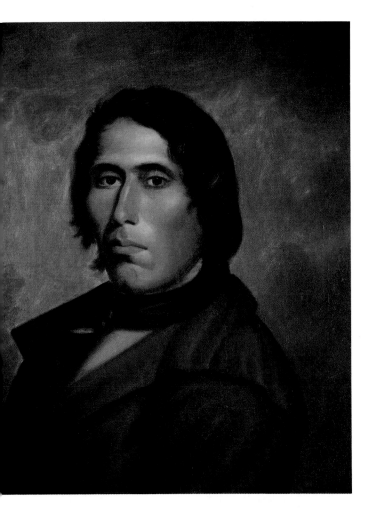

leading an army that included a large number of Creeks under McIntosh, as well as Cherokees and Choctaws, crushed the Red Sticks, led by Menawa, at the Battle of Horseshoe Bend. The militants refused to surrender and 700 or more died, trapped on a gooseneck of Alabama's Tallapoosa River. One of the few survivors of this battle on the oxbow was Menawa, though he had been shot more than a dozen times.

Another forced cession of Indian lands followed under the harsh terms of the Treaty of Fort Jackson, which the general imposed five months later. Creeks gave up their holdings in Alabama and along the northern fringes of Florida. Again dem-

Tenskwatawa, below, whose name meant "The Open Door," was Tecumseh's brother. A holy man and mystic who helped spread the gospel of a single Indian nation, Tenskwatawa also taught the value of traditional Indian ways, which were threatened at every turn by whites migrating west.

River in October 1813, Tecumseh sneered, "We must compare our father's conduct to a fat animal, that carries its tail upon its back, but when affrighted, he drops it between his legs and runs off."

Tecumseh fell soon after at the Battle of the Thames, and hope for Indian unity died with him. Yet the forces he had unleashed dominated events on the western frontier long after his death. His message ignited a civil war among the Creeks that pitted conservatives such as Menawa against pro-American progressives, including the mixed-blood leader William McIntosh, whom the Creeks later killed for signing a treaty with the United States.

Civil war was only part of the undoing of the once powerful Creek Confederacy; Andrew Jackson was the rest. The government sent him to avenge a massacre by the Red Sticks of 460 people at Fort Mims on the lower Alabama River. Old Hickory,

DEATH OF TECUMSEH
BATTLE OF THE THAMES OCT. 18, 1813

Tecumseh, above, meets his death in 1813 at the Battle of the Thames in Canada. With him died the Indians' best hope of unifying the tribes. After the War of 1812, government land grants, as at left, gave soldiers land on the frontier. Many Americans believed that during the war the British paid bounties for scalps of United States citizens. The propaganda tract, opposite, contributed to this belief.

onstrating an inability to distinguish long-term consequences from short-term benefits, 1,000 Creeks and Choctaws joined Jackson and opposed their Florida kinsmen. The resilient Menawa, one of Jackson's aides in the invasion of Florida, was told that he would be able to remain on his lands in Georgia, and yet he, too, was eventually removed and died in Oklahoma Indian Territory. Jackson did keep his promise in another instance, allowing a tiny remnant of the once great Creek people to remain in southern Alabama near Atmore, reward for services rendered at Horseshoe Bend.

The Treaty of Ghent, signed December 24, 1814, ended the War of 1812 and crushed any remaining vestiges of Indian nationalism. Diplomats an ocean away once again determined the fate of North America's Indians. As late as April 1814, British agents had assured them that the king, "always true to his promises," would not quit the fight until their rights and independence had been restored. The pledge proved meaningless: the British did suggest establishing an Indian barrier state, but the idea quietly died during the course of negotiations. The treaty itself contained only one reference to the Indians, a vaguely worded section promising restoration of all their pre-1811 rights. When all was said and done, the only real losers in the War of 1812 were the Indians. "From 1815 on," declares historian William T. Hagan, "the red man had to deal strictly on American terms."

For generations and with varying degrees of success, the Indians of North America had been able to balance tribal interests against European demands. Both the Revolution and the War of 1812 changed all that. Most of the eastern tribes were in various states of disarray, although Ojibwas, Crees,

Choctaw Chief Pushmataha, above, and his warriors fought against the Creeks on the side of Andrew Jackson in 1811. Although hardly an admirer of Indians, the future president paid high compliments to his Choctaw ally. Political cartoon circa 1830 depicts Jackson as the Great Father to Indians, themselves shown here as dolls or puppets subject to his will, opposite. He sent thousands of real Indians packing to Oklahoma.

Menominees, Sioux, and Winnebagos—those living in the far northern woodlands—managed to retain a degree of cultural integrity.

The midwestern tribes, which had borne the brunt of the fighting after the Revolution, were in particularly desperate straits. To the west lay the Mississippi River, to the east the oncoming settlers by the hundreds of thousands. As the Sac and Fox tribes under Chief Black Hawk were about to discover, resistance now represented tribal suicide.

Equally precarious was the situation of the southeastern tribes. Clinging tenaciously to ancestral homelands in the heart of what was to become the Confederate States of America, the Cherokees, Creeks, Choctaws, and Chickasaws stood in the path of an advancing agricultural frontier. This phenomenon was fueled by a combination of high profits and cheap labor, the legacy of Eli Whitney's cotton gin and African slavery. The fact that many leaders of the so-called "civilized" tribes were more white than Indian and were slave-owning cotton barons in their own right merely added an ironic twist to their fate.

Only tribes living in the heartland of the Far West still enjoyed what could be called a traditional way of life, after giving due allowances for the changes being wrought by the horse, gun, metal tools, and other goods that were reaching them by means of age-old trading networks. Yet, however remote the tribe, it could not long escape the juggernaut of white expansion westward after the War of 1812.

Jefferson, the architect of Manifest Destiny, envisioned the Louisiana country as a haven for eastern Indians. He realized that it would only be a matter of time before the southern states would demand the expulsion of their Indian populations, and he hoped their removal across the Mississippi, a program his presidential successors warmly embraced, would be a happy compromise. Jefferson simply failed to anticipate the speed with which the West would be explored, mapped, settled, and exploited. He had good reason to believe as he did: the colonists had taken seven generations and 200 years to breach the Appalachian barrier. At that rate, Jefferson expected, the settlement of the wilderness from Ohio to the Pacific would take 40 generations. Hardly four were needed. Figuratively speaking, the United States had the particularly energetic tiger of Manifest Destiny by the tail, or vice versa.

First to suffer the consequences of the Louisiana Purchase were tribesmen of the Midwest. Some of them had long received goods and support from Spanish officials who had taken over St. Louis from the French. "They seemed to us like brothers, and always gave us good advice," declared Black Hawk, the Sac war chief. He learned of the land sale in 1804, during his annual summer visit to St. Louis. Everyone seemed sad and gloomy, he recalled. Upon seeking the cause of this unhappiness, he learned that the Americans were coming to take control of the city. "This news made me and my band exceedingly sad, because we had always heard bad accounts of the Americans from Indians who had lived near them. We were very sorry to lose our Spanish father, who had always treated us with great friendship," he said.

Unfortunately for the southeastern Indians, the Spanish were soon evicted from Florida as well. East and west Florida had long concerned the new republic because its coves and inlets were ideal havens for pirates. Runaway slaves and hostile Indians found the swampy terrain and Spanish officials equally protective. More than a decade of negotiations for Florida's purchase had produced indifferent results, but Jackson's victory over the Creeks in the War of 1812 accelerated the pace.

The Treaty of Fort Jackson established a new border between Spanish Florida and the United States and forced hundreds of angry Creeks to join their Seminole relatives. When southern planters occupied the former Creek country, their slaves took advantage of the nearby Spanish colony and

found refuge with the Seminoles and Creeks already living there. The planters asked the federal government to intervene because the Indians thwarted their efforts to recapture slaves.

An opportunity for federal action arose when Neamathla, a Creek chief, warned the Americans not to cross the Clinch River or cut a stick of his timber. The United States took this as a declaration of war and attacked Neamathla's village. Indians retaliated by ambushing a boatload of soldiers and dependents, killing or capturing 45 of 51 passengers. Andrew Jackson, now commander of federal forces in the Deep South, responded with an invasion of Florida. By the time the dust settled, Jackson had executed two British subjects and two chiefs, captured two cities, and evicted the Spanish government of Florida.

Jackson's invasion set the Indians back only slightly, for when soldiers arrived they simply faded into the Everglades to await a more opportune moment for revenge. It took a political disaster rather than a military one to cost them their Spanish benefactors. After neglecting its northernmost colonial outpost for three centuries, Madrid decided to sell Florida rather than lose it through seizure. On February 22, 1819, in exchange for five million dollars, Spain ceded to the United States all her holdings east of the Mississippi as well as all her claims to the Oregon country. The agreement also defined the limits of Spanish territory between the Mississippi River and the Pacific Ocean, thus opening a corridor to the Far West.

Expansionists now declared that the Indians had no right to stand in the way of progress. According to this view, which was quickly accepted, the eastern Indians now had but two alternatives: either become yeoman farmers and adopt the white man's way of life or retire across the Mississippi River to join their wild brethren.

The philosophy of the white advocates of removal was well expressed by William Henry Harrison following his victory over Tecumseh. Speaking of the land west of the Appalachians, he asked, "Is one of the fairest portions of the globe to remain in a state of nature, the haunt of a few wretched savages, when it seems destined by the Creator to give support to a large population and to be the seat of civilization?"

ᏣᎳᎩ   ᏧᎴᎯᏌᏅᎯ.

CHEROKEE PHŒNIX.

VOL. I.   **NEW ECHOTA, WEDNESDAY JUNE 4, 1828.**   **NO. 15.**

EDITED BY ELIAS BOUDINOTT
PRINTED WEEKLY BY
ISAAC H. HARRIS,
FOR THE CHEROKEE NATION.

At $2 50 if paid in advance, $3 in six months, or $3 50 if paid at the end of the year.

To subscribers who can read only the Cherokee language the price will be $2,00 in advance, or $2,50 to be paid within the year.

Every subscription will be considered as continued unless subscribers give notice to the contrary before the commencement of a new year.

Any person procuring six subscribers, and becoming responsible for the payment, shall receive a seventh gratis.

Advertisements will be inserted at seventy-five cents per square for the first insertion, and thirty-seven and a half cents for each continuance; longer ones in proportion.

☞All letters addressed to the Editor, post paid, will receive due attention.

ᏣᎳᎩ ᏧᎴᎯᏌᏅᎯ ᎠᏂ ᎾᏍᎩᏗᎧᎢ. ᏉᎡᏗᎶᏂᎯ ᏔᎯᎵ ᎤᏴ ᏒᎨᏓᎵ ᏆᎾᏗ. ᏏᎭᎴ ᏂᎭᏝᏯ ᏑᏔ ᎠᏑᏈ ᏦᏣᏱ ᏆᎾᏗ, ᏔᏇ ᏔᏍᎣᏛ ᏕᏣᎧᏌᏂ. ᏔᏇ ᏨᎴᏛ ᏔᏬᎳ ᏔᏰ ᏕᏣᎧᏌᏂ, ᎧᏔ ᏗᎥᏓ ᏩᏉᏒ ᏆᎾᏗ. ᏕᏣᎦᏌᏂ ᏅᎶ ᏯᏫ ᏕᏣᎧᏌᏂ, ᎤᏴᎵᏔ ᏓᏒ ᏩᏉᏒ ᏆᎾᏗ. ᏣᎤᏎ ᎤᏣᎳᏂᎰᎵᏌᎥ, ᏭᎳᏛ ᏗᏩ ᏪᏣᎵ ᏆᎾᏗ ᏗᏝᏂᏐᏂ, ᏔᏇ ᏔᏍᎣᏛ ᏙᎵ ᏣᎩᏌᏂ. ᎧᏔᎶᏃ ᏓᏒ Ᏼ ᏏᏉᏣᎵᎠᎥᎧᏘ. ᏳᎡᏗ ᏗᏣᎧᏌᏂ.

AGENTS FOR THE CHEROKEE PHŒNIX.

The following persons are authorized to receive subscriptions and payments for the Cherokee Phœnix.

HENRY HILL, Esq. Treasurer of the A. B. C. F. M. Boston, Mass.
GEORGE M. TRACY, Agent of the A. B. C. F. M. New York.
Rev. A. D. EDDY, Canandaigua, N. Y.
THOMAS HASTINGS, Utica, N. Y.
POLLARD & CONVERSE, Richmond, Va.
Rev. JAMES CAMPBELL, Beaufort, S. C.
WILLIAM MOULTRIE REID, Charleston, S. C.
Col. GEORGE SMITH, Statesville, W. T.
Rev. BENNET ROBERTS—Powal Me.
Mr. THOS. R. GOLD, an itinerant Gentleman.

LAWS
OF THE CHEROKEE NATION.
[CONTINUED.]

New Town Nov. 14, 1825.

Resolved by the National Co and Council, That a men drawn up and presented, th United States' Agent for to the Congress of the U claiming, & respectfully allowance of interest years annual instalmen sand dollars per 'annu the treaty of Tillico, 1804, which has rece ed on the part of the and that the proper p that this nation had here ed of the United States the fulfilment of the trea terest, also to accompany rial.

Be it further resolved, Tha munication be addressed to the ted States' Agent, for this n touching the non-compliance, on part of the Unicoy turnpike compa to make the annual payments, pro ed under the articles of agree granting the opening said road, request that measures may b to coerce the said Unicoy t

of said river opposite to Fort Strother, on said river; all north of said line is the Cherokee lands, all south of said line is the Creek lands.

ARTICLE 2. WE THE COMMISSIONERS, do further agree that all the Creeks that are north of the said line above mentioned shall become subjects to the Cherokee nation.

ARTICLE 3. All Cherokees that are south of the said line shall become subjects of the Creek nation.

ARTICLE 4. If any chief or chiefs of the Cherokees, should fall within the Creek nation, such chief shall be continued as chief of said nation.

ARTICLE 5. If any chief or chiefs of the Creeks, should fall within the Cherokees, that is, north of said line, they shall be continued as chiefs of said nation.

ARTICLE 6. If any subject of the Cherokee nation, should commit murder and run into the Creek nation, the Cherokees will make application to the Creeks to have the murderer killed, and when done; the Cherokee nation will give the man who killed the murderer, $200.

ARTIC
Creek
will
to
do
ma

from the time o
Hickory gro
Fort Jacks
at the time
this date.
sioners

William Hambly,   (Seal)
his
Big ✕ Warrior,   (Seal)
mark.
WITNESSES.
Major Ridge,
Dan'l. Griffin.
A. M'COY, Clerk N. Com.
JOS. VANN, Cl'k. to the Commissioners.

Be it remembered, This day, that I have approved of the treaty of boundary, concluded on by the Cherokees, east of the Mississippi, and the Creek nation of Indians, on the eleventh day of December, 1821, and with the modifications proposed by the committee and council, on the 28th day of March, in the current year. Given under my hand and seal at Fortville, this 16th day of May, 1822.
CHARLES R. HICKS, (Seal)
WITNESS,
LEONARD HICKS.

WHEREAS, The treaty concluded between the Cherokees and Creeks, by commissioners duly authorised by the chiefs of their respective nations, at General Wm. M'Intosh's on the eleventh day of December, (A. D.) one thousand eight hundred twenty one, establishing the dary line between the two na as this day been laid before bers of the national com the head chiefs and mem uncil of the Cherokee na ml. Hawkins, Sah,naw, e,ho,mot,tee and In,des. chiefs duly appointed and d by the head chiefs of the ation, for a friendly explan full understanding of the con ons to be placed on the differ icles contained in the aforesaid , and to make such alterations ay be conceived necessary for peace and harmony and friend existing between the two na ns; therefore, WE THE UNDER GNED, in behalf of our respective tions, do hereby enter into the lowing agreement; viz: he first Article of the aforesaid establishing the boundary be he two nations from Buzzard n the Chattahoochee river, in ne to Coosa river, opposite th of Wills creek, thence river opposite to Fort hereby acknowledged and be permanent. d 3d articles, maki citizens of both l within the limi ning the lin reof shall apel the mits of it, man, ridge, abbit, mer, owning, ulah, Smith, wal,loo,kee,

mitting murder on the subjects of the other, is approved and adopted; but respecting thefts, it is hereby agreed that the following rule be substituted, and adopted; viz: Should the subjects of either nation go over the line and commit theft, and he, she or they be bpprehended, they shall be tried and dealt with as the laws of that nation direct, but should the person or persons so offending, make their escape and return to his, her or their nation, then, the person or persons so aggrieved, shall make application to the proper authorities of that nation for redress, and justice shall be rendered as far as practicable, agreeably to proof and law, but in no case shall either nation be accountable.

The 10th article is approved and adopted, and all claims for thefts considered closed by the treaty as stipulated in that article.

The 11th article is approved and adopted, and it is agreed further, the contracting nations will extend their respective laws with equal justice towards the citizens of the other in regard to collecting debts due by the individuals of their nation to those of the other.

The 12th article is fully approved and confirmed. We do hereby further agree to allow those individuals who have fell within the limits of the other, twelve months from the date hereof, to determine whether they will remove into their respective nations, or continue and become subjects of that nation; and it is also agreed that in case the citizens of either nation, who may choose to remove into the nation of the other and become subjects, such person or persons shall be required to produce testimonials of their good character from the councils of their respective nations and present the same before the councils of the other nation; & should the chiefs thereof then think proper to receive and admit them, it may so be done.

In behalf of our respective nations, WE DO HE ADOPT the above modi anations of the of th the treaty es tab between th addi

ll
KILLER,
rk.
Going Snake,
Chickasawteehee,
RIDGE, Speaker.

ᎠᏍᏆᏴᏃᏟ, ᏭᎠᏉᎵᏃ ᏣᎥ ᏍᎭᏣᏪᏬᎢ ᎤᏔ ᏰᏍᎠᏰᎵ ᎢᎠᎾᏗ.
ᎤᏂᎪᎠᏎ ᏗᏍᏆ ᎤᏍᏪᎣᎢ, ᏣᏂ ᏦᎡᏦ, ᏆᎴᎪᎪ ᏗᏍᏆ ᏔᏂᎪ. ᏐᎢᏞᏯ.
ᏉᏝᏀ ᏣᎷᏍᎧᏇ, ᏓᎴᏨᏗᏔ, ᏗᏴᎡᏐᎦᏐ, ᎱᏇ.
Ꮢ. ᎳᎠᏎ, ᎵᏌᏉᎴᏯ ᏗᏍᏆ ᏔᏂᎪ.
ᏏᏉᏦ, ᎵᏌᏉᎴᏯ ᏗᏍᏆ ᏆᏉᎢ.

ᏔᎢᎵ, 14 ᎤᏟᏍᏕ, 1825.

ᏦᎵᏂᎵᏯ ᏗᏍᏆ ᏓᎧᏙᏴᎢᎣᏯ ᎤᏘ ᎠᎵᏬᎣᏓ ᏗᏫᏂᎪᏩᎣᏐ ᏔᏯᏯᏌ, 24 ᏗᏏᎫᏔ 1804 ᎬᏔ ᏒᏩᏒᏔᏌ ᏓᏅᏍᎶ ᎤᏮ ᏔᎧᏑᏴᏂ ᏗᏍᎦᏟ ᏗᏍᏆᏌᏎ, ᏗᏗᏌ ᏂᏍᏗᎧᎵᎣᏛ ᎬᎢᏒ ᎳᎮᎳᎠᎢ ᎢᏬ ᎬᏝᏌᏯ ᎢᏴ ᏒᏣᏂᏛ ᏣᎥ ᎬᎭᎵᏐᎵ ᎯᏍᏛ ᎠᎵᎧᎵᏂ, ᏔᏯᏯ ᏖᏗᎦᏫᎮᏎ ᎢᏑᏥᎢ ᏗᏌ ᎤᏱᏛᎵ ᎧᎠᏒ, ᎤᏝᎤᏍ ᏗᎧᏙᎵᏂ ᎢᏚᏎᏘ ᎤᏤᎷᏐ ᏔᏯᏯᏌ ᎤᏑᎬᎦ. ᏔᎵᏁᎬ ᎤᏗᏞᎧ ᎬᏫᏙᏈᎦ ᏣᎥ ᏔᏇ ᏔᏍᏔᎳ ᏗᎢᏬᎵᎢ, ᏔᏇ ᏏᏇᏳᏒᎯᎵ ᏣᎥ ᎤᎳᏎᏚ-ᎵᏄ, ᏔᏯᏯ ᏔᏇ ᏗᏩᎭᏌᏂ ᏘᎴᏓᎵᏯ ᏗᏫᎯᏌᏂ ᎤᎴᏎ ᏔᏇᏒ ᎤᎢᎵᏔ. ᏗᏗ ᎠᎳᏔᎳ ᏗᏜᏞᏄᏐ ᏣᎥ ᏗᏴ ᏗᏝᏐ ᏗᏥᏞ ᎳᎥᏑᎾᏐ 1819.

ᏗᏢᏯ,   ᏣᏂ ᏦᎡᏦ.
     ᏐᎢᏞᏯ.
     ᎤᏃᏨᏟᏔ,
     ᎲᏇ.
Ꮢ. ᏖᏍᏛ, ᏗᏍᏆ ᎵᏌᏉᎴᏯ.
ᏏᏉᏦ, ᎵᏌᏉᎴᏯ ᏆᏉᎢ.

ᏔᎢᎵ, 14 ᎤᏟᏍᏕ, 1825.

ᏦᎵᏂᎵᏯ ᏗᏍᏆ ᏓᎧᏙᏴᎢᎣᏯ ᎤᏘ ᎠᎵᏬᎢ, ᏣᏂ ᏦᎡᏦ, ᏘᏬᎬᏃ, ᏍᏩᏴᎬᏃ, ᏣᎥ ᎬᎦᎠᎳ ᎠᎵᏁᎵᏈ ᎤᏴᎫᎴᏍᏔ, ᏣᎥ ᎤᎣᏝᏌᎳᏌᎵᏫ ᏗᎷᏂᏐᏏ ᎤᎮᏐᎦᏌ ᎠᎳᎲᎥᎢ, ᏣᎥ ᏔᏇ ᏗᏩᎭᏌᏐᎵ ᏒᏒᏔᏐ ᏬᎠᏐᏘᏛᎠᎢ. ᏇᏈ ᏗᏩᏌ. ᎤᏨᎴᎠ ᎳᏯᏯᏌ ᏗᏔ ᏏᏥᏅ ᎵᏍᏪᎠᏬᎴ ᏈᏏᏈᎵᎪᏌ ᏣᎥ ᏚᏂᎤᎵᏯ, ᏗᏗ ᏔᏇᎵ ᏖᏍᏓᎮ ᎤᏇᎠᎵ ᏣᎥ ᏖᎥᎵᎥ ᏘᏏ ᏔᏬᎤᏥ, ᎲᎵᏐᎬ ᎠᏔᎵᎵ ᏔᏍᎦᎵᏟ ᎧᏂᎤᏏᏯ, Ꮙ ᏈᎶᏈ ᎲᏒ ᏔᏇ ᎤᏇᎯᎧᎵᏐᎵ, ᏗᏗ ᎮᎵᏐᎬ ᏔᏇ ᎤᏝ ᏖᎥᎳᎵᏐ ᎫᏗᎪᏍᎶᏌ ᏔᏯ ᏏᎵ ᏗᏍᏆᎳᎥᏐ.

ᏆᎵᏌᎳ ᏗᏍᏆ ᏓᎧᏙᏴᎢᎣᏯ, ᏣᏂ ᏦᎡᏦ, ᏘᏔᎦᏘ ᏗᏍᏆ ᏓᎧᏙᏴᎢᎣᏯ. ᏐᎢᏞᏯ.
ᏅᎨ ᏓᏒᎵᏍᎦᏐ, ᎤᏃᏨᏟᏔ, ᏗᏴᎡᏐᎦᏐ. ᎲᏇ.
Ꮢ. ᏖᏍᏛ, ᎵᏌᏉᎴᏯ ᏗᏍᏆ ᎲᏇ.
ᏏᏉᏦ, ᎵᏌᏉᎴᏯ ᏗᏍᏆ ᏆᏉᎢ.

ᏔᎢᎵ, 14 ᎤᏟᏍᏕ, 1825.

ᏦᎵᏂᎵᏯ ᏗᏍᏆ ᏓᎧᏙᏴᎢᎣᏯ, ᏗᏔ ᎠᎵᏬᎢ, ᏈᎭᏂᏯ ᏬᏟᏐᎨᏪ ᏕᏦᏐᏘ, ᏗᏗ ᏥᏏᎡᏄ ᏙᎭᏂᏯ ᏗᏗ ᏗᏕᎬᏇᎵ ᎳᏅᏩᎳᏐᎵ, ᏗᏗ ᏙᎵ ᏟᏯ ᎬᏔ ᏔᎢᎵ ᏍᏌᏔᎢ, ᏣᎥ ᏭᏇ ᏗᎹᏴ Ꮪ ᏏᏇᏟᎵ ᏆᎾᏗ ᏏᏍᏔᏂ. ᏗᏢᏯ ᏗᏍᏆ ᏆᏉᎢ. ᏣᏂ ᏦᎡᏦ, ᏘᏔᎦᏘ ᏗᏍᏆ ᎲᏇ. ᏐᎢᏞᏯ.
ᏅᎨ ᏓᏒᎵᏍᎦᏐ, ᎤᏃᏨᏟᏔ, ᏗᏴᎡᏐᎦᏐ. ᎲᏇ.
Ꮢ. ᏖᏍᏛ, ᎵᏌᏉᎴᏯ ᏗᏍᏆ ᎲᏇ.
ᏏᏉᏦ, ᎵᏌᏉᎴᏯ ᏗᏍᏆ ᏆᏉᎢ.

ᏔᎢᎵ, 14 ᎤᏟᏍᏕ, 1825.

ᏒᏇᏯ ᏗᏍᏐ ᎡᎦᏬᏈ ᏗᏂ ᏌᎵᏂᏔ, ᏗᏗ ᎠᎵᎬ ᏗᏂᏌᎦᎶᏟ ᏦᎡᏦᏐ ᎡᎦ ᎡᎥ ᎬᏔ ᎵᏔᎳᎳᏘ Ꮜ ᎬᏘᏞ ᎵᏏᎦᏴ, ᏗᏗ Ꭼ ᎧᎥ ᏗᏘᎵ ᎲᏍᎦᏲ ᏈᏍ ᎤᏨᎵᏛ ᏗᏔᏌᎲᎵ ᏗᏔᏌᏀᎡ ᎶᏘᏞ Ꭾ ᏋᏟᏒ ᏗᎴᎤᏔᎵ ᏗᎡᏍᏌ Ꭼ ᎬᏯ, ᎠᏓ ᎬᏯᏐ ᎲᎨᏟ ᏗᏍᏆᏐ ᏙᏋᎴ, ᏗᏗ ᎬᎢ ᏓᎬᎥᎵ ᏔᎳᏐᎶ ᏣᎥ ᎤᏔ ᎦᎬᎢ ᏔᎢᎵ Ꮜ ᏍᏕᏩ ᏗᏘᎡ ᏔᏍᏆ ᏗᏍ Ꮤ-

One of the best retorts to such rhetoric came from Shulush Homa, a Choctaw chief with a wit as sharp as his quill pen. Writing to John C. Calhoun in December 1824, he remarked, "It has been a great many years since our white brothers came across the big waters and a great many of them has not got civilized yet; therefore we wish to be indulged in our savage state of life until we can have the same time to get civilized . . . [and] for that reason we think we might as well enjoy our right as well as our white brothers."

Efforts to reform the Indians, as humanitarians were wont to describe the process, had begun almost as soon as the first English settlers reached the shores of North America. Although such efforts almost always resulted in failure, the quest for the magic formula by which "Indianness" could be eradicated continued until well into the 20th century. Since most reformers were clergymen, Indians attending school in this period usually received religious instruction as well as drill in letters and numbers. Domestic duties were stressed for girls and manual arts and farming for boys. A legislative committee expressed the movement's underlying concept: "Put into the hands of their children the primer and the hoe, and they will naturally, in time, take hold of the plough . . . and they will grow up in habits of morality and industry. . . ."

Perhaps the most ardent and influential early advocate of this view was Thomas L. McKenney, the first head of the Bureau of Indian Affairs. A pompous humanitarian, McKenney was the principal architect of the government's reform and removal programs which, with the allotment program enacted in the late 19th century, rank among the most pernicious and culturally damaging pieces of legislation ever inflicted upon America's Indians. Although benign in intent, these programs often left the tribes bereft of culture, land, and dignity and, except in rare instances, still as "Indian" in attitude and belief as ever. When McKenney launched the government's first systematic reform program, established by the Indian Civilization Act of 1819, he firmly believed that it would take only one generation to educate and "civilize" America's Indians. Thomas McKenney based this belief on his experience with James L. McDonald,

Sequoyah, a Cherokee silversmith, opposite, developed an alphabet for his people after 1821. Thousands of his kinsmen soon learned to read and write their own language: the first bi-lingual tribal newspaper, the "Cherokee Phoenix," appears behind the drawing of Sequoyah. His 86 symbols were adopted from the Greek, Hebrew, and English. The alphabet lives on; a modernized version is displayed by Cherokee teacher Durbin Feeling and his grandson, Ryan, above.

a mixed-blood Choctaw boy whom he took into his Georgetown home in Washington, D.C., and raised for several years.

By the time McKenney met McDonald, the boy had already received more than a decade of schooling, so he was by no means a typical Indian. McKenney used the gifted Choctaw as a guinea pig for his reform experiments. McDonald wore the finest clothes; attended school in Georgetown, where he excelled in Latin, Greek, and mathematics; and served as McKenney's ready-made example of the educated Indian's potential.

Although the young man longed to return to his home in Mississippi, he let McKenney send him to

Under armed guard, tribes of the
Old South were all but herded
west across the Mississippi River
in the first half of the 19th century. Here, a group of Cherokees is
depicted during a day's travel.
Sixteen thousand Cherokees were
moved during 1838 in what
19th-century historians called The
Trail of Tears. As many as a quarter
of the travelers may have died.
While most tribes were removed
from the East to Oklahoma's Indian
Territory, some were marched
there from the Far West or settled
in areas often unsuited to occupations assigned to them by whites.
A few bands rebelled, fleeing the
reservations in generally hopeless
bids for freedom; some crossed into
Canada or Mexico.

Ohio to read law under John McLean, later a justice on the Supreme Court. He admitted in a moment of candor, "I have a partiality for a Farmer's life, and did I believe my choice unconnected with the interest of others I might probably give it the preference."

McDonald was admitted to the bar, becoming America's first Indian attorney, but he also crumbled emotionally under the burden he carried. Instead of emerging as the intellectual leader of the Choctaws, the Talleyrand of his tribe, the young man succumbed to alcoholism. In 1824, while representing a delegation of Choctaw chiefs in Washington to negotiate a treaty, McDonald's dissipation became public and greatly embarrassed his mentor, who responded by shutting the young man out of his life. "I have done all I could to save him," a self-righteous McKenney informed a mutual acquaintance. Patron and protégé remained estranged. In the summer of 1831, after a white woman rejected his proposal of marriage,

Central figure in the climactic wars of the Old Northwest (most of the present-day Midwest), Sac Chief Black Hawk, above at right, appears with his son Whirling Thunder in an 1833 painting by John Jarvis. Like Tecumseh a quarter of a century earlier, Black Hawk fought for tribal union and nationhood, but his Sac and Fox allies were forced westward. Easterners made Black Hawk into a media hero. Opposite, Sac, Fox, and Kansa chiefs of the 1860s meet with government officials to cede more land, this time west of the Mississippi.

McDonald either fell or jumped from a cliff to his death. McKenney claimed that it was his unhappy experience with McDonald that convinced him to support the idea of Indian removal.

To humanitarians such as McKenney, removal was not an alternative to civilizing the Indians but a prerequisite. Situated on land across the Mississippi River that would be guaranteed to them forever, the eastern Indians could remain isolated and undisturbed by the degenerating influence of the whites until they adjusted to a new way of life.

Removal advocates outlined a rosy existence for the Indians if they agreed to move. They would receive an equitable exchange of land, acre for acre; they would be paid for any improvements on the land they left behind; they would receive cash payments, supplies, and food. Best of all, the prospect of becoming a territory and eventually a state in the Union was held out to them.

Despite the promises and benevolent intentions, the eastern tribes were unanimous in their rejection of removal. Those most vehemently opposed to

the plan were the Cherokees, Creeks, Choctaws, and Chickasaws, the tribes toward which the program was primarily directed. Between 1789 and 1825, they had made 30 treaties with the United States, surrendering lands or agreeing to new boundaries. Having learned from their actions, they refused to consider any plan that called for further erosion of their homelands. As an indication of their resolve, the Creeks executed three chiefs in May 1825 for signing an agreement to sell tribal land to the state of Georgia; a fourth chief escaped the same fate only through the aid of a kinsman and a fast horse. William McIntosh fell at the hands of a war party headed by his enemy and rival, Menawa. The

Choctaws simply replaced the three full-blooded chiefs who governed their affairs with three educated mixed-bloods who, according to one government official, had "a purty good knowledge of the Laws of nations."

The most organized resistance to removal came from the Cherokees, by any standard the tribe best prepared to take its place as an equal partner in the democratic experiment. The tribe had its own written language, a special alphabet devised by George Guess, a mixed-blood genius better known as Sequoyah; its own newspaper, the *Cherokee Phoenix*; tax-supported schools; and a written constitution adopted in 1827, which provided the tribe

Seminole warriors of Florida evaded and punished United States troops, as opposite, in three conflicts from 1817 to 1858, wars that they won in the field but lost at the negotiating table. Effective guerrilla action was the Seminole specialty. Their leader, Osceola, was subsequently seized in violation of a truce, and died in prison only a few days after George Catlin had painted his portrait, left, in 1837. Escaped slaves found refuge with these southern Indians and often married into the tribe. Below, Black Seminoles appear in festive wedding dress.

with a code of laws, a court, and a bicameral legislature. A foreign visitor would have had difficulty distinguishing a Cherokee settlement from any number of rural white communities that were composed of well-tended farms, handsome plantations, and a slave-holding class of planters. Cherokee settlements even included a few Christians, who honored the Sabbath and read the New Testament (which had been translated into Cherokee).

The only flaw in this idyllic scene is that the Cherokees were Indians and the land they occupied was fertile and coveted by whites. Moreover, in 1802 the federal government had promised much of the Cherokee domain to the state of Georgia to resolve a dispute that had lingered since the American Revolution. The agreement called for the federal government to free Georgia of its Indian population "as soon as the same can be peaceably done on reasonable terms."

Under the able leadership of John Ross, the Cherokees used every weapon in the legal and moral arsenal of the United States in an effort to retain their eastern homelands. Despite the vigorous assistance of sympathetic Congressmen and three favorable decisions by Supreme Court Justice

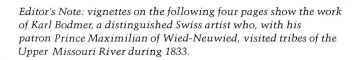

Editor's Note: vignettes on the following four pages show the work of Karl Bodmer, a distinguished Swiss artist who, with his patron Prince Maximilian of Wied-Neuwied, visited tribes of the Upper Missouri River during 1833.

Markings, feathers, and relics worn by Four Bears, a Mandan, left, stand for war wounds or battle feats. Owl feathers at the back of his head indicate membership in a tribal fraternity, the Society of the Dog.

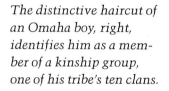

The distinctive haircut of an Omaha boy, right, identifies him as a member of a kinship group, one of his tribe's ten clans.

John Marshall, their efforts finally came to naught. Senator Theodore Frelinghuysen of New Jersey ended a two-day plea with the words, "Is it one of the prerogatives of the white man, that he may disregard the dictates of moral principles, where an Indian shall be concerned?"

Speeches and court decisions foundered on the southern-planter sympathies of President Andrew Jackson, who simply ignored the Supreme Court's ruling that federal law and not Georgia law should determine the fate of the Cherokees. The result was the infamous Trail of Tears, an expression derived from "The Trail Where They Cried," the Cherokee name for the forced removal of 15,000 people across the Mississippi River.

The Cherokees were but one of a dozen tribes forced to begin life anew in a country so strange that it might as well have been across an ocean as across a river. The trek and resettlement were horrors for every Indian who experienced them— whether Ottawa, Potawatomi, Wyandot, Shawnee, Kickapoo, Delaware, Peoria, Miami, Sac and Fox, Chickasaw, Choctaw, Creek, or Seminole—and a

scar on American honor, if only because of the worthless treaties and their broken promises.

Except for members of the Five Civilized Tribes, few Indians fully understood the documents they signed. The language barrier brought confusion even in the rare absence of any intention to deceive. In addition, most interpreters were poorly educated mixed-bloods whose comprehension of treaty proceedings was minimal at best.

The government's use of blandishments and coercion in the guise of treaties eventually convinced Indians to leave their homelands. The treaties salved federal consciences and suggested that the resettlements were accomplished through negotiations in which both parties shared equally. In retrospect, eastern tribes appear surprisingly submissive to the removal program, though many tribes split into factions. Of course, the Indians had no choice, as they had learned from previous experiences of defiance.

Black Hawk had attempted passive resistance. At issue was a treaty several Sac and Fox leaders signed under dubious circumstances while visiting

Woman of the Crow Nation, left, wears painted buckskin clothes. Turtle, right, arrived in St. Louis with other Sac and Fox men during 1833 to plead for the release of Black Hawk, the Sac chief captured the previous year.

St. Louis in 1804. Although the treaty provided for the sale of their land, one proviso allowed the tribe to continue using it until the federal government needed it, certainly a confusing arrangement at best. A quarter of a century later, the government called upon the tribe to honor its commitment.

Not only did Black Hawk refuse, but he spoke for all Indians when he declared in his remarkable autobiography, "What do we know of the manners, the laws, and customs of the white people? They might buy our bodies for dissection, and we would touch the goose quill to confirm it and not know what we were doing. This," he admitted, "was the case with me and my people in touching the goose quill the first time."

In 1831, when he and his followers returned to their village on the Rock River in Illinois for the spring planting season, they found it occupied by white settlers who claimed ownership. The whites were scared, the Indians angry, the outcome predictable. To call what happened a war stretches credulity, for at most 70 whites lost their lives, whereas nearly all of the Indian group of 500 men, women,

145

and children perished. As the commanding general boasted in his official report, "It is believed that not an individual comprising the band of Black Hawk . . . escaped being either killed or captured." Many of the terrified Sac and Fox people met death trying to escape across the Mississippi River under musket and cannon fire. Those who did not die in the water fell under the tomahawks of their Sioux enemies, whom the government had recruited as auxiliary soldiers.

"The whites ought not to have permitted such conduct, and none but cowards would ever have been guilty of such cruelty, which has always been practiced on our nation by the Sioux," remarked Black Hawk, who survived, but ended his days as a bitter, brooding man. Although shamed for having brought such anguish to his people, Black Hawk was lionized as the noble savage incarnate by eastern authors and artists, who vied to write his history and paint his portrait.

The Florida Seminoles struggled against removal more effectively. A coalition of refugees from several southern peoples—primarily the Oconees, Yamasees, and Creeks—the Seminoles may have

numbered 5,000. For 20 years they engaged the U.S. Army in an expensive and brutalizing campaign fought more for political than military reasons. Even bloodhounds and trickery, as in the capture of Chief Osceola under a flag of truce, failed to bring the tribe under government control.

The federal treasury probably expended a million dollars a man for the 50 or 60 Seminole warriors killed in battle, a price that does not include the lives of the 1,500 white soldiers who died so that perhaps 4,000 Indians could be transported west of the Mississippi. This hemorrhage of wealth, honor, and blood accommodated plantation owners by eliminating a haven for runaway slaves. Knowing the white man's language, settlements, and ways, black escapees made excellent spies and scouts. Some further bolstered their loyalty to and status with Indians by marrying into the tribe. The ex-slaves accompanied their Seminole kinsmen and friends to the West as part of a negotiated settlement, much to the dismay of their former masters.

Under the best of circumstances, the removal program would have been fraught with problems. Aside from the questionable wisdom of uprooting

Karl Bodmer's artwork of the Bison Dance of the Buffalo Bull Society, opposite, captures all the force of a Mandan ritual. Four years later smallpox nearly obliterated the tribe. Distant Bear of the Piegan Blackfeet, left, wears a topknot and face paint that may mark him as a medicine man. Two Ravens of the Hidatsa, below, shows the ceremonial rattle and ornate headdress of a leader of the Dog Society. The neck sash might be staked down in battle to prove that he would stand his ground.

thousands of people from their homes in the name of humanitarianism, the western tribes understandably resented and opposed the intrusion of their eastern brethren. Comanches, Osages, and Pawnees viewed the intruders as legitimate objects of plunder. Only a string of freshly built military posts and an issue of recently minted muskets allowed the travelers to keep the Plains tribes at bay.

Perhaps the most celebrated intertribal encounter took place on the Kansas plains near Fort Riley in 1854, when 1,000 Comanche, Kiowa, Cheyenne, and Osage warriors surprised 100 Sac and Fox buffalo hunters. New, reliable rifles enabled the latter to repel several massed charges by the ill-armed plainsmen, who lost 26 men and dozens of horses before quitting the field in disgust.

Little more than a decade after the Louisiana Purchase, the future caught up with tribes of the territories that became Texas, Arizona, New Mexico, and California. Here, beyond the area affected by the purchase, Indians and Spanish encountered the advance guard of American Manifest Destiny. At the time, Napoleon's invasion of the Iberian Peninsula preoccupied Spain to such an extent that it could spare little time for the needs of its New World empire, which it ultimately lost through a series of independence movements, including the one in Mexico in 1821.

Mexico's revolution against Spain upset delicate political relationships for Indians of the Southwest, and sporadic warfare again engulfed the region. Mexico ceased to provide the goods and services that had kept nomadic and militant tribes of New Mexico under modest restraint during Spanish colonial rule. Apaches, Comanches, and Utes from today's Arizona and New Mexico began to launch raids south into Mexico. With incursions occurring all along the northern frontier of Mexico, citizens reeled from abuse and pillage, which officials were powerless to halt. One famous "visit" to San Antonio involved 200 Comanches, who remained six days and entered and plundered private homes at will.

The people of San Antonio were fortunate compared with their compatriots. One official, writing in 1835, estimated that the "barbarians" had killed more than 5,000 Mexicans and friendly Indians since Mexican independence and the departure of Spanish forces. War broke out between the United States and Mexico in 1846, and yet Hispanic frontier communities feared the Indians at their doorsteps far more than American soldiers down the road. As one Mexican legislator described Indian dominance of the Mexican frontier, "We travel the roads . . . at their whim; we cultivate the land where they wish and in the amount that they wish; we use sparingly things they have left us to use until the moment that it strikes their appetite to take them for themselves."

America's westward expansion further hobbled Mexico's ability to cope with the rising belligerence. Unscrupulous Anglo-American traders furnished guns and whiskey to Indian raiders and bought livestock and other property stolen from Mexicans. American settlement disrupted northern Mexico; the closer the Americans, the easier for Indians to unload their plunder and buy guns and ammunition. Mexican officials in Texas believed that the American government deliberately encouraged Indian attacks so that farmers would plead for the protection of the U.S. Army.

Westward expansion had a domino effect on tribes in its path, tumbling many of them into northern Mexico. Ironically, even members of some of the eastern tribes found their way into east Texas and northern Mexico. Rather than wait to be moved again at government request, displaced Cherokees, Choctaws, Creeks, Delawares, Kickapoos, and Shawnees decided to cross the southern frontier. Mexican officials welcomed them in the hope that they would serve as a buffer against the Americans and the militant tribes on the northern frontier.

The course of Manifest Destiny unfolded in much the same way in California, though the Indians put up less resistance. The Spanish mission system had collapsed within 15 years of Mexico's independence. From its peak population of 23,000

Indians and 21 missions in 1833, the system declined, the result of a Mexican law requiring the exodus of all Spanish-born padres. Even more devastating was a decision to secularize the missions. The government had apparently intended gradual change with minimum disruption to the Indian neophytes. In practice, though, secularization bore a striking resemblance to the process by which the Cherokees, Chickasaws, Creeks, and Choctaws of Old Dixie were pauperized during the removal program.

When given a choice, most California Indians preferred working for the missions to owning and managing the land themselves. However they may have labored on behalf of the padres, they refused the overseers who replaced them. Some Indians joined traditional Indian communities, others moved into nearby towns, and the rest hired themselves out to the private farmers and ranchers who had appropriated mission lands for themselves. With the demise of the missions, extinct by 1846, the California Indians lost their only chance for survival. The American whirlwind swept them into oblivion.

Writing in 1840, one of the last Spanish padres lamented, "All is destruction, all is misery, humiliation and despair." His words provide as suitable an epitaph for California's Indians as for its missions.

America's westward expansion also disrupted the traditional economy of distant California. American fur trappers found their way across the mountains into California's fertile valleys soon after Mexican independence. They were struck by

Seneca Chief Ely Samuel Parker, shown in uniform at left, served the Union cause with distinction during the Civil War. He not only penned the final copy of the surrender terms at Appomattox Courthouse but later became the first Indian to serve as Commissioner of Indian Affairs. Reacting to Civil War strife, Kickapoo Indians of Texas moved south of the border. During the early 1900s, other Kickapoo families, such as those shown at right, traveled to join their Mexican kinsmen.

the abundance of horses and cattle. Jedediah Smith, for one, purchased domesticated California horses for ten dollars and later sold them for $50 at the annual trappers' rendezvous in the Rockies.

Navajos, Utes, Nez Percé, Yakimas, and even Delawares and Shawnees joined in the brisk horse-trading business. A few Indian raiders worked in concert with white middlemen who sold horses to the throngs of eager American pioneers. In 1840, Ute leader Walkara and mountain man "Pegleg" Smith obtained 1,200 horses from one raid on Mission San Luis Obispo. Walkara raided even after the Mexican War and sold his take to the Latter-Day Saints. The Mormons desperately needed horses to help them raise their earthly kingdom in the inhospitable environs of the Great Salt Lake.

The Mexicans derived one big benefit from the Treaty of Guadalupe Hidalgo (1848), which otherwise stripped them of California, New Mexico, and Arizona. Not only could Mexicans living on the United States side of the border now expect American protection, but the United States was liable for damages caused in Mexico by Indians living in the United States.

This bit of news annoyed the Comanches, Navajos, and Utes. Grumbled one Apache when informed by an American official of the ban on raiding, "We must steal from somebody; and if you will not permit us to rob the Mexicans, we must steal from you or fight you." This was no idle threat, as the Americans who so eagerly pushed into the recently acquired Southwest soon learned.

The Mexican War also forced federal officials to re-think their Indian policy. Many factors dictated this: territorial acquisitions, the gold rush, California statehood, and the opening of the Overland Trail. Officials quickly realized that the days of the West as an Indian sanctuary were numbered. Simply pushing the Indians backward or removing them as the line of settlement approached only delayed an inevitable decision. A consensus in favor of containing Indians on reservations began to form.

Although the concentration of Indians had been tried with indifferent success on one or two occasions, government officials now embraced this policy warmly. Commissioner of Indian Affairs Luke Lea informed Congress in 1850, "Any plan for the

civilization of our Indians will, in my judgment, be fatally defective, if it does not provide in the most efficient manner . . . for their concentration." His sentiments were echoed three years later by his successor, George W. Manypenny, who opined, "The emigrants and settlers were formerly content to remain in the rear, and thrust the Indians before them into the wilderness; but now the white population overleaps . . . the homes of the Indians, and is beginning to inhabit the mountains and valleys beyond; hence removal must cease, and the policy abandoned."

This pragmatic shift in policy is dramatically reflected in the numerous treaties negotiated in the decade of the 1850s. The change in policy had disastrous effects on the Indians in the new state of California, where a series of 18 land-cession treaties were negotiated between March 1851 and early 1852. Native peoples signed away rights to approximately 75 million acres in exchange for reservations totaling 8.5 million acres and support services and supplies.

However, California legislators wanted the Indians removed from the state and opposed the assignment of any lands to the tribes. Treaties sent up for ratification in the U.S. Senate were rejected. Classified as confidential, these propositions were filed away by clerks and forgotten by legislators. Meanwhile, Congress passed laws in 1851 and 1853 that effectively deprived the California Indians of all their rights to land. Bereft of homes, unprotected by treaties, the Indians became wanderers, hounded and persecuted by whites. Finally, in 1860, Congress established four small reservations, which sup-

ported only a minor percentage of the Indian population. More than 80 percent of California's tribal population vanished from 1851 to 1900, and by the turn of the century only 17,000 Indians remained.

Almost all treaties negotiated in the 1850s provided both for the protection of travelers and the reduction of tribal land holdings to more compact areas. A series of treaties negotiated in 1855 with the Blackfeet, Nez Percé, and other tribes of the Far Northwest specified that "citizens of the United States may live in and pass unmolested through the countries occupied and claimed by them." These tribes also agreed to allow the construction of roads "of every description" and the establishment of telegraph lines and military posts. A treaty with the Choctaws and Chickasaws that same year gave the United States "or any incorporated company" the right of way for a railroad.

Little wonder, then, that a spirit of apprehension

Tired of sporadic fighting between Plains Indians and whites, Chief Black Kettle of the Cheyenne, seated below at center, came to Denver, Colorado, during September 1864 to seek U.S. Army protection. A Cheyenne war shield appears at left.

and militancy pervaded the western tribes. Yet although most leaders feared federal motives and seethed with discontent, they also realized their helplessness. This changed, however, during the Civil War. When the United States reduced western garrisons and focused its military might on crushing the South, several western tribes seized the opportunity to lash out at encroaching farmers and miners. Others, including the Cherokees, Chickasaws, Choctaws, Creeks, and Seminoles, joined the Confederate States of America.

That the Five Civilized Tribes would ally themselves with the Confederacy was perhaps inevitable. What choice did they have? The land they occupied adjoined Confederate states and many of their mixed-blood leaders were slaveholders sympathetic to the southern cause. The Confederate states offered them a better deal than did the United States: the tribes could send representatives to the Confederate congress and had the right to tax traders within their boundaries. The Confederate government also promised compensation for damages caused by intruders.

As in previous North American conflicts, Indians actively participated on both sides with their manpower, in this case, especially important to the South. Fifteen thousand Indian soldiers fought primarily in the western theater, with Pea Ridge in Arkansas their most significant battle.

At least 3,000 Indians fought for the North, including 135 Oneida volunteers from Wisconsin. Only 55 Oneidas returned, a mortality rate of nearly 60 percent. General Ely S. Parker was the most prominent Indian soldier for the Union. A New York Seneca and a close associate of General U.S. Grant, the renowned Parker was related through his mother to both Red Jacket, the Seneca orator, and to Handsome Lake, the prophet.

Just as the national conflict turned white brother against white brother, divided loyalties tore apart the fabric of tribal unity and internecine violence flared. General Stand Watie of the Cherokees, commander of the last Confederate combat unit to surrender to Union forces, was the brother of Elias Boudinot, the *Cherokee Phoenix* editor who had been assassinated by followers of John Ross in the turbulent years after removal. Watie's avenging

forces burned the home of John Ross, principal chief of the Cherokee pro-Union faction.

Brutality and bloodshed erupted in the hinterlands. The Santee (Eastern Sioux of Minnesota) had already witnessed the steady loss of their lands to white settlement. Rumors circulated that their annuities would be cut off and their rations reduced greatly, and when tribal leaders asked a local trader for more food, he told them to eat grass. In this emotionally charged climate, four young warriors killed a white family.

Fearing massive retaliation by the army, tribal leaders persuaded Chief Little Crow to strike first, although, having visited the national capital and the mighty arsenals in the East, he knew better. The Sioux had no hope of ultimate victory, though the uprising claimed the lives of more than 500 white Minnesotans, including a certain trader whose mouth was stuffed with grass.

The army responded swiftly and ruthlessly, with General John Pope concluding the conflict within a month of his taking command. Having just suffered an embarrassing defeat at the Second Battle of Bull Run, Pope perhaps hoped to win back lost laurels, and thus showed no mercy. "It is my purpose," Pope informed his superiors, "utterly to exterminate the Sioux if I have the power to do so. . . . They are to be treated as maniacs or wild beasts, and by no means as people with whom treaties or compromises can be made." A year passed before the starving Little Crow was killed by a Minnesota farmer who found the chief and his son picking berries.

In the meantime, a military commission had condemned 303 of Little Crow's followers to death. Despite intense pressure from the Minnesota congressional corps, President Abraham Lincoln commuted the death sentences of all but 38 of the Indians, who were executed in a mass hanging in the public square of Mankato on December 26, 1862. Lincoln had urged caution lest innocent Indians be punished. It was later revealed that at least one of the executed had actually saved lives by warning white friends to seek safety.

The scene of phenomenal growth during the gold and silver rushes of the 1850s, Colorado Territory experienced the second serious outbreak of violence.

In their tens of thousands, miners had elbowed their way into the mineral fields, dislocating and angering the Cheyennes and Arapahos, who now sought to take advantage of reduced military garrisons during the Civil War. Tribesmen attacked wagon trains, mining camps, and stagecoach lines. One white family died within 20 miles of Denver.

The governor of Colorado Territory called out volunteer militiamen under Colonel J.M. Chivington to stem the mounting violence. Though Chivington had once belonged to the clergy, his compassion for his fellow man did not extend to Indians. Having chased the elusive "hostiles" for several weeks with little more than saddle sores to show for his troubles, Chivington decided to attack a Cheyenne vil-

Black Kettle's peace bid at the Denver conference failed when Col. John M. Chivington of the Third Colorado Cavalry mounted his surprise attack at dawn against Black Kettle's people at their camp on Sand Creek. Chivington and his troops killed men, women, and children and took many scalps. The colonel, formerly a preacher, faithfully carried out the directive of his superior officer, Maj. Gen. Samuel R. Curtis, U.S. Army, who said "I want no peace until the Indians suffer more." The war that resulted threatened to engulf the northern Plains.

lage on Sand Creek. Its peace-seeking chief, Black Kettle, believed that he and his people enjoyed the protective custody of the commander at Fort Lyon, some 40 miles away.

As Chivington's troops charged the sleeping camp at dawn on the morning of November 29, 1864, Black Kettle rushed from his tent and raised first an American flag and then a white flag. Chivington wanted a victory, not prisoners, and so men, women, and children were hunted down and shot. When asked at a subsequent military inquiry why children had been killed, one of the soldiers quoted Chivington as saying, "nits make lice."

The colonel was as thorough as he was heartless. An interpreter living in the village testified, "They were scalped, their brains knocked out; the men used their knives, ripped open women, clubbed little children, knocked them in the head with their guns, beat their brains out, mutilated their bodies in every sense of the word." As many as 200 of the 500 Indians in the village died that day. Black Kettle was not one of them, however. He survived, only to be killed in a similar attack several years later.

While the Sand Creek Massacre outraged easterners, it evidently pleased many people in Colorado Territory. Chivington later appeared on a Denver stage where he regaled delighted audiences with his war stories and displayed 100 Indian scalps, including the pubic hair of women.

If Chivington hoped to restore calm by destroying Black Kettle's village, he failed. An avenging wildfire swept the land and peace returned only after a quarter of a century of attack and retribution that shattered the far-flung warrior societies. Peace cost western tribes dearly, with nearly all native peoples having been defeated, demoralized, and degraded.

Sequestered after the bloody uprising of 1862, 1,700 Sioux raise their tipis within the stockade of Fort Snelling in Dakota Territory. These people, who had not participated in the outbreak, were subsequently relocated to a reservation in Nebraska.

Americans, seen in the colored lithograph of California's Grass Valley, below, streamed into Indian country in the 1840s and 1850s to dig for gold or to settle. In 1849 alone, California's non-Indian population rose from 20,000 to 100,000, equal to that of the Indians. By 1900 whites had killed or expelled 80 percent of the Indians.

156

Loss of the West

Frederic Remington's "Conjuring Back the Buffalo," left (inset), portrays the spiritual desperation of the Plains Indians, who sought to sustain their nomadic lifestyle on ever-shrinking lands.

To many white Americans, the Plains tribes appeared invincible as long as they could hunt the buffalo. Nobody believed this more steadfastly than the soldiers who chased the Indians, and that is why western army officers issued free ammunition to the hide hunters. Whittling away at the Indians' resource base was far more effective than direct military confrontation, and far less risky, since the Sioux, Comanches, Cheyennes, Arapahos, and others could field some of the finest horse soldiers known to history.

The memorable hunting-and-raiding culture of the Plains arose and passed away within two centuries, an epoch during which a magnificent landscape provided both strength and refuge for shifting populations. These spread northward into Canada from a secure domain centered in Montana and the Dakotas, where buffalo and other game flourished on the northern Great Plains and in broken high country near the Rockies.

Open warfare between whites and Indians began in Wyoming Territory in 1854. A foolish young army officer from Fort Laramie ignited the violence by trying to intimidate Sioux villagers charged with stealing a stray cow from a passing wagon train. The Grattan Massacre, as it is known, was but one of a succession of such incidents, which included the Fetterman Fight and culminated in Custer's Last Stand. All of these, particularly the defeats of white forces, have added to the romantic lore of the West and have been retold in countless books and motion pictures.

Interest switched back to the East and South during the Civil War, but the allure of the West returned, stronger than ever, after Appomattox. A rising tide of white migration coursed across the Plains as America not only entered a new era but consciously shaped a more complex society. The Homestead Act of 1862 fueled this acceleration in settlement by dispensing land to newcomers for a nominal fee after five years of residence.

The transcontinental railroad sped more and more people—the Pullman Pioneers—into the open lands. Safely and conveniently, passengers and freight could move from coast to coast in six days. The supply of settlers was endless: in the two decades after 1850 more than five million people had

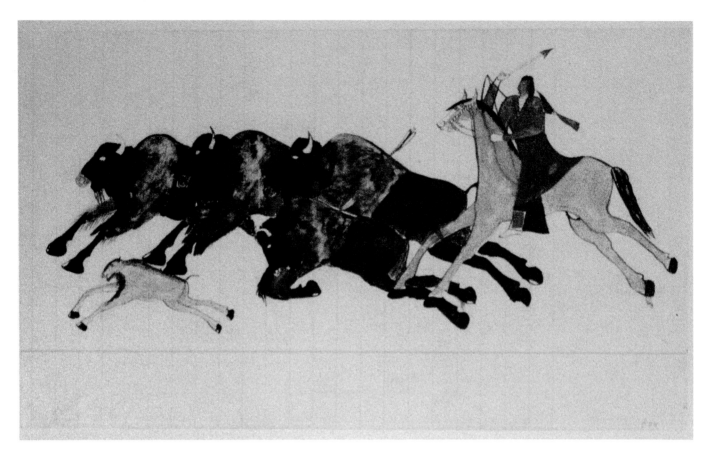

arrived in the United States, a land whose total population in 1870 was about 38 million. Immigration increased and goods were supplied almost without limit. The same Civil War that had enlarged the eastern industrial base also forged a mighty arsenal and fostered a professional military cadre that yearned for promotion through combat. The stage was set for action at a time when few in government took Indian likes and dislikes seriously.

Since the military had dealt so forcefully and effectively with the Santee Sioux in Minnesota, the Cheyennes and Arapahos in Colorado Territory, and the Navajos in New Mexico Territory, it was believed that recalcitrant tribes anywhere could be contained with ease. Westerners, in particular, had little sympathy for any policy that appeared to coddle Indians, who must, they felt, yield peacefully or face the consequences. Graffiti found scrawled on Indian skulls often encapsulated western attitudes. One such inscription read, "I am on the reservation at last."

Anti-Indian sentiment was not confined to pioneers of the early frontier period. As late as 1894 the prominent satirist William Nye expressed the conventional contempt for the Indian in his irreverent *History of the United States*. "The James Fenimore Cooper Indian was no doubt a brave and highly intellectual person, . . . a bronze apollo who bathed almost constantly and killed only those white people who were unpleasant and coarse." But the "real Indian," according to Nye, "has the dead and unkempt hair of a busted buggy-cushion filled with feathers. He lies, he steals, he assassinates, he mutilates, he tortures. We can, in fact, only retain him as we do the buffalo, so long as he complies with our laws."

The person charged with implementing the military solution to the western Indian problem was General John Pope, whose rigorous treatment of the Santee Sioux in Minnesota had endeared him both to settlers and to his military superiors. Commanding the entire western theater during the spring of 1865, he mounted a massive assault against the Plains Indians. Three separate armies with a total of 6,000 combat troops moved against the Comanches and Kiowas on the southern Plains and against the Arapahos, Cheyennes, and Sioux in the central and northern sectors.

Pope angered the Indians, embarrassed the army, and taught both sides a valuable lesson. Simply feeding the troops and supporting unwieldy military columns absorbed so much energy that the army had little left over for fighting. Tribal war parties quickly realized this, and experienced little

By 1884, when Gros Ventre artist New Bear drew the dynamic hunting scene, opposite, the buffalo had vanished from the Plains. Beginning in the early 1870s, the guns of professional hide hunters and even those of railroad passengers, as shown above, increased the killing to a million buffalo each year. At right, mountains of hide at Dodge City, Kansas, await shipment to leather factories in the East. With the buffalo gone, the Plains tribes could no longer sustain themselves.

or no difficulty in locating or eluding forces sent to engage them. Later, blustery autumn weather and a blast of sleet further hampered Pope's military effectiveness. One unit of volunteers not only lost most of its horses and mules but also came perilously close to losing people through exposure and starvation.

Indians so inclined had a field day at taxpayers' expense. Arapaho, Cheyenne, and Sioux war parties on the central Plains took revenge for the atrocities committed against Indians at Sand Creek in Colo-

rado Territory in 1864. They burned ranches and stage stations, disrupted telegraph service, twice terrorized the town of Julesburg, and generally played havoc with unwary travelers who came their way. One war party even succeeded in derailing a steam engine employed by construction crews on the transcontinental route. Southern Cheyennes still tell the story of a luckless telegraph operator killed in one raid. Aware that white people somehow talked over the line, members of the war party stuck a piece of telegraph wire in the victim's ear "so he could hear better in the afterlife."

All this bad news filtered back to Washington. For a while, at least, peace at any price seemed preferable to continued humiliation, even if certain guilty Indians escaped punishment. Pope was still in the field when government officials extended olive branches to the militants by asking them to assemble for a grand conference at Fort Laramie in the spring of 1866. "A lasting peace" was the order of the day, and a group of friendly Indians who spent their time lounging around Fort Laramie—the "Laramie loafers," as they were sometimes called—was enlisted to stir up interest.

Several thousand Sioux and Cheyennes eventually met with President Andrew Johnson's representatives, led by Indian Commissioner N.G. Taylor. Foremost among the militants was Red Cloud, the Oglala war chief whose name, along with those of Crazy Horse and Sitting Bull, was to become a household word in the decades following the Civil War.

Red Cloud seemed more interested in the promised presents and food than in negotiation. Tribes on the northern Plains were already suffering because of attrition of the buffalo herds upon which they were so dependent. As one official at Fort Laramie noted of Red Cloud and his people, "Nothing but ocular demonstration can make one appreciate their destitution, and near approach to starvation."

The government did not wish to purchase their country, the Sioux were told. It simply wanted to make peace and obtain permission for white travelers to use the Bozeman Trail, a new road through the Powder River country. A promise that all travelers would stay on the road and not do any hunting was, one official later admitted, "well calculated, and . . . designed to deceive."

Not easily fooled, Red Cloud noted that travelers already used the road. He suspected the worst when Colonel Henry B. Carrington and a battalion of infantry marched into Fort Laramie in the midst of the proceedings. Carrington carried orders to build a string of posts along the Bozeman Trail to protect pioneers from Indian attack. Red Cloud refused an introduction and then rebuked Carrington, saying, "Great Father sends us presents and wants new road, but white chief goes with soldiers to steal the road

before Indians can say yes or no!" With that, Red Cloud stalked off the treaty grounds, taking most of his warriors with him.

Commissioner Taylor continued with the conference and persuaded the remaining chiefs to sign an agreement allowing use of the Bozeman Trail. It concerned him little that the signatories were primarily Laramie loafers and a handful of leaders not affected by the proposed right-of-way. "Satisfactory treaty concluded with the Sioux and Cheyennes. Most cordial feelings prevail," he immediately wired his superiors in Washington.

The extent of the cordiality—or rather, the lack

White settlement clashed with the nomadic lifestyle of the Plains tribes and brought war to much of the West by the 1860s. Viewed by Indians as trespassers, frontiersmen such as Ralph Morrison, right, often died violent deaths. He was killed in 1868 by Cheyennes near Fort Dodge, Kansas. A Sioux and Cheyenne war party, above right, destroyed an army detachment on Wyoming's Bozeman Trail in 1866. Military motifs of the old days, in a modern painting, above, include an army button and a Cheyenne war shield.

Sioux, opposite, met with representatives of the U.S. Army, including Generals William S. Harney and William T. Sherman, in 1868, to demand the army's departure from the Powder River country of Wyoming and Montana. Only then would a treaty be accepted. Pictured above, from left to right, Red Bear, Pecks His Drum, and Old Man Afraid of His Horses appear with others who signed the Treaty of Fort Laramie.

thereof—soon became evident as Red Cloud's war parties harassed travelers and the garrisons building Bozeman Trail forts. Fort Phil Kearney, Carrington's headquarters, sustained more Indian attacks than any other post in American history. Actually, Red Cloud never attempted a direct assault on the fort proper, with its log palisade, but continually sent war parties against the work crews cutting trees on the slopes of nearby mountains.

An attack on a wagon train bringing logs to build up Fort Kearney provided Red Cloud his finest moment, and enabled the bold young Crazy Horse to join the pantheon of American Indian heroes.

On that fateful December day in 1866, Carrington allowed Captain William J. Fetterman and a combined force of cavalry troopers and infantry out of the fort to chase away what seemed to be a raiding party of Sioux and Cheyenne warriors who had attacked the wood train within sight of the garrison. Crazy Horse lured the relief column over a nearby hill and into a fatal ambush.

Brash and impetuous, Civil War veteran Fetterman disdained the fighting abilities of the Plains Indian. Certain that he could overtake Crazy Horse, whose pony appeared to limp, Fetterman dashed over the hill and led his small command into the hands of 2,000 warriors. Within minutes, only a dog that had followed the troopers remained alive; it, too, was shot when a warrior yelled, "Do not let even a dog get away!"

Eighty horribly mutilated corpses carried a clear message from Red Cloud's warriors. One corpse, that of a civilian who had joined the column to test his new repeating rifle against Indians, bristled with 105 arrows. Probably terrified at the rather unlikely prospect of being taken alive, Fetterman and his second-in-command committed suicide.

Red Cloud's stunning victory brought instant and surprising results. Rather than seek revenge, the federal government decided to improve the way the nation's Indian affairs were being managed. Appointed in 1867, a peace commission toured the Plains and concluded that most instances of Indian violence had been provoked by whites. At the commission's urging, the army closed the Bozeman Trail and abandoned the offending forts, one of the few instances in the history of relations between whites and Indians in which the white man retreated.

Some scholars now suggest that the entire Bozeman saga may have been orchestrated by monied interests, empire builders who might have wished to distract Red Cloud and his warriors from the work crews constructing the transcontinental railroad. Whatever the details, in hindsight it is clear that rails were about to render trails obsolete.

For Red Cloud, his victory offered the old story of winning the battle and losing the war. The Treaty of Fort Laramie, signed in 1868, negated the earlier agreement approving the trail but also established a great Sioux reservation west of the Missouri River in Dakota Territory. By assenting to the treaty, the chiefs agreed to settle near agencies and accept reservation life. True to his word, Red Cloud quit the warpath, but also forfeited the respect of those leaders who had refused to sign the treaty.

The Fetterman debacle also aided implementation of President Ulysses S. Grant's "Quaker Policy," so-called for its key feature, the appointment of clergymen and nominees of religious organizations as Indian agents. Few could fault the reasoning behind the policy, as corruption among civilian Indian agents was notorious. Otherwise, why should the low-paying agencies be such attractive political plums? Typical of venal officialdom was Upper Arkansas Indian agent Samuel G. Colley. Within two years of his appointment in 1861, he and a son had parlayed a herd of 30 cows into a small fortune of $25,000. For years, humanitarians and reformers had been seeking to correct the abuses in the federal system relating to Indians, and now it seemed the time had finally arrived.

Although the reformers prevailed throughout the Grant administration, their approach was no panacea, and the proselytizing of some high-minded but overzealous agents antagonized the tribes. Religious groups squabbled over the division of the reservations, and some of the smaller denominations lacked qualified volunteers. Agency administration soon returned to business-as-usual, with the worst abuses corrected by reform legislation introduced before 1900.

Grant's peace policy also had its shining moment, the all-too-brief tenure as Indian commissioner of a New York Seneca, Ely S. Parker. In this case, cronyism worked: Parker had served as Grant's military secretary during the Civil War and was one of the ablest and best-educated people ever to head the Bureau of Indian Affairs. He was also the first Indian to hold the post of commissioner.

Parker opposed the treaty-making system because he believed it was based on an erroneous assumption that the tribes were sovereign nations. His recommendation to abolish treaties coincided with a drive in the United States House of Representatives for more participation in Indian affairs. As matters stood, ratification of all treaties was the Senate's prerogative. Though existing treaties remained in force, this practice was terminated in 1871; subsequently, new-style "agreements" became

law only when ratified by both the House and the Senate. Running afoul of the Board of Indian Commissioners, another component of Grant's peace policy, Parker was unjustly charged with fraud and resigned to return home and await his exoneration.

The Board of Indian Commissioners, reputedly weak and ineffective, still retained enough clout to stir up many a hornet's nest by exposing waste, fraud, and abuse. Established in 1869 to control the corruption associated with Indian affairs, the board consisted of ten high-minded, unpaid philanthro-

Hoping to awe Indians, the government invited many to Washington, D.C. Red Cloud, below, a Sioux chief, made 12 trips. Potawatomi, Pawnee, Ponca, and Sac and Fox leaders see the White House in 1857, right.

pists whose primary task was to oversee fiscal matters within the Bureau of Indian Affairs. They had their work cut out for them, particularly regarding a key component of the peace policy, that of Indian delegations. As the commissioners explained in their 1872 annual report, "It would cost less to carry every warrior of the untamed tribes on a tour through the States than [to incur] the expense of one campaign against a single tribe."

No one could refute such logic, because most Indians who had been east prior to the Civil War had remained peaceful, doubtless shocked by the huge cities, the abundant technology, and the crowds they encountered everywhere. An agent accompanying Red Cloud and Spotted Tail on an eastern excursion in 1870 overheard several of the Indians discussing the great numbers of whites in evidence. The astonished warriors at first believed that they were seeing the same people in each city. Chicago's population had somehow scampered ahead of them to Washington, Philadelphia, and then New York. The delegates were convinced that

B-4669

An early-19th-century war-medicine shield, below, of Crow Chief Arapoosh, depicts a vision of the moon in a human form, and recalls a time when tribes had distinct social clubs of warriors who competed to be the bravest in battle. War costumes indicated the vision-spirit protection of the warriors. A fight between Sioux and Crow forces, opposite, drawn by a Crow named Above in 1884, may be his recollection of an encounter.

white people had developed the means of moving whole cities, much like the Sioux themselves transported their tipi villages from one site to another.

Each delegation's tour followed a similar script. The bewildered Indians met with government officials, endured guided tours of arsenals, battleships, and forts, and then appeared before the President, whom they addressed as the Great Father. This title of respect implied no subordination: "Great White Father" was never used, the testimony of motion pictures notwithstanding.

Besides discovering the folly of military defiance, delegates were also expected to accept the superiority of civilized life. Yet this aspect of delegation policy was a signal failure, as few Indians returned home wanting to trade places with their white brothers. Ten Bears of the Comanches expressed "a big disgust at the noise, confusion, and crowds of the city." Chief Spotted Tail of the Brulé Sioux, for his part, much preferred watching women to surveying the cultural attractions specially arranged for his delegation. Why, he asked at one point, did President Grant have only one wife when he could choose from so many pretty women? By the time he reached New York City, even feminine beauty failed to hold the chief's attention, and he slept through a carriage ride along Broadway.

The officials who arranged the delegate tours were perplexed. "It is a curious, and almost painful fact," admitted the agent who accompanied Spotted Tail, "that nearly all these Indians were often so home-sick that they would urge the agents to move on, as fast as possible, toward their wild homes in the remote west."

No warrior left Washington unimpressed by his military education, however. Huge shore guns shook the earth as they hurled thousand-pound projectiles at an unseen target in the distance and rapid-fire Gatling guns blazed away, fed by an inexhaustible mountain of ammunition. Such force and abundance lay beyond any Indian's wildest dreams. Most amazing of all were the tens of thousands of muskets and rifles at the Washington Arsenal, "a forest of guns," as one astonished visitor muttered.

On another note, as the Board of Indian Commissioners quickly learned, the delegations yielded a swindler's harvest. "It is no easy matter for an Agent to visit Washington and get off whole," admitted a government clerk in 1874. "The town is full of sharks who make Indian delegations and their Agents a summer prey." The delegates often stayed at the finest hotels, ate the best food, and patronized such cultural events as the opera and the theater. Yet they were exploited and manipulated beyond belief; both agents and merchants cheated and almost always got away with it. Shopkeepers charged the government inflated prices for inferior products, while agents authorized payments for services and merchandise never received.

Only a blind accountant could have missed the mistakes in the expense vouchers submitted to the Bureau of Indian Affairs for payment. Probably the worst excesses involved three delegations—Utes,

Sioux Chief Gall, left, and his adopted brother, Sitting Bull, refused to move to a reservation as the 1868 Fort Laramie treaty dictated. Led by Gall, Rain in the Face, below, and others, the Indians won a stunning victory at the Battle of Little Bighorn on June 25, 1876. White Man Runs Him, opposite, led Crow scouts who reconnoitered for Col. George Armstrong Custer and the Seventh Cavalry before the Little Bighorn disaster.

Crows, and a joint Cheyenne and Arapaho group—that visited Washington during the summer of 1872. The 15-member Ute delegation traveled to Mount Vernon aboard a Potomac River excursion boat and was charged for 24 tickets and lunches. How did 15 people eat 24 lunches? A wit in the auditor's office thought that such appetites demonstrated "the wonderfully bracing effect of a short voyage on the Potomac."

More significant were this same delegation's clothing bills, totaling $8,225.40. Each of the delegates supposedly purchased several business suits, numerous pairs of boots, hats, shirts, liberal supplies of underwear, sleeve buttons, shirt studs, suspenders, ladies' kid gloves, balmoral skirts, pulse warmers, and a variety of other incidentals. One auditor noted that all this indicated "quite a civilized taste on the part of the poor Indian." One of the offending Indian agents asked what difference it made. He added that the Indians enjoyed themselves and the only money wasted was their own.

Surely some of those purchases found their way into the hands of wives, friends, and even enemies back home. The Indian way of life demanded, and often still demands, that good fortune be shared with the entire tribe. News of the trip, though, was far more difficult to accept than the gifts themselves. Many fellow tribesmen refused to believe the wondrous tales of the returned delegates. A member of the Assiniboine tribe murdered his chief, The Light, after listening to his travel stories. Sitting Bull himself discounted the fabulous tales of Sioux delegates as figments of the imagination induced by the white man's powerful "medicine." Only after his startling victory at the Battle of the Little Bighorn did Sitting Bull go and see for himself, and then not as a member of a delegation: at the urging of "Buffalo Bill" Cody, Sitting Bull joined the Wild West show.

Quaker Indian agents, delegations to the East, and empty promises could not long restrain Indian resentments of their treatment by whites, which finally erupted in the early 1870s. No corner of the Great West at that time escaped the wrath of angry tribesmen who lashed out in a final, desperate attempt to keep the white man at bay.

Few peoples ever fought harder to maintain their traditional way of life than did the Sioux and their Cheyenne and Arapaho kinsmen. And although Red Cloud signed the Treaty of Fort Laramie in 1868 and accepted the reservation, many other Sioux leaders had not. Sitting Bull, Crazy Horse, and Gall all roamed at will on unceded Indian lands. The construction of the Northern Pacific Railroad through Dakota and Montana territories, the heart of Sioux country, triggered the next confrontation.

The military decided that a new fort was necessary to guard the railroad and that the ideal site for the structure lay somewhere in the Black Hills, a sacred precinct in the southwestern portion of the great Sioux reservation. Colonel George Armstrong Custer led an expedition into the Black Hills to establish a precise site for the fort and, in the process, discovered gold. Prospectors soon overran the country, and the army faced a losing battle trying to keep them off Sioux land. When a move to purchase the Black Hills failed in 1875, the commissioners recommended government action against the Sioux and their allies for failing to meet the terms of the Treaty of Fort Laramie in 1868 by stray-

ing off the reservation. This pretext for rounding up the likes of Sitting Bull was subject to debate, as the treaty plainly allowed for hunting rights in the unceded lands. Regardless of the merits of the case, the federal government acted against the "hostiles" and ordered the person who precipitated the crisis —Custer—to apprehend Sitting Bull and take him to the reservation.

Few people know that Custer had hired four Sioux, thirty Arikaras, and six Crows as scouts. One of those Crow scouts was White Man Runs Him, grandfather of Joseph Medicine Crow, the tribe's official historian. As White Man Runs Him later told his grandson, the Crows informed Custer that Sitting Bull's village was too large for the Seventh to attack and asked him to await reinforcements. Custer refused, however, lest the Sioux escape and deprive him of the victory he so desperately wanted and anticipated. When Custer later noticed one of

"After the Battle," a painting by J.K. Ralston, depicts warriors and family members collecting arms, clothes, and other items carried by the soldiers during the Battle of Little Bighorn, popularly known as Custer's Last Stand. Sioux contingents under Gall and Crazy Horse and Cheyennes under Lame White Man wiped out five companies of the Seventh Cavalry who had attacked their village on the Little Bighorn River. White encroachment on the Black Hills of South Dakota—considered sacred by the Sioux—had made an Indian war inevitable.

the Crow scouts taking off his uniform and putting on traditional dress, he asked the scout why he was changing. Speaking through an interpreter, the young man replied, "We are all going to die today, so I intend to meet the Great Spirit dressed as an Indian, not as a white man." This comment so angered Custer that he immediately fired his Crow scouts; thus none of them died with Custer.

The Crow scouts and other tribal guides often worked for more than money; they were part of a legacy of intertribal warfare that predated the arrival of white men on the Plains. Fighting alone, the outnumbered Crow people had long managed to hold off their traditional Sioux and Cheyenne enemies and thus protect their beloved lands. Hardy, brave, and cunning, they also saw a way to even old scores by embracing the white man as an ally against the Sioux.

The Crows still suffered from Sioux aggression as late as the 1860s and 1870s, and understandably viewed the United States Army as a weapon in their centuries-old struggle for survival. Unfortunately, in helping the United States defeat their Sioux

enemies, the Crows consigned themselves to the same destiny as the Sioux. In the end, both tribes accepted the inevitable—life on a reservation. Unlike the lands assigned to many other tribes, however, the Crow reservation included at least part of an ancestral homeland.

The Little Bighorn victory over Custer on June 25, 1876, proved the undoing of the Sioux and their allies. Just as America was trumpeting its rise to world power, a hodge-podge of undisciplined aboriginals had demolished one of the nation's most glamorous and efficient fighting units. Imagine the shock and embarrassment that Custer's defeat caused Americans on the very eve of the centennial celebration of their independence. The army went after Sitting Bull and friends with a vengeance; before 1877 was done, most of the militants were either on reservations or with Sitting Bull in Canada, where a few diehards remained until 1883.

A particularly cruel fate befell the Northern Cheyennes wintering over in Wyoming during late 1876. Their camp became the target of 1,000 cavalrymen, who ejected them and destroyed their tipis, clothing, and food supply on November 26. Eleven Cheyenne babies froze to death that night. Crazy Horse aided the survivors, but they surrendered in the spring, expecting reservation life but not relocation 1,000 miles from their northern-Plains homeland. Their own trail of tears lasted 70 days and led them to what is now Oklahoma. The government subjected them to a new program designed to concentrate as many groups as possible in the restricted space of the Indian Territory, to which two dozen tribes eventually were moved.

Rather than die by degrees, 300 Northern Cheyennes under chiefs Dull Knife and Little Wolf made a desperate dash for Montana. They lacked tents and sufficient food. Although only one in five was a warrior and all were poorly armed and mounted, they eluded several army battalions sent to stop them. They reached the Dakota country in December 1878 and split into two groups, some joining Little Wolf to winter deep in the Wyoming wilderness and others, thinking themselves safe, surrendering with Dull Knife at Fort Robinson, Nebraska. When the latter party learned it would be sent back

Still encased in a boot, right middle, the leg of a cavalry trooper marks a site missed by the 1881 party that interred other remains on the Little Bighorn battlefield in a mass grave. Finds of bullets and cartridge cases plotted on a map, bottom right, reveal Indian and army positions on the terrain. A cartridge case, shown at far right of the map, split open when a standard army round was fired in an Indian weapon of larger caliber. A detailed archeological survey of the site in 1984 and 1985, right, turned up more than 4,000 artifacts. Identification of cartridge cases and bullets indicates that the Sioux and Cheyenne warriors not only outnumbered the soldiers but also possessed more than 300 modern repeating rifles. Opposite, soldiers return to the Montana site in 1879 to rebury remains.

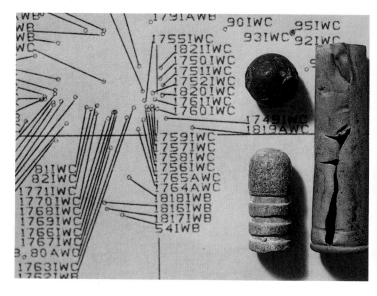

to Oklahoma, it refused, and authorities confined the Indians to unheated barracks without food or water. During the night of January 9, 1879, the imprisoned Cheyennes made a suicidal break for freedom. Of 149 held in the barracks, 64 died. Most of the others, many gravely wounded, were recaptured.

Iron Teeth, who was among those at Fort Robinson, later told of her experience. Her husband had died in the 1876 attack on their village at the Powder River in Wyoming, but she had survived and, with her five children, had traveled to Oklahoma and then participated in the escape. When the large group split up, a son and a daughter joined Little Wolf. She and the remaining children, including a grown son, followed Dull Knife to Fort Robinson. During the breakout, she kept one daughter with her and hid in a cave until caught. Armed with a pistol, her son Gathering His Medicine packed the youngest girl on his back and found another cave. When soldiers tracked him through the snow, Gathering His Medicine told his sister to stay hidden while he challenged them. "Lots of times," Iron Teeth admitted, "as I sit here alone on the floor with my blanket wrapped about me, I lean forward and close my eyes and think of him . . . fighting the soldiers, knowing that he would be killed, but doing this so his little sister might get away in safety. Don't you think he was a brave young man?"

A small group of Poncas led by Standing Bear also fled Indian Territory, where they had been beset by illness and death. The Ponca leader, deter-

Guns as well as more traditional arms were necessities for the well-equipped Indian fighting man of the Great Plains. Trade with whites brought steel weapons, but most of these soon bore decoration. From times before the American Revolution, warriors coveted the flintlock trade musket, upper right. The 1866 Henry repeating carbine, upper left, was the type of weapon that won the Battle of Little Bighorn. A Cherokee chief made the underhammer pistol, at center, in 1845. The Hawken Plains rifle, also at center, served frontiersmen and Indians alike. Lines of brass studs adorn a Sharps rifle.

mined to bury his son on the tribe's former land in Nebraska, traveled with 30 followers to the Omaha Reservation, where a military unit commanded by General George Crook detained them. Two lawyers came to Standing Bear's aid before Crook could return the Poncas.

Crook was served with a writ challenging the right of the government to hold the group. When the United States attorney responded that as wards of the government these Indians were not "persons within the meaning of the law," a legal battle ensued. *Standing Bear* vs. *Crook* proved to be a precedent-setting civil-rights case, and in 1879 the judge ruled that an "Indian is a person within the meaning of the law." Standing Bear and his followers continued their journey to the Niobrara River country, where they remained.

The Indians of the northern Plains probably experienced the greatest overall violence in the period after the Civil War, and their situation was by no means unique. The military, under famed frontiersman Christopher "Kit" Carson, rounded up the Navajos of the Southwest and forced them on their "Long Walk," a 300-mile trek to an inhospitable reservation on the Pecos River in New Mexico. Here, 2,000 Navajos died of smallpox. The survivors finally were allowed to return to their own country after a delegation to Washington pleaded the tribe's case and pledged that it would mend its ways. That the Navajos managed to come through such trial and tragedy with a minimum of cultural loss was primarily due to their pastoral and agricultural way of life, practiced in an area shunned by white settlers. The 1868 treaty providing for their reservation was one of the last ratified by the Senate.

Indians of California were far less lucky. "*Genocide*," writes historian William T. Hagan, "is a term of awful significance, but one which has application to the story of California's Native Americans." Scattered in small bands that lacked both numbers and political unity, the California Indians were easy prey for whites who were anxious to strike it rich in the years following the discovery of gold. Prospectors and miners drove the Indians from ore-rich streams and valleys. Claiming that they stole livestock and produce, ranchers and farmers hunted

Warrior-in-exile Chief Joseph of the Nez Percé, seated (above left), was photographed with Gen. John Gibbon near Lake Chelan, Washington, in 1889. The epic flight of the Nez Percé tribe across three states and 1,700 miles in 1877 cost them more than 300 lives. Many more died in exile in Kansas and Oklahoma. Though they fled to avoid confinement, they were ultimately settled on an Idaho reservation, where the warriors at left were photographed in 1906. The girl, above, in traditional garb was pictured at the same site in 1982.

them down with dogs. Diseases and a state law that permitted whites to maintain Indians as indentured servants hastened their disappearance. The law was little more than a license to enslave Indian women and children.

The experiences of the Modoc and Nez Percé tribes are indicative of the trials of Indians in the Northwest. Forcibly removed from California to Oregon, the Modocs would be largely forgotten today were it not for their encounter with the army, which was sent to forcibly return them to the reservation. For six months a handful of poorly equipped warriors occupied the Lava Beds, terrain in northern California that resembles a moonscape. Led by a man known to whites as Captain Jack, they defied ranks of soldiers many times their own number. Scores of similar incidents marked the progress of Indian-white relations in North America, of course, but this one stood out because the Modocs killed two men under a flag of truce, one of them the only general to die at Indian hands.

Captain Jack and three other Modoc leaders paid with their lives. After their execution,

officials severed their heads and shipped them to Washington for study by phrenologists intent on discovering the cranial characteristics that had governed their supposedly criminal behavior. These relics, symbols of Manifest Destiny's dark side, remained in the nation's capital until 1984, when the Smithsonian Institution returned them to the Modoc people for burial.

Another freedom fight, the Nez Percé War of 1877, ranks close to Custer's last campaign in terms of historical interest and military tactics and strategy. Unusual restraint by the Indian belligerents marked this entire campaign. Warriors tried to spare civilian lives and even tended wounded soldiers who fell into their hands. Indeed, never in the 75 years since they had befriended explorers Lewis and Clark had the Nez Percé people been known to take the blood of a single white man. Sadly, such relations changed after white squatters insisted that the government move the Nez Percé onto a reservation at Lapwai, Idaho, as specified in an 1855 treaty.

Although many members of the tribe made the move, Joseph, Looking Glass, White Bird, and others refused. They represented "pagan" or "non-Christian" elements of the tribe and, since they had not signed the agreement, did not consider themselves bound by it. Violence broke out when three young men killed four settlers. Uncertain about what to do, the defiant group of Indians finally decided to flee their homeland and seek refuge in Canada with Sitting Bull. Thus, in mid-July 1877, they began an epic trek. Eight hundred Nez Percé joined the four-month odyssey that took them over the Bitterroot Mountains into Yellowstone National Park (where they frightened groups of tourists and killed two people), and on to the Bear Paw Mountains and a campsite less than 40 miles from the Canadian border. They conducted themselves with considerable dignity along the way, committing few atrocities and paying for the supplies and ammunition they obtained from farmers and merchants. They fought and defeated several numerically superior forces attempting to intercept them. No wonder embarrassed military commanders began to believe they were chasing a "red Napoleon."

Nomadic herders and raiders of the Southwest, the Navajos prospered with horses and sheep obtained from the Spanish, right. Conflict with American settlers trespassing on traditional Navajo grazing lands brought Christopher "Kit" Carson and federal troops in 1862. The tribe was forced to march more than 300 miles to Fort Sumner in Bosque Redondo, New Mexico Territory, above left, where they suffered from hard labor, disease, exposure, and crop failure. At left, Navajo woman with cradleboard at Bosque Redondo. In 1868 the tribe was allowed to return to a reservation carved from their homeland.

As part of a coming-of-age rite, White Mountain Apache Cora Knight, above, is showered with pollen. Opposite above, Hopi dancers perform during the Niman Kachina at Shongopavi Pueblo, Arizona Territory, in 1901. Kachinas are supernatural guardians of the Hopi. Fertility Symbols, opposite below, by Hopi artist Waldo Mootzka, honors pollination of the corn, central to traditional Hopi life.

It is doubtful whether Napoleon himself could have done much better at escaping, given the handicaps facing the Nez Percé group. Women and children outnumbered the men three to one. Not only were the whites against them, but many of the tribes to whom they appealed for assistance turned on them. Warriors from several tribes joined in the chase, partly attracted by the desire to steal some of the fine Appaloosa horses for which the Nez Percé breeders were justifiably famous. The fight also afforded these warriors a rare opportunity to once again earn war coups (traditional honors for specific feats performed in battle), even if it meant doing so on behalf of the United States Army.

The Nez Percé party might have escaped, had it not paused for rest before crossing into Canada. Surrounded by an overwhelming force armed with cannons, the group had three options: surrender, fight, or break away during the night, leaving the elderly and wounded behind. For five days they kept the whites and allied Indians at bay. During that time, White Bird and 300 followers slipped into Canada. On October 5, 1877, Joseph finally ended the struggle.

"I am tired of fighting," he reportedly told Colonel Nelson A. Miles in a speech that smacks of journalistic embellishment. "Our chiefs are killed. Looking Glass is dead. Toohoolhoolzote is dead. The old men are all dead. It is the young men who say yes or no. He who led the young men [Joseph's brother Ollokot] is dead. It is cold and we have no blankets. The little children are freezing to death. . . . Hear me my chiefs! I am tired. My heart is sick and sad. From where the sun now stands, I will fight no more forever."

Because of the surrender speech, Joseph has received much of the credit for the gallant retreat of the Nez Percé people. Actually, the key decisions had been made by a group of leaders, but most of them had either been killed or had crossed into Canada, leaving Joseph behind.

Captain Jack and Joseph share certain similarities—their English names and their faithfulness to their people and to themselves. Had Captain Jack not been executed, they would have also shared the same destiny. Both the Modoc and Nez Percé peoples were exiled to the Indian Territory, perhaps

the worst fate of all for those whose only real crime was a desire to keep their homeland.

Only scattered bands of one tribe remained at war with the United States by the 1880s. These Chiricahua Apaches had managed to withstand the forces of change in the Southwest for more than three centuries by farming tiny plots and raiding the Spanish and, later, the Mexicans. Wily, tough, and implacable, the Chiricahuas were conquered with the assistance of fellow tribesmen enlisted in the belief that only an Apache could catch an Apache. One reason for the Chiricahuas' success at escape and evasion was their ability to use the international boundary between the United States and Mexico as a shield. Depending on who was chasing them, Apache war parties enjoyed relative safety by crossing to the other side of the border when threatened. The game ended only after arrangements were made for troops of either Mexico or the United States to disregard the border when in hot pursuit of Apache raiders.

Highly effective in small units, the Apaches were regularly able to achieve stealth and surprise in their raiding operations. Beginning on March 21, 1883, for instance, a Chiricahua named Chatto led a force of 25 from Mexico into Arizona for six days. The several military units that rode out never sighted him. He and his men slipped back into Mexico after covering more than 400 miles, killing 26 people, and losing only one of their own.

General Nelson Miles, the officer responsible for Joseph's surrender a decade earlier, determined the strategy that brought the Apache wars to their conclusion. The diehards had maintained their independence by visiting relatives on Arizona reservations, gaining refuge, rest, moral support, and occasional reinforcements. Miles finally deported all the Chiricahua Apaches to detention camps in Florida. To close every loophole, he even bundled off men who had fought with the United States Army against their untamed kinsmen. The women and children went, too, but were placed in a different camp. Geronimo, last and most notorious of the Apache raiders, surrendered only a few weeks after the Chiricahuas were shipped by train to Florida in August 1886.

Except for a few incidents, all armed hostilities ceased after Geronimo's surrender. However, the brutal and sometimes bloody struggle left many western Indians embittered, since they were forced to accept a way of life they neither wanted nor understood, and were often given land that was useless for either white man's work or traditional Indian ways of life. Reservation soil might also be culturally sterile, with ancestors buried elsewhere and old landmarks left far behind.

In contrast, the Indians of Canada experienced little of the rancor or social and cultural deprivation that characterized relations with the tribes south of the international border. Only on two occasions did major hostilities open up between whites and Canadian Indians: in Manitoba during 1869, and in western Saskatchewan during 1885. Each incident was brief and relatively bloodless; each was led by Louis Riel, a Métis, or mixed-blood, anxious to establish a form of self-government for the Métis and their full-blooded kin of the western provinces. His execution after the second rebellion ended further difficulties between the Canadian government and its native peoples.

An interesting sidelight to the Riel rebellion of 1885 illustrates the differences that have marked Indian-white relations on each side of the border. A year after termination of hostilities, the Canadian government invited leaders of several powerful western tribes to visit Ontario and meet the prime minister. The purpose of the delegation was not to frighten the Indians into remaining peaceful, a primary motive behind the policy in the United States, but to thank the chiefs—three Bloods, two Piegans, and four Crees—for remaining loyal during the rebellion.

Canadian Indian policy was not necessarily more humanitarian than American policy, although probably wiser and certainly productive of

Exiled warriors Geronimo, at left below, and Naiche, son of Cochise, pose on a ranch in Oklahoma.

far less bloodshed. Although the Indians of Canada lost as much land as their kinsmen south of the border (only six million acres remained to Canada's Indians in 1923) the Canadians did not dislocate their native peoples. Official policy kept the numerous Indian bands as widely scattered as possible, in contrast to the American policy of concentration. This was done so that Canadian Indians could retain their traditional hunting economy, which made state support considerably cheaper. Though preservation of Canadian Indian culture was not a goal of the framers of the policy, nonetheless this purpose has been well served for more than a century.

Six million acres held by Indians in 1923 were divided among 2,200 reserves scattered across the Canadian wilderness. The philosophy behind the policy was well expressed by an official of the Canadian Indian Department in 1880. "I regard the Canadian system of allotting reserves to one or more bands together, in the localities in which they have had the habit of living, as far preferable to the

Painted by Chiricahua Chief Naiche in the 1890s, an Apache girl's puberty rite ceremony comes to life on doeskin, below.

American system of placing whole tribes on large reserves. . . . Moreover, the Canadian system of band reserves has a tendency to diminish the offensive strength of the Indian tribes, should they ever become restless."

It is doubtful such a policy could have worked in the United States. America's burgeoning population had filled nearly all usable space and the federal government seemed unable or unwilling to protect what little land remained to America's Indians by 1890. Canada, on the other hand, had a relatively small white population. Canada's approach to Indian life and culture, among other things, represented a matured English colonial policy with an older egalitarian base inherited from the French. After rejecting British guidance, Americans followed the dictates of the common man and evolved a populist policy that sometimes verged on genocide before 1900 but, later, allowed for independent tribal development.

The situation stabilized for Indians in the United States after they had lost the West. In a sense, though, wars continued, and these were fought on cultural and political fronts and against new foes, including humanitarians, educators, speculators, and bureaucrats. Each group claimed friendship with the Indian, yet each contributed in some measure to the continued degradation of the tribes. Indians of the United States won their victories through adaptation to new times and new challenges, and yet they kept the ancient and unbroken traditions that have sustained their peoples in the New World for 20,000 years or more. The chapters that follow outline that heroic struggle for cultural continuity and a renewal of self-reliance.

Chiricahua Mountains, below, of southeastern Arizona, hid Apache raiders until the army drove them out in 1886. At left, two boys, a black and a white, were captured by the Apaches to replace war losses.

Era of Internal Exile

Brulé Sioux leader Spotted Tail, left, poses with his sons at the Carlisle Indian Industrial School, Carlisle, Pennsylvania, in June 1880. Spotted Tail was a reluctant advocate of accommodation with whites, whose numbers and might he witnessed during trips to Washington as a spokesman for his people. Above, a bisque-headed doll nestles in a Kiowa toy cradleboard decorated with colored glass beads. Such dolls were prized by Indian children of the Great Plains during the late 19th century.

The period between 1880 and the First World War was one of stress and confusion for America's Indians. Having defeated them militarily, the U.S. government tried to defeat them politically, economically, and spiritually. Traditional ways were seriously challenged, deeply eroded; yet the pride of many Indians survived and was even strengthened.

The campaign started in Washington, D.C., when the government, allying itself with powerful eastern church groups and humanitarian organizations, launched a massive campaign to transform the Indians. The goal was to eradicate "Indianness" and to assimilate Indians into white society. Those involved believed that their aim could be accomplished only by altering tribal society and abolishing native religions.

Simply put, the credo of the humanitarians was "To reach the full-blooded Indian send after him a full-blooded Christian." Furthermore, give each Indian an allotment of tribal land. The reformers believed that private property lay at the heart of civilization. Ownership of land would provide Indians with the basic incentive to begin farming and to adopt all the other trappings of civilized life.

Allotments had been attempted on a minor scale —and had failed—as early as the 1850s. Yet the advocates insisted that such a program, modified and with suitable guarantees, could be made to work. Therefore, during the 1880s, the movement for allotments gained a ground swell of support, linking both eastern and western interests. Westerners welcomed the program because they stood to gain directly. Surplus lands belonging to individual tribes that had received their allotments were to be sold and opened to white settlement.

Already beaten in battle, dispirited, trapped between two worlds, nearly all Indians now were confronted with a new way of life they neither understood nor wanted. The western tribes sought escape through religions preached by three dreamer-prophets who appeared in the waning years of the 19th century and attempted to revitalize native cultures.

"Dreamers" was a term given by whites because two of the Indian preachers based their doctrines on spirit-world experiences induced by trances.

These two—Smohalla, a Wanapam, and Skolaskin, a Sanpoil—lived and died within 300 miles of each other along the Columbia River in the plateau country of the Pacific Northwest. Of the two, Smohalla was far more important, although both preached similar messages combining elements of Christianity with traditional tribal beliefs. Both emphasized adherence to traditional dress and lifeways. This speech by Smohalla, reported by an army officer in the 1880s, reflects their viewpoint:

You ask me to plow the ground! Shall I take a knife and tear my mother's bosom? Then when I die she will not take me to her bosom to rest.
You ask me to dig for stone! Shall I dig under her skin for her bones? Then when I die I can not enter her body to be born again.
You ask me to make hay and sell it, and be rich like white men! But dare I cut off my mother's hair?

Such teachings remained popular in the North-west well into the 1890s. The Indian Shaker Church, founded in 1881, was an important off-

By the close of the 19th century, the millions of rolling acres of grasses, forbs, and shrubs comprising the Great Plains, right, were empty of bison and antelope. The Plains tribes, who had roamed the prairie since time immemorial to hunt the bison, were banished to reservations. The Plains awaited the plow. Below, in a scene by no means typical of the time, Indian farmers on North Dakota's Fort Berthold Reservation pose with their traction engine, diskers, and seeders around 1910.

shoot of the movement, and numerous other sects appeared. Smohalla's religion gained national attention when Chief Joseph of the Nez Percé announced that he and his band were believers.

Wovoka, a Paiute living on the Walker River Reservation in western Nevada, founded the major nativist religion to appear at this time, the influential and widespread Ghost Dance. While delirious with fever during an eclipse of the sun in January 1889, Wovoka claimed, he had been carried into heaven where he spoke with God and saw departed Indians living in peace and happiness.

God gave Wovoka a message to take back to earth, he said. Indians could enjoy Wovoka's paradise if they remained at peace, lived honest and industrious lives, and performed the special dance God had taught his prophet. After Wovoka displayed

apparent supernatural control of the elements, his fellow Paiutes followed him with enthusiasm and his message spread to nearly every reservation in the West.

The Ghost Dance religion has come to be most closely associated with the Sioux. Their emissaries, as well as those of other tribes, went to Wovoka to learn firsthand. Returning home during March 1890, the Sioux messengers carried marvelous stories about the Indian messiah, but they changed his peaceable teachings and launched a militant and explicitly anti-white movement.

Wovoka, they said, promised that during the spring of 1891 the whites would disappear, that dead Indians would return to life, and that buffalo would once again fill the Plains. For this to happen, however, Indians everywhere had to practice the

In an undated photograph from the late 19th century, Sioux in the Dakotas wait to receive government rations, left. The issuing of rations began after treaties were implemented in 1868 and 1876 to confine the tribes to reservations. To bridge the gap between hunting and farming, agents handed out beef, flour, and other necessities, often with indifferent regularity, causing much hardship. Agents punched ration tickets, below, issued quarterly. These are for the Pine Ridge Agency, 1882, 1883, and 1884.

On beef day at Cut Meat, Rosebud Agency, South Dakota, in 1893, Sioux butcher cattle distributed by the government agent. Reluctant farmers, some Sioux became successful cattlemen until World War I, when they sold off their herds.

No.245. MODERN INDIAN HOME. PHOTO. BY J. A. ANDERSON.

Ghost Dance. The Sioux needed little urging.

It is difficult for us today to appreciate their trauma: living upon barren and isolated tracts of land, enduring economic and emotional poverty, and confronting tremendous pressures on their traditional culture. No longer could they hunt the buffalo or practice their old religion or fight. Instead, the government ordered them to become farmers, raise crops and cattle, and send their children away to boarding school so they could become educated Christians.

Total dependence on government rations further undermined traditional Indian self-reliance. Compounding their miseries, the government in 1885 had taken a census of the Sioux, discovered that their population was less than expected, and immediately reduced rations. The disastrous winter of 1886 followed, killing off a third of their cattle. The summer of 1890 was especially severe. Drought and heat thwarted efforts by farmers to raise crops.

"The Sioux country in that year was a veritable dust bowl," wrote Elaine Goodale, a white teacher on one of the reservations. "The pitiful little gar-

dens curled up and died in the persistent hot winds. Even young men displayed gaunt limbs and lack-luster faces. Old folks lost their hold on life, and heart-broken mothers mourned the last of a series of dead babies."

Little wonder, then, that the Sioux were ready to grasp at anything that offered them hope for a better life: in this case, a wondrous life. Within a remarkably short time, large numbers of tribesmen on Sioux reservations in both Dakotas embraced the new religion. Ghost Dancing became a widespread and daily phenomenon. Dancers would sit on the ground facing a small tree. Then, following a brief ceremony and the eating of sacred food, they would rise, join hands, and begin singing as they circled the tree. The songs, like this one recorded by Smithsonian ethnologist James Mooney, evoked vivid images of the old way of life:

The whole world is coming,
A nation is coming, a nation is coming,
The eagle has brought the message to the tribe.
The father says so, the father says so.

Over the whole earth they are coming,
The buffalo are coming, the buffalo are coming,
The crow has brought the message to the tribe,
The father says so, the father says so.

Dancers moved slowly and sang softly at first, but the tempo increased. Faster and faster the circle moved until the dancers would become so dizzy and tired that some would collapse, falling into a trance. This was the goal of each dancer. Enraptured, the person's spirit would visit Wovoka's paradise and greet dead relatives and friends. Those who did not faint would wait for the others to awaken and relate their wonderful tales. Some Sioux dancers claimed their spirits had received special powers that would enable them to kill whites.

This religion's spread greatly alarmed Indian agents who viewed Ghost Dancing as a threat to their authority and a harbinger of armed conflict. Many such men, products of the patronage system at its worst, were inexperienced, ineffectual, and unprepared for crisis. Typical was the Pine Ridge

agent, Daniel F. Royer, whom the Sioux dubbed Young-Man-Afraid-of-Indians. On December 15, 1890, when Ghost Dancers defied him and his Indian policemen, Royer telegraphed the Commissioner of Indian Affairs, "Indians are dancing in the snow and are wild and crazy. . . . *We need protection and we need it now.*"

Five days later, infantry and cavalry units equipped with both Hotchkiss rapid-fire cannons and Gatling machine guns rattled onto the Pine Ridge and Rosebud reservations. Rather than restore order, the soldiers greatly escalated the danger of a confrontation. In fact, the presence of the military pushed the Ghost Dancers into armed defiance of

Under strong pressure from government agents to build houses and take up farming, many Sioux, like this man and child of the Rosebud Reservation in South Dakota, opposite, tended tiny plots in season and lived in houses in the winter, returning to traditional tipis in the summer. Below, Sioux girls pose in uniforms at the Rosebud Agency in 1926.

the government. Large numbers of them gathered in the badlands in the northwest corner of the Pine Ridge Reservation where, by their dancing, they threw themselves into a frenzy.

When Sitting Bull, then in retirement on the Standing Rock Reservation, threatened to join the dancers, government officials decided to have him arrested. This, too, was bungled. On the morning of December 15, forty Indian policemen approached Sitting Bull's cabin and sparked a fierce gun battle in which the old chief, seven of his followers,

and six policemen died. Only the timely arrival of reinforcements saved the policemen from annihilation.

Government overreaction took its toll once again. Even before the attempted arrest, disillusioned Ghost Dancers had relented and retreated. The onset of winter and threat of starvation had sapped their militancy and all of the separate groups were bound for their reservations by the end of December. In fact, further bloodshed probably would have been avoided had not troops of the Seventh Cavalry intercepted one of the last bands of returning Ghost Dancers.

Led by Big Foot (also known as Spotted Elk), this ill-starred group included some of the most militant dancers. In all, Big Foot's people—men, women, and children—numbered 350. Most were Miniconjou Sioux, with members of other bands. After the death of their chief, 38 followers of Sitting Bull had also joined these Ghost Dancers.

A former delegate to Washington, Big Foot was revered by his tribe as one of its greatest chiefs. The people were cold, hungry, disheartened, and Big Foot had fallen gravely ill with pneumonia and rode in the back of a wagon. They were fewer than 30 miles from Pine Ridge Agency when eight troops of the Seventh Cavalry—Colonel Custer's old outfit—appeared, to escort them to the army camp on Wounded Knee Creek. Big Foot was given a large army tent and a camp stove and made as comfortable as possible. Although the Indians had offered no resistance, the army decided to disarm them in the morning.

When morning came, the Sioux found themselves in the middle of a military park consisting of 500 soldiers and a battery of four Hotchkiss cannons. The Indian men were assembled in front of Big Foot's tent and told to surrender their guns. This order further angered and frightened them, because they suspected that the soldiers planned to kill them once they were disarmed. As squads of soldiers searched the Indian tents for weapons, other troops approached the men who stood in a rough line, their blankets clutched tightly about them. An already tense situation was made worse by Yellow Bird, a medicine man and staunch Ghost Dancer.

"Do not be afraid," he exhorted the warriors, many of whom were wearing ghost shirts—ritual garments believed to afford protection against injury. "I have received assurance that their bullets cannot penetrate us; the prairie is large and the bullets will not go toward you; they will not penetrate you."

At this moment someone fired a gun. The compound became a frenzied battleground as the Indian men, after grappling with the surrounding soldiers, rushed towards their wives and children.

Students assemble in front of the Pine Ridge Agency Boarding School, Dakota Territory, in 1884. Reservation schools and national boarding schools such as the Carlisle Indian Industrial School enrolled nearly 22,000 students by 1900; most aimed at suppression of Indian ways and integration of students into white society. An 1884 Leslie's Illustrated Newspaper *depicts a Carlisle student visiting her home at Pine Ridge— and unwittingly hints at the difficulties such students would face upon return to their homes.*

Boys from several tribes make up
a baseball team, above, at the
Hampton Institute in Virginia,
founded in 1868 to educate freed
slaves. Richard H. Pratt, later the
founder of the Carlisle School,
convinced Hampton principal
Samuel C. Armstrong to accept
Indians in 1878. Opposite, Carlisle
students accompany their teacher
on a field trip. Right, by their beds
in a barracks-like dormitory at the
Phoenix Indian School, girls from
various Arizona tribes kneel to
pray in 1900.

When the Indians broke free of the troops, the artillerymen opened fire with their cannons which, when massed, could deliver 50 explosive shells a minute. Although they later claimed they tried to avoid harming women and children, it was almost impossible to sort them out in the melee.

When Yellow Bird and a few of the warriors took cover in the Indian camp and began shooting at soldiers, artillery quickly reduced the tipis to lodgepole skeletons. Then the focus of the shooting shifted to a nearby ravine where surviving Indians—men, women, and children alike—sought shelter. The artillerymen moved their cannons and soon raked this area with fire. Although a few Indians tried to resist, most simply ran until they succumbed to their injuries or to exhaustion. By noon, most of the shooting had stopped and the task of collecting the dead and wounded began.

Due to a blizzard, three days passed before the army returned to Wounded Knee to bury the Indian dead. The burial party interred 146 on the battlefield—84 men and youths, 44 women, and 18

Winnebago artist and Carlisle graduate Angel De Cora illustrated fellow Carlisle student Francis La Flesche's memoir of his experiences with this scene, above, in which Brush, an experienced student, comforts the recently arrived La Flesche. The Middle Five: Indians Boys at School was published in 1900. New students, such as the Sioux boys at Carlisle, opposite, were allowed to keep their traditional dress only long enough for a "before" photograph to be taken. Three years later, the same boys pose in uniform, left.

children. Fifty-one Indian casualties, including a woman with 14 wounds, were taken to Pine Ridge where seven more people died. Many more corpses were taken from the battlefield by relatives after the soldiers left, and a few people escaped unharmed. The exact toll will never be known.

As for the soldiers, they counted 25 officers and enlisted men dead—some of whom were trapped in a deadly cross fire and killed by their fellow troopers—and 37 other casualties. One wounded soldier was killed by a badly injured woman who crawled from the village with a butcher knife in her teeth and stabbed him to death before another soldier shot her.

A photographer from Chadron, Nebraska, accompanied the burial party, as did Charles Eastman, a Santee Sioux himself and the physician at Pine Ridge. The first body they encountered, that of a woman, lay under the snow a full three miles from the scene of the fighting. "From this point on," Eastman recalled, "we found them scattered along as they had been relentlessly hunted down and slaughtered while fleeing for their lives."

Far worse was the sight awaiting them at the camp—scraps of burned canvas clinging to tent poles, scattered belongings and bedding, and mounds of snow, each hiding one or more hapless victims. Incredibly, the burial party found several half-frozen survivors, most of them infants shielded from the elements by their mothers' bodies.

"It took all my nerve to keep my composure in the face of this spectacle," Eastman remembered, "and of the excitement and grief of my Indian companions, nearly every one of whom was crying aloud or singing his death song." This was, Eastman later confessed, "a severe ordeal for one who had so lately put all his faith in the Christian love and lofty ideals of the white man."

Nearly a century has passed since that fateful day, yet the fascination with Wounded Knee remains strong. Indeed, historians still differ over its causes and significance. Some have accused the Indians of plotting a murderous assault on their captors; others have condemned the army for senseless atrocity. Neither opinion is without fault, of course, but some guilt must be associated with the decision to disarm the freezing and frightened

Indians, and some with Yellow Bird's incitement of the dancers.

Wounded Knee was an instant media event because reporters from three newspapers accompanied the Seventh Cavalry that awful day. Other correspondents, including Frederic Remington, the famous reporter-artist for *Harper's Weekly*, waited only 20 miles away at Pine Ridge Agency where they thought the real excitement would occur.

The photographs provide another compelling reason for the intense interest in Wounded Knee. This was the only fight between Indians and whites whose aftermath was recorded by the camera. Because of those photographs, Wounded Knee has a freshness and permanence that will forever scar the American conscience. Images of Big Foot and the others, dead in the snow, will haunt many Americans for all time.

Potential for similar incidents existed on reservations all across the northern Plains during these years of trial and transition. The adjustment was particularly difficult for the boys and young men. No longer were they permitted to earn honors by counting coup, capturing horses, or going on the warpath. They were, remarked one observer, "warriors without weapons."

The frustration and resentment of these young men is poignantly illustrated by an incident that occurred on the Northern Cheyenne reservation at Lame Deer, Montana, just a few months before the massacre at Wounded Knee. The incident could have resulted in similar tragedy, in fact, had it not been for the coolness and sensitivity of the individuals involved. In early September 1890, a white rancher who lived on land adjoining the reservation went searching for a missing cow and surprised two young Indian men who were butchering it. The two men—Head Chief, aged 28, and Young Mule, aged 14—killed the rancher and so skillfully hid his body that four troops of cavalry and several companies of infantry from nearby Fort Keogh spent a fruitless week searching for it. Finally, Major Henry Carroll called a halt to the search and summoned the Cheyenne leaders to a council.

"You know who killed this boy, and you know where his body is. If you tell me, I'll give each of you five dollars," Carroll promised.

Gathered for a 1914 Philadelphia banquet of the Society of the American Indian are a number of prominent Indian members, white associate members, and their guests. Established in 1911 to assist Indian legal claims and promote reform of Indian affairs, the society withered by the mid-1920s due to factionalism and the lack of real resources and public support.

The use of the hallucinogenic plant peyote has played a role in the religious ceremonies of many Indian groups. Below, in a water-color by Shawnee Earnest Spybuck, members of the Delaware tribe of Oklahoma conduct a peyote rite around 1912. Omahas attend a peyote ceremony in an undated photograph, left.

The Indians did not want the money, but they were anxious to avoid trouble because tensions were high in the white community and violence could erupt at any moment. Yes, they knew what happened and who did it. To bring an end to the matter, the leaders offered gifts of ponies and money to the relatives of the dead man as atonement, which was the Indian way of resolving such matters. This could not be done, Carroll replied. The guilty parties must surrender and go to trial and the soldiers would fight anyone who might interfere with their capture.

After further deliberation, the Cheyenne leaders offered Carroll a unique proposal. The young men were not afraid to die, but they did not want to die by being hanged. "They will come tomorrow morning. They will come fighting. They will show you that Cheyennes are not afraid of your soldiers. If you want their bodies, you will have to kill them."

It happened the next morning as hundreds of Indians assembled on the hills overlooking the agency to witness the deaths of their two suicide warriors. Mounted bareback on splendid ponies, their bodies painted as for battle, each armed with

Prominent late-19th-century Comanche leader Quanah Parker, shown opposite around 1895 with two of his wives, To-narcy and To-pay, was the son of Comanche Chief Peta Nocona and Cynthia Ann Parker, a white woman taken captive as a child. Initially a war leader, Quanah Parker stopped fighting in 1875 and became an important figure of conciliation between Comanches and whites. However, he defied white opinion when he supported the use of the peyote plant in religious ceremonies.

Comanche leader and Court of Indian Offenses Judge Quanah Parker relaxes in his office. Although he lived in a 12-room house and amassed a considerable fortune through his dealings with whites, Parker was an effective spokesman for Comanche interests and never forgot his heritage. Below, Comanche girls sing hymns before the Quanah Parker Memorial in Oklahoma.

INDIAN POLICE FORCE, ROSEBUD AGENCY, S.D.

Mounted Indian police, above, parade on the Rosebud Agency, South Dakota. Below, Indian police reenact the arrest of Hunkpapa Sioux Chief Sitting Bull at his cabin on the Standing Rock Reservation, South Dakota, on December 15, 1890, which resulted in his death.

a rifle, the young men charged down one of the hills towards the waiting soldiers. Young Mule's horse was hit, and the lad pitched into an old buffalo wallow from which shooting continued. Unscathed, Head Chief dashed through the ranks of soldiers, wheeled his pony and charged again. This time, the soldiers hit their mark.

Attention turned to the fallen Young Mule. His mother pleaded with the soldiers to stop shooting and rushed forward only to find that her son was dead; the shots had come from his cloth ammunition belt which had been set afire by a soldier's bullet.

With tension so high among the assembled Indians, a clear potential for catastrophe existed. Further bloodshed occurred when an army physician went to examine Young Mule's body. The boy's distraught mother flung herself at the soldier and stabbed him in the back with a knife. Instead of overreacting, Carroll ordered his men away and told them to leave the Indians to their grief.

Such compassion and common sense were the exception, however. Humanitarian efforts, often

misguided, led to prohibitions against dancing, native religions, and other traditional practices which could have eased the transition into a new kind of life. Other than to force obedience, what reason was there for the Bureau of Indian Affairs to order all Indian males to cut their hair? This regulation offended those among some tribes who believed long hair was essential to the successful completion of certain ceremonies. Since some agents viewed long hair as a sign of passive resistance to their civilizing efforts, they enforced the directive even to the point of handcuffing Indian males in order to do so.

Particularly dehumanizing was the matter of rations, which were distributed periodically. Cattle were issued "on the hoof," but this ended when certain tribes took to killing them from horseback, a sad parody of their former hunts. Thereafter, only slaughtered livestock reached the Indians.

Whereas the men had once been the providers for their families, now the women waited in long lines at the agency on issue day to receive the family ration. When government officials thought to encourage self-sufficiency by slashing rations and forcing the Indians to provide more for themselves, they accomplished little more than to make everyone on the reservation hungry. Indians did as they always had done in time of need: they simply made do with what they had, sharing their dole equally.

The circus offered escape for a few. By the closing years of the 19th century, "Wild West" shows had become very popular and offered employment opportunities for Indians who welcomed the chance to "relive" aspects of their former life. "Buffalo Bill" Cody operated the most successful show and even managed to hire Sitting Bull for one season. This loophole in reservation life was relatively short-lived, however, because it obviously flew in the face of efforts to assimilate Indians into white society.

As the "vanishing" Americans were adjusting with varying degrees of success to life on reservations, word went out of the discovery of an unknown and "wild" Indian who had been found in northern California. Thus an amazing chapter opened in the history of the American Indian. This man, the last of his tribe, not only seemed to provide a portal into man's Stone Age past, but also

Yankton Sioux Standing Rock Agency Police Sergeants Red Tomahawk and Eagle Man, above, pose with rifles sometime around 1890. Sergeant Red Tomahawk shot and killed Sioux leader Sitting Bull during a dispute on the reservation in December 1890.

brought to public awareness the fate that befell many of the native peoples of California.

On the morning of August 29, 1911, barking dogs awakened employees of a slaughterhouse near Oroville, California. The animals had cornered a frightened, emaciated person dressed in little more than a poncho made from a tattered piece of canvas. He appeared to be an Indian, but he spoke a language completely foreign to all who heard it. Since the man defied either identification or classification, he was placed in the Oroville jail for safekeeping and until the authorities could decide what should be done with him.

Meanwhile, news of the wild man piqued the interest of anthropologists at the University of California at Berkeley. During their visit, these scholars determined that he was neither insane nor wild, but a mild, thoroughly frightened Indian who spoke a dialect of the Yana, a group believed long extinct. The excited academics received permission from the Bureau of Indian Affairs to take custody of the man, whom they housed in the university's newly built museum across the bay in San Francisco. Here he remained the rest of his life—four years and seven months. The anthropologists called him "Ishi," the Yana word for man, since his real name was never learned.

Ishi proved to be an encyclopedia of aboriginal information. He knew all the primitive techniques for survival in the wilderness, including the use of a hand drill to start fires. Metal tools were unknown to him but, utilizing bone and stone implements, he fashioned sturdy bows. Stone arrowheads were his specialty, which he shaped by the score and gave to delighted museum visitors for whom he performed on Sunday afternoons.

Ishi impressed everyone with his gentleness and warmth, greeting strangers and friends alike with a cheery, "Evelybody Hoppy?" He also adapted readily to life in the museum, perhaps not even realizing that he was a living display. He learned to speak broken English and write his name, a necessity for cashing his monthly 25-dollar paycheck, the "salary" he earned as assistant janitor. The anthropologists even took him on a field trip to his former hideaway, though much against his wishes. "That treep . . . crazy," he tried to explain.

Back home, Ishi astonished even the scientists by his ability to lure wild animals within range of his bow, including a deer which he brought down. During the four weeks they remained in his old haunts, Ishi harpooned fish, killed small game, and generally gave his companions a peek into a hunting-gathering way of life.

There is no happy ending to Ishi's story. Tuberculosis claimed him on March 25, 1916. Even in death, he could not find peace. Contrary to the

William F. "Buffalo Bill" Cody's Wild West show drew huge crowds to see his real cowboys and Indians. Below, in 1908, Omaha witnesses the Wild West reenactment of the 1869 Battle of Summit Springs, in which Cody had scouted for the army against the Cheyennes. Opposite, Indians visit Venice during the Wild West's 1890 European tour.

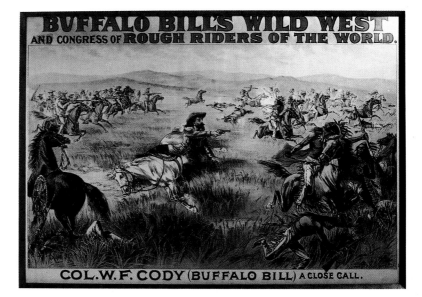

wishes of those closest to him, an autopsy was performed and his brain preserved. His body, however, was cremated according to the custom of his people. In his coffin lay a bow, five arrows, a basket of acorn meal, a purse filled with tobacco, some obsidian flakes, and various sea shells. The inscription on his urn, which is in the Mount Olivet Cemetery in San Francisco reads: "ISHI, THE LAST YANA INDIAN, 1916."

Ishi contributed much to our knowledge of aboriginal life. He perhaps deserves most credit, though, for the attention he focused on California's Indians, who lacked the organization and numbers to receive federal protection. Ishi's fate, in a sense, was the fate of all California Indians.

He was, in fact, the sole surviving Yahi, member of a tribal offshoot that probably never numbered more than 400 people. The Yahi were a subdivision of the Yana. The larger tribe originally occupied a tract of land, roughly 40 miles by 60 miles, hidden in the rugged foothills of Mount Lassen, east of the Sacramento River and south of the Pitt River.

For generations, the Yana had led a meager and isolated existence, living off the land and avoiding contact with the Spanish and all but their most immediate Indian neighbors. Their fierce independence kept their way of life virtually unchanged until the 1850s. Then the gold rush and California statehood placed them in confrontation with prospectors, ranchers, and other whites. The Yana retreated to the most inaccessible pockets of their original territory.

Even here, they could not escape the brutal ways of the newcomers. In 1846, the tribe numbered perhaps 2,000 people living in four distinct but culturally and linguistically related groups—the North, the Central, and the Southern Yana and their less numerous cousins, the Yahi. By 1868, hardly 20 years later, the principal bands of the Yana were gone, except for perhaps 30 individuals working on nearby ranches or married into other tribes. As far as anyone knew, the traditional Yahi were completely extinct.

Yet, somehow, some of them endured. Having been hunted like animals for more than two decades, the survivors—a dozen or so individuals at best—had simply gone into hiding. Their "long

concealment" began in 1872; it ended abruptly on November 10, 1908, when surveyors for a proposed dam stumbled across a Yahi camp virtually invisible in the dense brush. This was home to the last four traditional Yahi Indians—Ishi, then about 50; his elderly mother; an old man; and a younger woman, presumably his sister.

The Indians, except for Ishi's mother who was

William F. "Buffalo Bill" Cody takes a bow near the end of his long career as star and impresario of his world-famous Wild West "reenactments." Pony Express rider, scout, buffalo hunter, and showman in turn, Cody tried to be a friend to Indians, notably Sioux leader Sitting Bull, below, who traveled with Cody's show in 1885.

an invalid, fled in terror. Ishi never saw the old man or his sister again and it is believed they drowned trying to cross a nearby river. The surveyors, delighted at the opportunity to collect Indian artifacts, looted the camp of all its possessions, even the food, thereby sealing the fate of Ishi's mother. She died a few days later. Ishi survived alone for two years before hunger finally drove him into Oroville and the 20th century.

Not all Indians were as determined to resist assimilation. Even within some of the most conservative tribes, individuals attempted to accept the new way of life. One of the more acceptable alternatives was that of agency policeman. Such persons were used not only to maintain order but also to encourage acculturation. The men enjoyed wearing the uniform and being part of quasi-military units reminiscent of the soldier societies of the Plains tribes. Those organizations, too, had performed police and military functions in the pre-reservation days. Congress authorized Indian police in 1878, and within two years units had been established on 48 of the 60 agencies in the United States.

Indian policemen were expected to embody the new way of life, keeping only one wife at a time, wearing short hair and white men's clothes, and eventually accepting an allotment of land. That they wore their uniforms proudly and took their duties seriously is obvious from the attempt to arrest Sitting Bull.

Chief Running Crane and his son Wades-In-Water of the Blackfeet exemplify the sincerity and determination of such earnest individuals. Their combined careers spanned more than 50 years. Running Crane was appointed sergeant of police on the Blackfeet Reservation in 1880 and subsequently became judge of the Indian Offenses Court. His son, who became a policeman in 1913, closed his career a quarter of a century later as chief of police on the same reservation.

For much of this period, the son's wife, Julia, had been a member of the Browning, Montana, police force. The only Indian policewoman in the United States in her day, Julia also retired in the early 1930s, after 25 years of service. According to the agency medical examiner, who wrote to the Commissioner of Indian Affairs on their behalf, they

Tipi Heraldry

"The Indian is essentially religious and contemplative, and it might almost be said that every act of his life is regulated and determined by his religious belief. It matters not that some may call this superstition. The difference is only relative."
    James Mooney,
    Smithsonian Ethnologist 1886

Journalist and staff member of the Smithsonian's Bureau of American Ethnology, James Mooney realized that Native American culture was alive and still adapting even as others lamented its imminent demise. From 1885 until his death in 1921, Mooney made field trips, amassed notes, and wrote for the BAE on the Arapahos, Cheyennes, Kiowas, Kiowa-Apaches, and Eastern Cherokees.

Mooney began his detailed study of the Kiowa tribe during 1894, becoming interested in their heraldry as painted on shields and

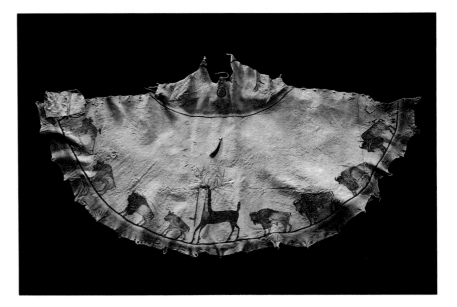

tipi covers and in pictographic calendars used by storytellers to recall events in the tribe.

Decorated shields identified members of warrior societies, each of which possessed distinctive rules, rituals, and history. Painted tipis, the property of famous families, commanded special places within the camp circle, and

became prized legacies. The tipi skin was renewed yearly at a feast in which 20 to 30 men would copy the old design onto the new cover.

For the Tennessee Centennial Exposition held in Nashville in 1897, James Mooney hired Kiowa artists to construct a camp circle of 28 painted tipis built to scale, complete with miniature shields.

Twenty-eight-inch-tall Buffalo Picture Tipi, above, is decorated after an heraldic design associated with a Kiowa named Never Got Shot, who also possessed a personal buffalo-shield insignia. The model is made of buckskin and colored with commercial paints. Bear Tipi design, left, originated as an image seen in a dream by Kiowa warrior Bear Bringing It.

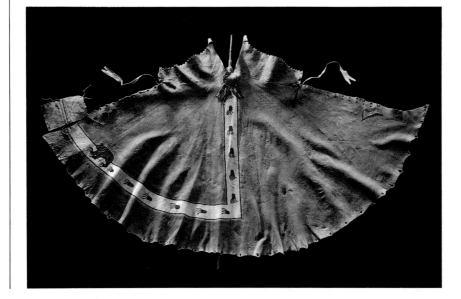

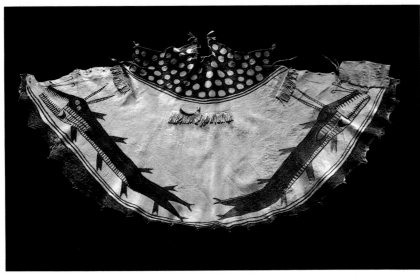

Ethnologist James Mooney, above center, with mixed-blood Arapaho Jesse Bent, right, and Indian boardinghouse owner Ben Beveridge, was largely sympathetic to the plight of reservation Indians as their culture was stripped from them. Kiowa-designed Underwater Monster Tipi model, left, was collected by Mooney between 1891 and 1904.

Borne on its vision of a heaven like the world the tribes had known before the whites, the Ghost Dance ceremony swept across the Plains around 1890. In colored inks on buckskin, above, a pictograph of a Ghost Dance by a Ute named Yellow Nose shows the dance as practiced by the Cheyennes and Arapahos. Opposite, Arapaho women sing and dance with upraised arms while other Ghost Dancers watch. In dance-induced trances, the participants believed their spirits would visit the paradise promised by prophet Wovoka.

were wonderful examples of the modern Indian. Although Running Crane could not as yet speak or write English, he had learned to sign his name. The medical examiner enclosed a specimen of his writing to show the commissioner in Washington the progress the 60-year-old policeman was making with the language.

It was particularly important to the old man that the commissioner knew he kept President Harding's photograph on his bedside table. There he could see it the last thing at night and first thing in the morning as a reminder "that he must do as Washington want[ed] him to do."

Both the son and his wife had "good hearts" for their fellow Blackfeet and did all they could to encourage them to follow the white way. They even spent their own money to buy delicacies for those who were ill. Wades-In-Water assured the commissioner that he was always faithful in his duties and that he was living the good life as taught him by his father, Running Crane, "who was ever the friend of the white people." One of the couple's most prized possessions was a photograph of them with the Commissioner of Indian Affairs.

Courts of Indian Offenses were associated with the Indian police and were intended to discourage the practice of traditional religion, polygamy, and other pursuits deemed inappropriate. The judges were also to be models of civilized behavior, but the tribal leaders capable of fulfilling that role were usually conservatives whose lifestyles were not exactly what government officials had in mind for role models. Typical was Quanah Parker of the Comanches, a former war chief who became a founder of the Native American Church and a prosperous Oklahoma cattleman. In many respects the ideal choice to be a judge, he also had "five undisputed facts," as one witty government official

described Quanah's wives. Judge Parker lost his job when he refused to set aside four of them.

Once on reservations, the Indians came under the control of the reformers, whites who persuaded Congress to enact a three-prong program intended to de-tribalize and Americanize the individual Indians. Foremost was a policy referred to as "severalty." Simply put, it meant dividing up the reservations and allotting land to individual tribal members. A second goal was citizenship, including the rights and responsibilities thus entailed. The third and, as events proved, least successfully realized goal, was the destruction of Indian culture, to be accomplished by an extensive and largely coercive government school system.

Severalty was an idea as old as the nation itself, but it became an unstoppable force after the Civil War. Humanitarians and reformers across the country gained the upper hand and effectively promoted their belief in the concept of private property as the heart of civilized life. Among their number was the Sioux agent who sent this ditty to the Commissioner of Indian Affairs in 1886: *We'll have a little farm, a horse, a pig, and cow; And she will mind the dairy and I will guide the plow.*

As envisioned by proponents of the Dawes Severalty Act of 1887, all land in Indian hands was to be apportioned to individuals with the title held in trust by the federal government for 25 years. Heads of families were to receive 160 acres with lesser amounts going to other tribal members. All land-owning Indians were to be granted citizenship.

A sinister aspect of this seemingly utopian legislation was the proviso that unassigned lands, over and above the allotments, were to be opened for sale and settlement. Indeed, cynics saw the legislation as little more than another land grab. Why else, they pointed out, were westerners so anxious to support it?

Perhaps the most forthright statement during the debates on severalty came from members of the Committee on Indian Affairs in the House of Representatives who were opposed to the proposed legislation. "However much we may differ with the humanitarians who are riding this hobby, we are certain that they will agree with us in the proposition that it does not make a farmer out of an Indian to give him a quarter section of land."

In their opinion, the congressmen continued, the real purpose of severalty was to take more land from the Indians. "If this were done in the name of greed, it would be bad enough; but to do it in the name of humanity, and under the cloak of an ardent desire to promote the Indian's welfare by making him like ourselves, whether he will or not, is infinitely worse," they wrote.

Friends of the Indians such as Captain Richard H. Pratt, founder of the Carlisle Indian Industrial School, supported the policy, even suspecting that the Indians, having lost their property, would be forced to work for others out of desperation and poverty. Soon, however, long-silent critics would find a voice as shortcomings became apparent.

Whatever its justifications, allotment, like prohibition, was a noble experiment that failed. The policy's chances for success were not helped by the fact that it was implemented in the days when the Indians of the northern Great Plains were being placed on reservations. Certainly, the timing could not have been worse for the Sioux and Cheyenne who had no agricultural experience and whose land was better suited for stock raising than for farming.

In 1894, President Grover Cleveland addressed the problem. "In these days when white agriculturalists and stock raisers of experience and intelligence find their lot a hard one, we ought not to expect Indians, unless far advanced in civilization and habits of industry, to support themselves on the small tracts of land usually allotted to them."

Interestingly, the so-called Five Civilized Tribes from the Southeast—probably those best prepared for severalty—fought allotment until they had exhausted every legal option open to them. They were among the last to be allotted. Why should they fear it so?

The outcome and true implications of the allotment program are revealed by a few simple statistics. The most telling: in 1887, Indians owned 138 million acres of land; in 1934, when the act was abolished, that total had dwindled to 52 million. The experience of the Chippewas is typical: 1,735 allotments were granted in 1871; in 1878, hardly 300 Chippewas retained their plots. Some had sold out, but most lost their land through some form of chicanery.

Federal laws seem to have been equally incapa-

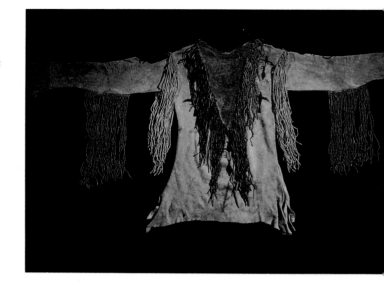

ble of protecting the lands of Indians who did not live on reservations. Land-grabbing was common in the Pacific Northwest where many people possessed individual holdings before passage of the Dawes Severalty Act.

Indians with properties were not required to move onto reservations until the government had paid them for houses or other improvements. To protect their holdings, however, the Indians needed to fulfill certain legal formalities, to get "good strong papers." Many failed to do so, believing the right of occupancy protected them or simply because they lacked money for the required fees.

Indians also regarded survey crews with suspicion and often refused to cooperate. Some Indians ignored boundaries or moved stakes and stone markers at will. The agent of the Colville Reservation in Washington State, for example, estimated that not one in 100 stakes was still in place on Indian lands after the survey had been completed in his region and that not one in ten farms was situated in accordance with the legal records. This was, of course, an open invitation for later encroachment and trespass by white neighbors.

Another agent in the Pacific Northwest admitted that Indians in his jurisdiction had been "cheated, frightened, cajoled, and bought out of their rightful possessions." The white individuals responsible, many of them "eminently respectable people," saw no wrong in this because "there is no other way in

The Paiute prophet or
"messiah" of the Ghost
Dance, Wovoka, poses
with cowboy actor Tim
McCoy on a Nevada
movie set in 1926. In 1889
Wovoka reported his
vision of a paradise free of
whites. Some believers
wore sacred shirts like the
one shown opposite to
make themselves invul-
nerable to bullets. White
authorities reacted harshly
to reports of unrest among
the northern Plains tribes
as the Ghost Dance reli-
gion swept through them
in 1890. The death of
Sitting Bull and the
massacre at Wounded
Knee followed.

No. 3564. "AT THE DANCE"
"Big Foot's Band" at grass Dance on Cheyenne
River, Aug. 9, 1890.
Photo. and copyright 1890, by Grabill, Dead-
wood, S. D., Dec. 29th or 30th. Nearly the
entire number were killed at the battle of

*Members of the Miniconjou Sioux band led by Big Foot
assemble for a dance on the Cheyenne River, South
Dakota, in August 1890, above. Most of those present in
the photograph were killed or wounded on December 29,
1890, at Wounded Knee, South Dakota, when men of the
Seventh Cavalry, opposite, attempted to disarm the band
during a period of extreme tension over the Ghost Dance.*

which lands can be obtained within a reasonable time; . . . the government forces honest people to commit perjury."

One of the easiest and most effective ways to disassociate Indians who did have "good strong papers" from their property was marriage. It was widely believed that severalty encouraged miscegenation and that the whites who participated in such liaisons were the real beneficiaries of the allotment system.

Typical was this letter received by an agent for the Flathead reservation in Montana: "Is there any Indian girls with money which would married a white gentleman in every respect, but . . . needs the money to get a new start." Intermarriage was certainly an effective way to achieve assimilation, but inevitably such unions resulted in further erosion of the Indian land base.

Guardianship was another effective means of appropriating Indian lands. This device proved especially popular in Indian Territory, where it was

an easy matter for a white person to secure custody of an incompetent adult or orphan in order to gain control of the Indian's property. One outsider claimed 161 Indian children as his wards. His attempt failed, but other whites successfully persuaded Indians to have them as beneficiaries of their wills, and mysterious deaths followed. As historian William T. Hagan so aptly puts it, "Severalty may not have civilized the Indian, but it definitely corrupted most of the white men who had any contact with it."

The question of inheritance further complicated

the allotment system. At the time the severalty act was passed, Indian populations were falling at a rapid rate. Literally as well as figuratively, the first Americans were becoming the "vanishing Americans." By the beginning of the 20th century, however, the figures began to increase, something reformers had not anticipated when they agreed to the sale of surplus Indian lands. Thus, more and more people inherited the small allotments that remained in Indian hands.

A Nez Percé friend of the author claims he is one of 81 heirs to a 60-acre tract of land on his Idaho reservation. It is common to find more than 100 heirs for similar small plots. The usual solution is to lease the land to a white farmer or rancher and divide the income among the heirs. The few cents each claimant receives does little to offset the economic difficulties experienced by most Indian families today.

Indian education, another plank in the platform of the reformers, had been attempted with indiffer-

ent success since the colonial period. The reservations finally provided the means of reaching and controlling the bulk of Indian school-age children. In 1870, Congress made the first appropriation for Indian schools. In 1926, more than a half century later, 12,191 of 83,765 school age children were still not attending (2,500 of those children were on the Navajo reservation). The system that year included 18 nonreservation boarding schools, 59 reservation boarding schools, 140 day schools, and 81 mission schools (18 under contract to the Bureau of Indian Affairs). The annual cost was $6 million.

The reformers most favored the nonreservation boarding school, with one of the most successful established at Carlisle Barracks in Pennsylvania by Captain Richard H. Pratt, a former cavalry officer turned reformist. The flagship of the government boarding schools, Carlisle flourished from 1879 to 1918, when it and other similar schools fell out of favor. Offering little more than an eighth-grade education, Carlisle taught skilled trades, farming,

and home economics. Its students, however, were usually of college age, and the football team played a formidable schedule against Notre Dame and other collegiate powerhouses of the day.

Although inspired by the best of intentions, such schools sometimes created more problems than they resolved. A classic example involves Plenty Horses, a young Sioux who returned to Pine Ridge Reservation nine days after the Wounded Knee massacre. Plenty Horses killed a cavalry officer to prove that school had not turned him into a white man. Indicted for murder, he was eventually acquitted by the United States Supreme Court on grounds that

the killing had occurred during time of war.

Citizenship for Indians was relatively meaningless because few of them had the opportunity or knowledge to exercise their rights. Contrary to popular belief, the vast majority of Indians had become enfranchised before 1924, when Congress enacted formal legislation. Many had already gained such status through the Dawes Act and related laws. Other Indians became citizens as a reward for military service during World War I.

In many respects, the Great War proved a watershed for America's Indians. They established a remarkable record of patriotism and selflessness

Buried the Dead
at the Battle of Wounded Knee S.D.
by Right led Jan 1st 1891 by the
North Western Photo Co.
Chadron Neb
No1

Miniconjou Sioux Chief Big Foot lies dead in the snow of Wounded Knee, South Dakota, opposite. He was among the first to die in the fusillade that exploded on December 28, 1890, when fearful Miniconjous refused to surrender their weapons to some 500 artillery-equipped troops ordered to disarm them. Above, a mounted officer surveys the field three days after the one-sided battle. Civilian grave diggers bury the Miniconjou dead in a mass grave hacked from the frozen earth, left.

Birds Eye View of
Indian Village at Pine Ridge, S.D.

during a conflict which they had no readily apparent reason to join or recognize. Nonetheless, they contributed to the victory beyond their numbers and resources.

Several tribes made it "their" war as well. Most notable was the Onondaga Nation of the once feared Iroquois Confederacy. It unilaterally declared war on Germany, citing the ill-treatment accorded tribal members performing with a Wild West show who were stranded in Berlin when hostilities began. A few weeks later the Oneida Nation followed with its own declaration of war.

Although most Indians in 1917 were not liable to the draft, they enlisted in amazing numbers. Even

before the draft, more than 2,000 had volunteered for the American and Canadian armies, many of them eager to gain "war honors" and maintain the warrior tradition of their tribes. All told, 17,213 Indians registered for the draft: of these, 6,509 or 37.6 percent were inducted. Their percentage of inductees was more than twice the national average. Even the Passamaquoddies of Maine, one of the smaller tribes in the United States, fielded 500 volunteers, including their chief, Peter Neptune.

Perhaps more telling, only 228 of the 17,213 Indians who registered for the draft claimed an exemption, and most of those were forced to do so because of age. The Bureau of Indian Affairs later

Area photographers sold views of the aftermath of the disastrous action at Wounded Knee, South Dakota, such as those on preceding pages and opposite. Here, an unidentified band camps under the eyes of the army in 1891. One young survivor, orphaned by the massacre, was adopted by Brigadier General L.W. Colby and reared as Marguerite Colby, above.

declared that of the 10,000 Indians who actually served in the army, and 2,000 in the navy, fully three out of four were volunteers.

Indians also contributed on the home front. More than 10,000 joined the Red Cross, and Indians purchased a total of not less than $15 million in Liberty Bonds, a per capita subscription of $50.

Typical of the Indian attitude is the story told of a 75-year-old Ute woman who attended a Red Cross meeting on her reservation. Each finger a person held up meant a $10 donation to the Red Cross. The old woman held up five fingers, which was recorded as $50. A few days later, when she limped to the agency headquarters to sign her contribution form, she became indignant when the interpreter explained she had donated $50.

"I want to give $500," she said. When the superintendent told her she had only $513 to her credit on the agency records, the old woman smiled: "Thirteen dollars left? That's enough for me."

The Indians volunteered and they fought, accumulating casualties and decorations that belied their small numbers. The first decorated war hero from South Dakota was Chauncey Eagle-Horn, who was killed in France. His father had fought Custer. Joe Young Hawk, the son of one of Custer's Arikara scouts, was wounded and taken prisoner by the Germans but later escaped after killing three of his guards and capturing two others.

Perhaps the most brilliant record of the Indian volunteers belongs to Private Joseph Oklahombi, a full-blood Choctaw in the 141st Infantry. His exploits rivaled those of the more famous Sergeant Alvin York. Oklahombi received the Croix de Guerre from Marshal Philippe Pétain for scrambling across 200 yards of barbed-wire entanglements, wrenching a machine gun from its crew, and then using it to capture 171 German soldiers. He held the position for four days while withstanding a constant artillery barrage, including gas shells.

German fear of the "American savages" accounts for some of the success of Indian soldiers. Having been introduced to Indians through Buffalo Bill's Wild West shows, German soldiers continually inquired about their fighting abilities and were convinced that they still wielded the scalping knife and tomahawk.

In traditional garb, a boy whirls in a dance at a 1985 pow wow on the Rosebud Reservation, South Dakota. Held at reservations around the country, pow wows are grand get-togethers where people of many tribes celebrate Indian culture past, present, and future.

Indians were particularly useful as messengers and telephone operators because the Germans were unable to understand their languages. In one regiment alone were Indians who spoke 26 different languages or dialects, with two Choctaw officers responsible for transmitting telephone messages regarding troop movements and other sensitive operations. One difficulty with the novel arrangement, a precursor of the well-known Navajo "code talkers" of World War II, was the lack of military words in the Indian vocabulary. Hence, "Big Gun" in Choctaw meant a cannon, "little gun shoot fast" a machine gun, "tribe" a regiment, "grain of corn" a battalion, "stone" a hand grenade, and "many scouts" a patrol.

One unanticipated benefit of participation in the Great War was the "education" the Indian soldiers received. Military service afforded them new contacts and experiences and made them dissatisfied with conditions at home. Indeed, wider involvement in the life of the country led to many changes for America's Indians in this period. By the 1920s, they came to realize that the philosophy of the reformers was badly flawed.

Severalty and the sale of so-called surplus lands had been an economic and psychological disaster for the Indians, while citizenship meant little to people who did not know how to use it. Education also proved an empty promise because educated Indians had few opportunities for meaningful employment. Meanwhile, many white Americans experienced a refreshing change of attitude about Indians. No longer was all Indian life seen as bad. More people in the United States and abroad began to seek out the remarkable beauty to be found in Indian art and culture. All this combined to launch another reform movement, one designed to salvage what remained of Indian culture and to allow Indians a hand in determining their own place in American society.

Fighting for Rights

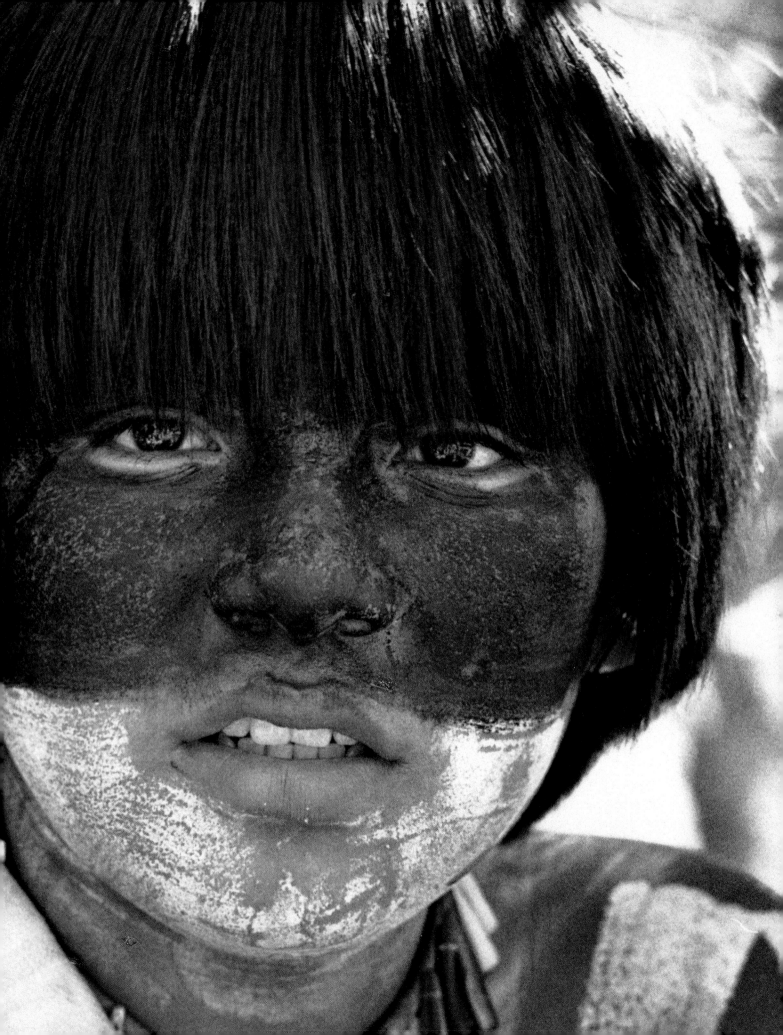

Red Power

Victimized and exploited for more than 400 years, American Indians probably reached the depth of their despair in the 1920s. The era between the World Wars, though, brought an awakening of pride within the Indian community that often expressed itself through federal military service and grassroots political activism. In the latter area, action replaced rhetoric on November 20, 1969, with the dramatic occupation of Alcatraz Island in San Francisco Bay by a group of Indians, most of them students of nearby colleges.

Alcatraz became a symbol as well as a cause as Indians demonstrated their pride and determination to the world. Not only did the events at Alcatraz electrify Indians across the country, but the occupation inspired widespread applause and sympathy from non-Indians both in the United States and abroad.

The occupiers possessed two tactical advantages: first, since they operated in the glare of publicity, the authorities were careful to avoid bad press; and second, they had a lively sense of humor—typical Indian humor, mordant wit liberally peppered with irony. Calling themselves "Indians of All Tribes," they issued a proclamation to the "Great White Father" informing him that they had "reclaimed" the island for all Indians by right of discovery. Nonetheless, they offered to pay a fair price—$24 in beads and cloth—the amount that had been paid for Manhattan Island three centuries earlier. Although at $24 the Indians realized they were paying more per acre for Alcatraz, they felt that some concession to increased land values was necessary. At $1.50 per acre, the price was still more than the 47 cents an acre that the federal government was currently offering California Indians as part of a settlement under the Claims Commission Act. The Indians also promised to give the island's white inhabitants a portion of the land for their own use "to be held in trust by the Bureau of Caucasian Affairs."

Alcatraz, the students pointed out, was ideally suited to become a reservation; previously it had been the site of a maximum-security penitentiary. The Indians also noted that the site was isolated, lacked adequate means of transportation, had no fresh running water, and no oil or mineral rights.

Overleaf: Hopi boy costumed for a warrior dance embodies the masculine virtues of physical and emotional strength. In the vanguard of ethnic activism, Sioux demonstrators, opposite, raise a flag to reclaim Alcatraz Island as Indian land soon after the federal penitentiary was closed in 1963. Beginning in November 1969, hundreds of Indians from different tribes occupied the island for 19 months, focusing public attention on the plight of the first Americans. Below, in January 1945, Pima tribesman Ira Hayes joined other Marines raising the American flag in victory over Mount Suribachi, Iwo Jima island.

Furthermore, the island was short of sanitation facilities, its inhabitants had a high unemployment rate, the soil was sterile, and there were no educational facilities. The population exceeded the land base, and most of the island's former residents not only had been kept there against their wishes, but had also been largely dependent upon others for their sustenance.

Should the government agree to the offer, the Indians promised to teach the white inhabitants Indian religion, education, and lifeways "in order to help them achieve our level of civilization and thus raise them and all their white brothers up from their savage and unhappy state." The occupants further presented some attractive plans for the island's future, including the establishment of a Center for Native American Studies, an American Indian Spiritual Center, an Indian Center of Ecology, the Great Indian Training School, and a cultural museum.

Alcatraz ushered in a new era of pan-Indianism. The students and their allies represented half a hundred tribes from across the United States and Canada. Ironically, many of them were enrolled in newly inaugurated programs of American Indian studies that encouraged ethnic pride and fueled the exuberance and vitality of pan-Indianism which so joyously came to light on Alcatraz. Indeed, the 80 or so Indians who captured the "Rock" on the evening of November 20 were soon joined by 100 or more who abandoned their classes and took up the cause of red power. Of 40 students enrolled in the Indian program at the University of California at Berkeley, for example, all but one joined the group at Alcatraz; a similar exodus occurred at San Francisco State University, which saw 28 of its 35 Indian-studies students leave for Alcatraz. Along with those who took up residence on the island, some 12,000 visitors also traveled to the rocky outpost during its year-and-a-half occupation.

Although the takeover eventually collapsed—a victim of transient leadership, internal dissension, and exhaustion—Alcatraz represented the beginning of an era of takeovers, confrontations, and militancy. While dwarfed by subsequent events, the non-violent occupation of this island remains a milestone in the Indian civil-rights movement, and

the declaration "I was on Alcatraz" established one's credibility among Indian militants for years thereafter.

As exuberant as was the mood on the "Rock," the road from reservation to self-determination had been a long and difficult one. Perhaps the toughest miles were covered during the 1920s, at which time Indian lands were shrinking at a startling rate, and tuberculosis and other diseases were ravaging tribes at a pace far in excess of that of the general population. All aspects of traditional religion and culture, including those of language and crafts, were under continued assault as undesirable vestiges of a pagan past that flew in the face of the mythic American "melting pot."

Despite having been assailed by both enemies and supposed friends, by 1920 Indians had neither vanished nor had they been assimilated. They had been forgotten. Ironically, having come to believe that they were foreigners in their own land, many Indians tried buying into the "American dream." The buckskins and beadwork reminiscent of another era were packed away; Indians now wore

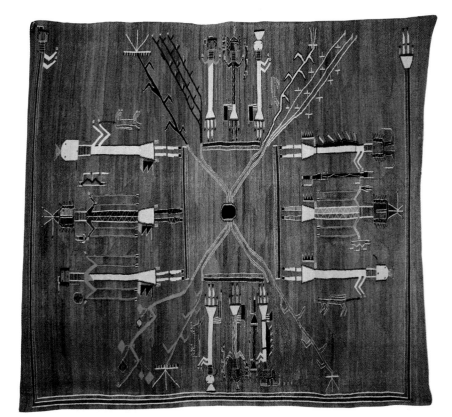

Navajo singer Hosteen Klah, opposite, was a respected conservator of his people's cultural heritage. To preserve for future generations the sacred rites of his tribe, Klah learned to weave the designs of ritual sand paintings. "Fringe Mouths," left, is a textile version of the sand painting used on the eighth day of the Nightway, a curing ceremony Klah learned during 26 years as an apprentice. Water at the center of the design is transformed into sacred plants. At the four sides, supernatural beings stand on rainbows. The Navajos employ complex chants and sand paintings to invoke the spirits of supernaturals.

close-cropped hair and store-bought clothes, and struggled to learn English. Some even changed their names—to Smith, Jones, and other equally mainstream examples.

These and other transformations wrought by Indians themselves often had their roots in military service. Thousands of Indian veterans of the Great War were certainly no longer content to accept the prewar status quo. Indian soldiers had worn their uniforms with pride and had fought and died for such ideals as freedom and democracy. No longer would they now be content, for instance, to obtain written permission from the agency superintendent simply to travel from one point to another, as had been required on the Crow Reservation in Montana prior to World War I.

The First World War also contributed to the change in attitude on the part of white reformers and social scientists who had grown cynical of prewar values. This was the era of the "Lost Generation," and, during those iconoclastic times, who could insist that the Indians' only salvation lay in slavish imitation of the precepts of their

white Christian advisors? Advocates of a secular solution to the Indian problem now urged their fellow Americans to open their eyes to the beauty of native religions in order to develop cultural sensitivity and understanding.

John Collier, spokesman for the new vision, started his career as a New York City social worker and came to dominate the nation's Indian affairs for 30 years. A bill introduced in 1922 by Senator H.O. Bursum of New Mexico catapulted Collier into national prominence. This legislation would have favored whites over the Pueblo Indians of the Southwest in disputes concerning land titles. Collier, who organized the American Indian Defense Association, successfully led the attack on the Bursum bill and then turned his attention to government Indian policy in general. Convinced that Pueblo communal existence could serve as a model for correcting the ailments of America's industrialized society, he fought against federal policies that threatened Indian cultural integrity. He campaigned for Indian religious liberty and against removal of Indians from the tribal setting, part of

World War II Air Corps trainees, left, perform an impromptu dance. Attending mechanic's school at Sheppard Field, Texas, were, from left to right, Abraham Little Beaver, Winnebago; Adam Bearcup, Sioux; Delray Echo-Hawk, Pawnee; and David Box, also Sioux. Thousands of Indians volunteered for service in the armed forces. Opposite, Henry Bake, at left, and George Kirk, Navajos in the U.S. Marine Corps, operate a radio in 1943 on Bougainville Island. More than 400 Navajo Marine "code talkers" helped to maintain security by transmitting orders in their tribal language. Below, "First Furlough," by Quincy Tahoma, depicts a code talker's return to the reservation.

a program known as allotment that Collier viewed as the primary cause of Indian poverty. "Indian idleness," he insisted, "is idleness of allotted Indians. Indian disinheritance, moving ahead faster each year, is almost exclusively a disinheritance of allotted Indians."

So effective was Collier that Franklin Delano Roosevelt, upon becoming President in 1933, appointed him his Commissioner of Indian Affairs. With that appointment began a New Deal for America's Indians, and the Wheeler-Howard Act of 1934 provided the cornerstone of Collier's program. Although far more mild than the bill Collier originally drafted, this Indian reorganization plan could be considered radical. With its passage, allotment ceased to be federal policy, and thus ended a sorry period in American Indian history, one which

had seen the tribal land base reduced from 138 million acres in 1887 to 52 million by 1934. Of the land remaining in Indian hands, fully half was desert or semi-arid.

The act also authorized Indian tribes to organize their own governments and to form corporations for tribal enterprises; it established an annual fund for land purchases and sanctioned the preferential employment of Indians by the Bureau of Indian Affairs. Furthermore, it allowed each tribe to vote whether or not to accept the act.

Collier followed this legislative success with the creation of the Indian Arts and Crafts Board, which was designed to encourage artisans and to keep imitations out of the marketplace. The board served both to stimulate economic activity on reservations and to keep alive the production of traditional arts and crafts.

Collier also struck a blow for religious freedom for Indians. Indian children at boarding schools were no longer required to attend Christian services, and traditional religious observances that had been outlawed on reservations were now permitted. Thus ended a prohibition that had been in effect since 1921, and that had forbidden dances that encouraged "acts of self-torture, immoral relations between the sexes, the sacrificial destruction of clothing or other useful articles, the reckless giving away of property, the use of injurious drugs or intoxicants, and frequent or prolonged periods of celebration which bring the Indians together from remote points to the neglect of their crops, livestock, and home interest."

Thanks to Collier, Indians could once again legally practice the Sun Dance and use peyote, a hallucinatory plant essential to ceremonies of the Native American Church. Produced by a cactus found in northern Mexico, the peyote "button" had long been used by Indians of the Southwest for religious purposes. Employed in this manner, with ingestion of the substance occurring in a socially controlled and supportive setting, peyote is thought to be non-addictive and free from such harmful side effects as violent or aberrant behavior. Peyote reportedly induces a spiritual rapport and beatific visions compatible with traditional Indian harmony with nature.

The peyote ceremony itself, brought to the United States in the 1880s, was warmly received by the defeated and dispirited buffalo-hunting Indians of the southern Plains. The movement helped adherents achieve a sense of racial solidarity and enabled them to cope with the disorientation caused by the demands of the new social order. Featuring the ritualized use of peyote in an all-night service that blends Christian and Indian elements, the religion closely resembled the nativist movements that preceded it. Quanah Parker of the Comanches, a major figure in the Native American Church, was instrumental in the religion's rapid spread across the United States.

Figures such as Collier and Parker managed to buy some time for the tribes while they regrouped and began to reassert their cultures. Reservations became safe havens and yet, even when they could, Indians did not wholeheartedly endorse a return to tribalism. The specific reasons and motivations are complex.

Some individuals, such as Adam Castillo, who edited *The Indian*, urged Congress to follow a path similar to that blazed by President Abraham Lincoln and "free" native peoples from federal bondage by abolishing the Bureau of Indian Affairs. Certain educated Indians, including Charles Eastman, Carlos Montezuma, and Alice Lee Jemison, viewed assimilation as desirable.

In one instance, demographics replaced debate. Thanks to the allotment policy, many whites and Indians had become neighbors, and widespread intermarriage had resulted. In the 20 years between 1910 and 1930, the number of full-blooded Indians in the United States decreased from 65 to 58 percent of the total Indian population, while the number of mixed-bloods jumped by 51 percent. Many Indians so involved simply did not want a return to the "good old days."

For this last reason, and many others, the Wheeler-Howard Act and John Collier's program provoked a storm of controversy even in Indian communities. Perhaps the primary difficulty was that of white men acting for Indians, and not Indians for Indians. In any event, tribes had two years to debate and to decide whether or not to accept the act. In the end, 181 tribes representing

129,750 Indians voted to accept; 77 tribes—86,365 people—rejected it. Fourteen more groups that failed to vote at all were placed under the act. Eventually, 93 bands and communities adopted constitutions and bylaws, with 73 receiving charters. One Pueblo leader explained the failure of his tribe to adopt a constitution in this way: "If we had a written constitution and laws, we'd always have to look up what we could do and then maybe [have to] ask a lawyer half the time."

Some groups, such as the Five Civilized Tribes of Oklahoma (woodland and riverine tribes removed from the Old South after the 1830s), were so fragmented and dispersed by 1934 that it was impossible to restore their tribal unity. The Navajo rejection of the Wheeler-Howard Act illustrates the countercurrents at work in several groups. Involving the largest tribe in the United States, it not only highlights the success that the reformers had in fact achieved within the Indian community but also points up the divisiveness caused by federal programs. The tribe's conflict was embodied in two powerful individuals, each representing a different way of life.

Jacob Casimera Morgan, a full-blood Navajo,

Source of sacred waters for tribal rituals, Arizona's famed Window Rock, opposite, became the seat of the Navajo tribal council in the 1930s. The council hogan, below, built under a federal work program, reflects traditional designs. Henry Chee Dodge, left, spent part of his childhood with other Navajos who had been removed from their homeland and interned at Bosque Redondo from 1864 to 1868. In 1923, he was elected chairman of the first tribal council and helped to change it into a strong central legislature. Dodge was reelected in 1942.

The Menominee Quest

by Ada Deer

Growing up on the Menominee Reservation in Wisconsin and living in a log cabin on the banks of the Wolf River, like my ancestors before me, I absorbed a deep love and respect for the land and for all living things—trees, plants, and birds, to name but a few. This legacy, so precious to all of us, is central to being Indian. This kinship with the land, strengthened through 5,000 years of residence in the same area, is a driving force in tribal life. The Menominees, Wisconsin's oldest continuous residents, successfully resisted the major federal policies of removal, allotment, and termination, all of which were designed to destroy tribes outright or to grab land, thereby dispossessing the Indians.

With the passage of the Menominee Termination Act in 1954, a tragic chapter in the tribe's history began (see page 243). Although designed to free us from federal supervision, termination was a cultural, political, and economic disaster. Our land, our people, and our tribal identity were assailed in a calculated effort to force us into the mainstream of society. Like me, other Menominees were wounded to the heart when, unannounced, bulldozers began slashing and clearing trees from our beautiful lake shores and slicing the land into lots to be sold. This was the spark that lit a fire of determined resistance in us all, resulting in the formation of DRUMS (Determination of Rights and Unity for Menominee Shareholders). DRUMS led a successful effort to reverse termination and,

with the signing of the Menominee Restoration Act on December 22, 1973, the future of the tribe, its land, and its people was assured. Working through the legal and political systems, we achieved a historic reversal of an ill-considered and damaging policy, thereby establishing precedents for other tribes in their struggles for self-determination.

Our experience has taught us that despite almost 300 years of disruption, tribal values run deep within each of us. We have two conclusions: first, *INDIANS*, remain true to your tribal values and traditions; second, the first Americans have a richness and depth of cultures which the world needs, and which our tribes will gladly share.

Ada Deer, left, one of the first organizers of Determination of Rights and Unity for Menominee Shareholders (DRUMS), worked to gain the support of interest groups and state and federal government officials, and to repeal the Menominee Termination Act of 1954. Tribespeople protest in 1971, above. The Menominees' federally recognized status as an Indian tribe was restored in 1973. Legal help for DRUMS was provided by the Native American Rights Fund (NARF), of which Ada Deer became the chairwoman in 1989.

came to espouse the assimilationist tenets of the most die-hard reformers. Born in 1879 to a family of traditionalists, Morgan attended boarding school off reservation in Grand Junction, Colorado, where he converted to Christianity. He entered Hampton Normal and Agricultural Institute in Virginia and graduated in June 1900. Now an apostle of assimilation and a zealous Christian, he considered Navajo culture and traditional religion repugnant and sought to "elevate" his people into the mainstream of white America.

Throughout his long and active life, he espoused the ideals and values of the white middle class. He lived outside the reservation, paid taxes, sent his children to white schools, dressed in a suit and tie, and drove a car. Morgan was also the first Navajo ordained as a Methodist minister. When the Navajos organized their first tribal council in 1923, he was elected as a delegate from the Shiprock District.

Opposed to him was Henry Chee Dodge, a tribal patriarch and traditionalist who dominated tribal politics from the 1880s until his death in 1947. A crusty, hard-drinking Catholic, Dodge symbolized the choice—at least as Morgan saw it—between the Indian who is totally oriented to tribe and the middle-class American. As the leader of the traditionalists, Dodge opposed the ideas and goals represented by Morgan and his fellow progressives. Morgan, in turn, felt that educated Navajos should run the reservation. Yet the traditionalists, mistrustful of their educated brethren, excluded most of them from jobs and power.

Morgan's experience was typical of Indians elsewhere who returned to the reservation from boarding school. Although the agency officials sympathized with their plight, the returning students enjoyed little standing with their people and were often shut out of tribal government. Little wonder, then, that Morgan viewed John Collier's new deal for Native Americans with alarm: Collier advocated the closing of the Indian boarding schools, religious freedom, Indian self-rule, and cultural preservation.

Morgan wanted none of that. In his opinion, boarding schools shielded Navajo youngsters from the degradation, disease, and ignorance of the reservation. Thus, Morgan fought vigorously to defeat the Wheeler-Howard Act, and accused Collier of trying to establish "human zoos" for the edification of tourists. Morgan warned that medicine men would replace teachers in reservation schools and that tribal customs would be perpetuated, not eradicated. He saw Indians returning to tribalism, "going back to the blanket." Due to his efforts a referendum was twice delayed and narrowly defeated, 8,197 to 7,679.

To most Navajos, however, the debate between the cultural pluralists and the supporters of assimilation mattered little. In the end, an issue emerged that struck at the heart of Navajo culture—their animals. Morgan associated Collier with an earlier program of livestock reduction by the government, a controversial and improperly handled attempt to reduce the size of Navajo sheep and horse herds in the 1930s. To the average Navajo, sheep and goats meant security and were treated like members of the family. Tying Collier to the destruction of their animals made Morgan unbeatable.

Also, times were changing, and by the end of World War II Collier had fallen out of favor with both the government and the intellectual community. Furthermore, the war itself had unleashed forces of change that continue to this day. First of all, mobilization for the war effort brought Indians off of their reservations and into nearby cities. In combat, servicemen learned that courage, judgement, and skill could prove more important than the color of one's skin or one's place in any peacetime pecking order. Indians in all branches also learned practical problem solving.

By war's end, public opinion had swung against the U.S. government's involvement in Indian affairs. This attitude was reinforced by the Hoover Commission, a body appointed in 1948 to improve federal efficiency. A new policy took shape, supposedly to benefit the Indians by freeing them from government domination while facilitating their assimilation into white society. The new guidelines clearly signaled that Collier's vision for a pluralistic society had been sacrificed to the dictates of expediency and economy.

Congress chose this new direction because it appeared that the Wheeler-Howard Act had not successfully alleviated the nation's Indian prob-

terminated in 1954, this northeastern Wisconsin tribe was fairly prosperous, with a magnificent stand of virgin timber on its 234,000-acre reservation. Although the timber was worth a fortune—appraised at $36 million in 1936—the 3,270 individuals on the tribal rolls endured a standard of living far below the national average. Nonetheless, on June 17, 1954, President Dwight D. Eisenhower signed the Menominee Termination Act. Members received a payment of $1,500—which was their money to begin with—then they were thrown upon their own resources. The tribe even had to pay the administrative costs of implementing termination.

Poverty was instant and became almost intract-

lem. Also, the Indians themselves were split on the merits of the Collier program. Even those who liked it, however, also welcomed the opportunity to get out from under federal control. Dillon S. Myer, spokesman for the new order and President Harry S Truman's choice for his Commissioner of Indian Affairs, had established and supervised the relocation camps for West Coast Japanese-Americans during World War II.

By the early 1950s, federal policy makers had adopted two new initiatives designed to bring Indians into the American mainstream. The first policy, that of relocation, favored the movement of reservation Indians to major urban areas, including Los Angeles, Chicago, Denver, and Dallas. The second policy, called termination, fostered the withdrawal of all federal support to the affected tribes whether or not they wanted or were prepared for this. In brief, terminated tribes were to become the responsibility of the states in which they were located, with their resources placed in private trust and their treaty rights abrogated. In all, about a dozen tribes and bands, including the Klamaths of Oregon and the Menominees of Wisconsin, were terminated before lawmakers realized where the policy was headed and abandoned it.

Termination proved to be a major disaster for the affected Indians, especially the Menominees. When

able. Few tribal members could afford to pay taxes or utility bills; their school and hospital failed to meet state standards and were closed, leaving them without an educational system and without dental and medical care (a tuberculosis epidemic broke out soon after termination); and their sewage plant had to be rebuilt. Menominee County immediately became the poorest of Wisconsin's 72 counties, with half its residents on welfare and a quarter unemployed. The sawmill, the Menominee tribe's major source of revenue, installed automated equipment to improve production and in the process added still more people to the ranks of the unemployed.

As the Menominee fiscal situation went from

Testing a truce in the three-month conflict at Wounded Knee, South Dakota, opposite, armed members of the American Indian Movement (AIM) ride a lawn mower around the village in March 1973. Left, in 1974, protest leaders Russell Means, seated at left holding a drumstick and Dennis Banks, in a vest, celebrate the dismissal of all charges arising from Wounded Knee. Indian activism grew increasingly militant in the early 1970s as tribal grievances went unanswered. In November 1972, above, 500 Indian protesters occupied the Bureau of Indian Affairs building in Washington, renaming it the "Native American Embassy."

"Just Like We Saw It in the Movies"

by Rennard Strickland

There is a story told about the shooting of one of John Ford's epic westerns in Arizona's Monument Valley. The cameras stop. The Navajos dismount and take off their Sioux war bonnets. One of the crew says to the Indians, "That was wonderful. You did it just right." An Indian replies, "Yeah, we did it just like we saw it in the movies."

The Hollywood Indian is rooted in 500 years of non-Indian portrayals of Native Americans. In this century, film has given light and motion to long-standing images of deeply entrenched stereotypes. With few exceptions, the screen Indian steps directly out of the travel-and-exploration narrative, the captivity-and-atrocity accounts, and such stalwart literary traditions as James Fenimore Cooper and the popular dime novels.

Two themes dominate Indian films, dual images rooted in the contradictory portrayals of the Indian as the noble red man or as the savage pillager. These themes have endured from the 1894 flickerings of Thomas Edison's *The Sioux Ghost Dance* through the 1989 Indian spiritual quest of *Powwow Highway*. Included in the spectrum of these two powerful Hollywood stereotypes of Native Americans are those of the Indian as lazy and shiftless drunk; the Indian as educated half-breed unable to live in either the red or white world; the Indian as noble hero; the Indian as friendly, loyal, trustworthy companion; the Indian as victim of evil white man; the Indian as stoic and unemo-tional; and the Indian as vanishing American.

Until recently, the one constant in the casting and screen portrayal of the Indian has been that the Indian is played by a white; whites have even acted as extras in war parties. In *One Flew Over the Cuckoo's Nest* (1975), however, Will Sampson, a Creek, proved conclusively that the Native American actor could convey a remarkable breadth and depth of emotional experience in even the most difficult roles.

The screen portrayal of the Indian is important not only from an academic perspective but from

Jay Silverheels, a Mohawk, portrayed Tonto in the 1956 film and
subsequent television series The
Lone Ranger, opposite. In Hollywood at that time, stereotypes were
common, cultural accuracy was
unimportant, and Indian roles
generally were not assigned to
Indian actors. Broken Arrow
(1950) starred Jimmy Stewart,
above (center), and Debra Paget
(at right); Jeff Chandler (at left)
played Cochise. The first western
to portray Indians as sympathetic
characters, Broken Arrow told
the story of the misunderstanding
and conflict that arose between
Arizona settlers and Chiricahua
Apaches. Will Sampson, right, a
Creek who played Crazy Horse in
The White Buffalo (1977), heralded
a movement toward using Native
American actors.

the viewpoint of its effect on the daily lives of Native Americans. This image transcends mere entertainment, for movies and television, in particular, profoundly influence the self-image of contemporary Native Americans.

The film Indian is pervasive. No Indian reservation is too distant, no native community too traditional to escape the power of film. Indeed, this power manifests itself in actions ranging from the smallest details of an everyday children's game of cowboys and Indians to the international arena, in which America's movie-star President gave stereotyped, Hollywood-rooted answers to Soviet students' questions about Native Americans.

Today, the American Indian is making a concentrated assault on the film industry. Talented and aggressive Native Americans are producing films that portray Indians in realistic situations, often using Indians as actors in contemporary roles. Among the best of these Indian-produced films is Bob Hicks' *Return of the Country* (1984), which satirizes the popular clichés of the Hollywood Indian.

These new Indian film makers and their Indian acting colleagues intend to change the old Hollywood images and to convert the screen Indian into a real Indian, so that "just like we saw it in the movies" will, for the first time, mean just like we are.

At right, Little Big Man *(1970), starring Dustin Hoffman (at left) and Salish Chief Dan George, featured Indians as the helpless victims of whites. According to Houma Indian film maker and television producer Chris Spotted Eagle, above, "Indian people have doubted themselves for so long . . . In my own small way I am trying to convince them that they are good and have something to contribute." Spotted Eagle's films, such as* Our Sacred Land *(1987), are about modern Indians.*

dire to desperate, the tribe began selling off its land. Particularly attractive to prospective buyers was waterfront property, and the reservation included several lakes noted for their excellent boating and fishing. Remarked one concerned federal official, "Once an Indian has sold his land and used up his money, he does not stop being an Indian. He simply becomes a landless Indian."

Had the course of events proceeded in this manner, the Menominee tribe would have been shattered, its culture destroyed. Recognizing their plight, tribal members turned to activism. In the winter of 1969, a group of Menominees founded DRUMS—Determination of Rights and Unity for Menominee Shareholders. Led by Ada Deer and Jim White, within two years DRUMS had enlisted the support of a tribal majority. Menominees picketed real-estate offices on the reservation in hopes of discouraging further land sales, conducted meetings to revive tribal spirit and pride, and marched to the state capitol to draw state and national attention to their plight. Zealous and tireless, Ada Deer and her fellow Menominees wanted nothing less than a complete repeal of termination, a goal finally achieved in 1973. Although the tribe was restored to federal status, decades will be required to heal the wounds the Menominees suffered during their termination, which Smithsonian historian Wilcomb Washburn aptly described as a "monumental miscalculation . . . growing out of a mixture of good will, ignorance, and greed in varying proportions."

The furor over termination also contributed to the creation of such militant organizations as the American Indian Movement (AIM) and the National Indian Youth Council (NIYC), which came to dominate Indian affairs on the national scene in the 1960s and 1970s. Inspired by the successful example of militants in the black civil-rights movement, Indian militants clamored for "red power" and "self-determination." The road to red power, as we have seen, inevitably led to Alcatraz Island and beyond.

One of those who traveled to the Rock was George Capture (who later reclaimed the traditional family name Horse Capture), a member of the Gros Ventre tribe from Montana who worked as a California state steel inspector for the Department of Water Resources. A four-year veteran of the U.S. Navy, married to a white woman, and the father of two sons, George Capture seemed perhaps the ideal product of the federal government's assimilationist policies.

His father, Joseph Horse Capture, a veteran of World War II, had moved the family from their home on the Fort Belknap Reservation to Butte, Montana, where he worked as a hard-rock miner. As George Horse Capture explains, "the move was my father's effort to assimilate his family into ' white society to escape racism and the restrictions it imposes." As part of the effort, Joseph Horse Capture never spoke his native language and shortened the family name to Capture. Such sacrifices did little to protect the family from prejudice, however. "Eventually my father took to drinking and the family broke up." When his mother remarried, George Capture joined the U.S. Navy.

Upon his discharge four years later, he returned to Fort Belknap, where he signed up for the Bureau of Indian Affairs' relocation program. "As a result, I found myself in Los Angeles in welding school in 1962. In the beginning part of this program, a male had to be a welder and a female a beautician."

The young man succeeded. From school he went to the Hunter's Point Naval Shipyard, where he advanced rapidly through the ranks from welder's helper to steel inspector. By 1968 he had become the youngest steel inspector in the Department of Water Resources—and its only Indian employee. He wore a three-piece suit to work, carried a briefcase, and drove a state-owned car. Fort Belknap had become a distant memory—until the events on Alcatraz jarred it back into focus.

As George Horse Capture recalls, "I heard the news over the car radio, and suddenly I felt I had to be part of it." Taking his two sons, he went to the island and got caught up in the excitement. "It became clear my direction in life must change. I was, after all, an Indian, and that realization felt good. I had looked over the white hill of success, saw the other side, and realized nothing was there." After much soul-searching, George resigned his position with the state government, enrolled in the American Indian Studies program at U.C. Berkeley, and adopted his traditional name, Horse Capture.

Photographed on South Dakota's Rosebud Reservation, a room in the house of Peter Swift Hawk reflects the complex world of modern native people.

Today he is curator of the Plains Indian Museum at the Buffalo Bill Historical Center in Cody, Wyoming, and assists Indian tribes across the country in preserving their Indian heritage. He is one of the very few Indian curators in a non-Indian-owned museum in the United States.

Alcatraz and the events that followed demonstrated that leadership in the Indian community was swinging rapidly from reservation to urban-based Indians. Indians on reservations were often preoccupied with issues of immediate and local

concern: unemployment, economic development, and the next election for the tribal council. Urban Indians, often separated from relatives and members of their own tribe, increasingly found companionship, ethnic identity, and support from Indians of other tribes, even from tribes that at one time had been traditional enemies. In Minneapolis the two dominant groups that came into contact were the Ojibwa and the Dakota, whose enmity for each other dated back to the pre-Columbian era.

Beginning in the 1920s, Indians from these tribes began moving to Minneapolis, but their great urban migration occurred during World War II, which saw the city's Indian population surge from 1,000 to as many as 6,000. While the Indians retained tribal associations, they also forged pan-

Indian organizations, such as the American Indian Association and the Tepee Order, a national fraternal society. Different tribes living in the Twin Cities—Minneapolis and St. Paul—soon discovered that they shared similar problems, anxieties, and experiences within the dominant white society; they also realized that they needed to devise new solutions to their problems.

In addition to creating a pan-Indian community, the Indians worked to awaken their white neighbors to the richness of Indian culture and to counter rising prejudice as Indians living in the Twin Cities and elsewhere fell victim to postwar housing shortages and increasing unemployment. Indian ghettos arose, along with their attendant evils—juvenile delinquency, prostitution, alcoholism and drug abuse. Urban Indians became politically active and, in addition to dealing with the problems of urban life, they sought to maintain their Indian identity and protect their rights and legal status with the federal government.

In 1946 an act of Congress established the Indian Claims Commission, a three-judge panel to hear and resolve claims against the United States presented by any tribe, band, or identifiable group of Indians who had grievances against the federal government growing out of treaties or similar contracts. Initially established for a period of five years, the commission generated so much business that it gained two additional judges and remained in existence until September 1978, at which time unresolved cases were transferred to the court of claims. During the 32 years of the commission's operation, more than 170 tribes and bands in the United States filed 370 petitions, which were then organized into 617 dockets. The resulting awards totaled more than $818 million, most of it paid out as reimbursement for Indian lands that had been obtained at less than market value.

Although the legal action under the Claims Commission Act benefited many tribes and individual Indians, it proved far more lucrative to the host of lawyers and expert witnesses who helped the Indians present their cases to the federal government. By the time everyone involved in the lengthy and litigious process received payment, little was left for individual tribal members.

Docket 332A, for instance, was filed on behalf of the Yankton Sioux Nation in August 1951, and pertained to lands lost through the Treaty of Fort Laramie, which had been signed less than a century earlier. In January 1969, the commission finally awarded the Yankton Sioux $1,250,000, which the government then placed in escrow. Four years passed while the tribe decided how to dispense the money. The net award, including interest, amounted to $1,611,303.54, which was dispersed as follows: $125,000 to attorneys; $15,000 for attorney expenses; $11,000 for the update of the tribal rolls; $50,000 to repay an expert-assistance loan; and $150,000 for fees paid to expert witnesses. Of the remaining $1,260,303, a quarter was set aside for tribal investments, and the rest—$945,227—was distributed in a $262 per capita payment to the 3,600 eligible Yanktons, of whom only 1,200 still lived on their South Dakota reservation.

Beyond such basic and practical concerns, many of them involving official tribal enrollment and ties to the rural reservations, urban Indians turned their attention to issues of local and national concern. As Ojibwa author Ignatia Broker, a member of the Twin Cities Indian community, suggests in her book *Night Flying Woman*: "maybe it was a good thing, the migration of our people to the urban areas during the war years, because there, amongst the millions of people, we were brought to a brotherhood. . . . And because we all were isolated in this dominant society, we became an island from which a revival of spirit began."

The revival of spirit that prevailed on Alcatraz had been largely lighthearted and symbolic. The spirit that emanated from the Indians of the Twin Cities was far more serious and even ominous. A white backlash against the Alcatraz demonstration and other examples of Indian activism soon brought incidents of violence. Indians were also inspired in their impatient quest for a political and cultural renaissance by two best-selling books— *Bury My Heart at Wounded Knee*, a decidedly pro-Indian account of the Indian wars by novelist Dee Brown, and *Custer Died for Your Sins*, by Dakota author Vine Deloria, Jr., whose insightful interpretation of events in American Indian history gave focus to the issues that emerged in the Indian community

during the civil-rights era. Evidence of the backlash was resentment towards Indian treaty rights and programs that appeared during the Nixon Presidency.

Violence surfaced in February 1972 when Raymond Yellow Thunder, an Indian cowboy, died in Gordon, Nebraska, after being beaten by white toughs. Only after hundreds of angry Indians protested Yellow Thunder's death did Gordon law officers investigate the circumstances surrounding the incident and file murder charges. Richard Oakes, a leader of the Alcatraz occupation, was shot to death in November of the same year at a YMCA camp. The worst violence, however, erupted in Washington State, where Indians and whites were in a virtual state of war over traditional fishing rights. Hank Adams, an outspoken and militant leader of the Indian fishermen, lost his sister-in-law in a shooting by unknown white assailants. When, in January 1971, would-be assassins shot him as well, local police claimed he had tried to commit suicide.

Out of this climate emerged the American Indian Movement, or AIM, which came to represent some of the best and some of the worst of the red-power movement. Founded in 1968 by Dennis Banks and George Mitchell, two Ojibwas from Minnesota, AIM grew out of a neighborhood organization that had formed to prevent what appeared to be discriminatory arrests—"preventive detention," it was called—of Indians by Minneapolis police. Once AIM members began following police patrols the number of Indians arrested dropped dramatically.

From its success with this program, AIM moved to larger issues such as unemployment, housing, and recreation facilities. Urban Indians complained that the BIA appeared interested only in Indians living on reservations, while city dwellers were abandoned to the whims of state and local jurisdictions. In an angry confrontation, AIM members told the Minneapolis area director for the Bureau of Indian Affairs that "Everything is for the reserva-

tion, but this is the largest reservation right here. When will you help the people living here?"

Although the protestors were arrested, their complaints were aired over radio and television: the red-power movement had been launched. AIM chapters opened in cities across the United States and Canada, and the organization emerged as the cutting edge of Indian militancy. The leadership included Banks, Mitchell, Clyde and Virgil Bellecourt, Ojibwas from Minnesota, and Russell Means, an Oglala Sioux from Pine Ridge Reservation in South Dakota. Clearly indebted to the examples established by the campus and black militants who had preceded them, the red militants used the media to maintain enthusiasm and popular support. Events were staged as much for their media potential as for their significance to the issues. Thus, the success at Alcatraz was followed by the capture of Mount Rushmore and Plymouth Rock, as well as by less newsworthy sit-ins and confrontations in such Indian urban centers as Denver, Detroit, and Milwaukee.

The red-power movement flourished for only a short time. By the mid-70s it had run its course, a victim of waning public interest and of dismay by both Indians and whites at the excesses that resulted from two demonstrations: the Trail of Broken Treaties and Wounded Knee II.

Seizing the opportunity presented by the 1972 Presidential election, AIM leaders proposed a march on Washington, D.C., by Indians from all corners of the country. The pan-Indian caravan threatened to remain in the nation's capital and hold rallies and religious ceremonies and lobby their Congressional representatives until federal officials took seriously a list of 20 grievances and demands drafted by Hank Adams. With the Presidential election just a few days away, the caravan leaders were optimistic that both political parties would curry their favor.

The demonstration was ill-fated from the beginning. The hundreds of Indians who descended upon Washington in early November 1972 found it easier to get in than to get out. Government officials refused to meet with them, black militants and community leaders resented their presence, and their promised logistical support—food, lodging,

Sewel Makes Room for Them was photographed sometime after 1974 in the isolated community of Spring Creek on the Rosebud Reservation in South Dakota.

funds—failed to materialize. Frustrated and desperate, the demonstrators went en masse to the Bureau of Indian Affairs building. After all, the bureau was supposed to help Indians, and help is what they needed. Before surprised officials could react, several hundred Indians had taken residence in the auditorium on the main floor. Officials had expected a demonstration, but thought it would take place at the Washington Monument, long known on the reservation circuit as the "Indian Shaft." At an impromptu press conference, however, caravan leaders announced that they would remain in the Bureau of Indian Affairs building until satisfactory housing arrangements were made.

Following a week of confrontation, hysteria, and near disaster, government officials and Indian demonstrators alike tried to devise a peaceful solution to the problem. At various times during the week, riot police were poised to assault the building, which the Indians had barricaded with office furniture. For weapons, the Indians had a few clubs, lances, and Molotov cocktails; and a pistol taken from a captured security officer.

The demonstrators subsisted on food, clothing, and bedding provided by various supporters from Washington and the surrounding suburbs. The confrontation ended when government negotiators agreed to give the demonstrators $65,650 to finance their transportation home. How much actually went for this purpose remains unclear. According to one popular theory, AIM leaders saved most of the money and used it to finance the subsequent takeover at Wounded Knee. Regardless, the demonstrators vacated the building and Washington, D.C., and left government officials to pick up the pieces.

The Washington incident left its legacy—relief that it was over and resentment of its excesses. Sadly, the occupation hurt some Indians: demonstrators at the Bureau of Indian Affairs destroyed and stole files, some containing irreplaceable documents of importance to individuals and tribes throughout the country. The resentment of these people, in turn, quickly eroded whatever moral support the militants might have enjoyed among reservation-based Indians.

In early 1973, only four months after the occupation of the bureau, AIM's seizure of Wounded Knee further weakened red power. The place itself, chosen as a major confrontation site because of its historic associations, was a cluster of houses and a Catholic church on the Pine Ridge Reservation. The encounter unfolded after AIM leader Russell Means demanded the recall of Pine Ridge Tribal Chairman Richard Wilson, charging that he was a stooge of the Bureau of Indian Affairs. Civil strife ensued when Wilson refused to step aside; the conflict ended in a standoff between heavily armed militants and federal authorities. During 70 days of confrontation, Wounded Knee had been destroyed, the church burned, two militants killed, and a federal marshall shot in the spine and paralyzed for life. Negotiating through the National Council of Churches, the Indians eventually withdrew, though violence continued for months and two FBI agents died in a shootout.

As the '70s progressed, most of the prominent protest leaders grew more interested in avoiding jail than in fomenting further unrest. Many Indians, however, continued to celebrate the red-power movement. The events at Alcatraz and Wounded Knee, the takeover of the Bureau of Indian Affairs, and the numerous other encounters did, in fact, spotlight legitimate Indian grievances. The clashes and the war of words also sensitized the general public to the Indian need for respect, educational and employment opportunities, and religious freedom.

Perhaps most important, red power reinforced Indian ethnic pride, a guiding light that had been eclipsed by events but not extinguished. As tribes across North America reasserted their deeply held values, the conviction grew that, if given half a chance, Indians could manage their own affairs and become a positive force in American life. Perhaps Vine Deloria worded this conviction best in 1966 when he was serving as executive director of the National Congress of American Indians. "Red Power," he wrote in 1966, "means we want power over our own lives."

Fritz Scholder painted "Last Indian With American Flag" in the 1970s. Descended from the Luiseño tribe of California, Scholder participated in the Indian cultural renaissance.

*Looking like typical American schoolchildren any-
where, Navajo youngsters mug for the camera against
the magnificent backdrop of Monument Valley, Arizona,
part of the tribe's 16-million-acre reservation.*

Horizons

The future begins today, and tribal concerns are the horizons, the challenges, that Indian peoples must meet and master if they are to endure for centuries to come. Many problems and perils are evident, and yet the situation of America's Indians may be the best it has been since 1492. Opportunities for effective social and political action have increased as the Indian population has grown. At least two million Native Americans will be living in the United States by 1992, a figure widely believed to equal or exceed the total for the same territory on the day that Columbus first stepped ashore in the New World.

In certain parts of the country, especially the Southwest, Indians could exert a formidable force in local and national elections if they exploited the majority status they enjoy in certain districts. Concern over energy, environment, and other issues of vital interest to the future of Indians has tended to overcome the old-time reluctance to join in the life of the society at large. Many years may pass, though, before the full potential of Indian participation in national issues is tested.

One aspect of Indian-white relations has changed dramatically: it has never been more fashionable to be an Indian or for a white person to have Indian friends. Large metropolitan newspapers often report issues concerning tribal groups. Indian entertainers and political figures appear on television. The pendulum could swing back toward the hostility of yesteryear, however. In fact, some individuals expect this to happen. Nevertheless, in times either of acceptance or rejection, the general public has gained little conception of the true nature and dynamics of Indian culture.

Indian culture has never been static. Indians readily adapt, changing to meet new challenges, and a tradition of pragmatism continues and even is accelerating today. Indians are becoming more mobile, better educated, and more involved in the wider implications of citizenship. For example, according to the latest statistics, only a quarter of all Indians live on reservations; in 1980, half did.

From the earliest days of intercultural contact, Indian peoples eagerly sought newer and better ways of doing things. Thus iron tools readily replaced stone tools, the gun supplanted the bow, cloth replaced leather, and canvas tents took the place of buffalo-hide tipis. Revealing examples of Indian adaptiveness can still be found in today's handicrafts. Dental floss has replaced sinew in beadworking, and one can now buy beaded tennis shoes as well as moccasins at pow wows and reservation gift shops. Plastic knives, forks, and spoons from fast-food shops do not always end up in a trash bin; some Indian craft workers are using them instead of bone for the breastplates and other items they sell to tourists. Furthermore, in the late 1980s, the rage among pow-wow dancers was to use the tin covers from Copenhagen-brand snuff cans as the

"jinglers" worn on their dance outfits. Such incremental change, a small-is-beautiful approach, has its place in cultural survival for Indians both on and off the reservation.

Yet Indians may need to make bigger changes to meet greater challenges. Resources for such costly programs as education and health care could be more difficult to come by in the future. The season of large social budgets and legislation favorable to Indians—the 1960s and '70s—is almost ancient history now, and nothing lies on the horizon to take its place.

America's Indians never experienced anything

like the legislative windfall of a few decades ago. Perhaps it was the tension and sense of urgency provoked by the events of the red-power movement; perhaps it was simply an effort by the white majority to rectify past injustices and to ensure that Indians at last could view themselves as equal members of the "Great Society," in the famous phrase of the Lyndon Johnson administration. Now that time, too, is past. In the era of self-empowerment, how will Indians work out their destinies in a national context of scarce funds?

A review of the extraordinary legacy of the Johnson and Nixon administrations may provide a hint of the direction the tribes would like to follow into the next century, a direction that may often involve acquisition of land and resources. In December 1970, legislation confirming the right of Indians to protect traditional religious areas enabled Taos Pueblo in New Mexico to reclaim its sacred Blue Lake and the 48,000 acres surrounding it. A year later, thanks to the Alaska Native Claims Settlement Act, the Indians, Aleuts, and Inuits living in our nation's largest state received legal title to 40 million acres of land and a billion dollars in compensation and mineral rights.

In June 1972, the Indian Education Act, sponsored by the U.S. Department of Health, Education and Welfare, established new Indian educational programs and authorized a National Advisory Council composed of Indians and Alaska natives to provide oversight and advice. In 1974, in *Morton v. Mancari*, the Supreme Court upheld the right of the Bureau of Indian Affairs to adopt a policy of preferential hiring of Indians. Such favorable treatment was not "racial discrimination," the justices ruled, but rather constituted "an employment criterion reasonably designed to further the cause of Indian self-government and to make the BIA more responsive to the needs of its constituent groups." With over 80 percent of bureau employees now Indians, native peoples can no longer claim that BIA stands for "Boss Indians Around," a common joke in the turbulent '60s.

Perhaps most important, in 1975 Congress passed the Indian Self-Determination and Education Assistance Act, a major step in giving tribes control over the federal education and health programs that

Nestled at the foot of northern New Mexico's Sangre de Cristo range, Taos Pueblo, opposite, is one of the oldest continually inhabited sites in North America. Residents of tightly knit communities such as Taos Pueblo have kept their way of life distinct from the larger culture more successfully than have many other groups. Above, San Ildefonso Pueblo resident María Martínez revived traditional polychrome pottery designs for which she became world famous. Here she surveys some of her work at the Museum of Anthropology in Santa Fe.

affected them. In theory, this meant that Indians would reap the benefits of better programs and that public funds would be well spent because the people most affected by the programs would be responsible for implementing them. And tribes have gained a few victories in this area of participatory social policy.

For the most part, however, Indians have been ill-equipped to exercise some of the responsibilities of self-determination. A number of money scandals have beset tribal governments across the country. Remarked one Indian tribal officer, "Looking for fiscal irregularities on an Indian reservation is like looking for rain in Seattle!"

Modern accounting techniques and old-fashioned Indian values remain far from reconciled. Indians,

for example, possess a strong tradition of generosity. Thus, if there is a financial need, it is filled, whether the funds available were intended for that purpose or not. "Commingling funds," says Cherokee attorney Joel Thompson, "may appear like fraud to non-Indians, when the underlying motivation was not personal gain but a desire to help someone in trouble." Naturally, federal officials are distressed at such behavior, but it is an integral part of the Indian value system. It is simply one of many areas in which the old and the new still come into conflict on an Indian reservation.

In the 1940s and 1950s, Bureau of Indian Affairs Commissioner John Collier and his successors hoped that tribal corporations would come to provide the economic base for Indian communities; in reality, this has seldom happened. Many tribes have seen their corporations collapse for one reason or another, but all too often from poor management. Furthermore, efforts to attract private industry to reservations have frequently failed because of such culturally determined pitfalls as "Indian Time," a phenomenon that is easy to define—Indians often miss or show up late for appointments—but difficult to explain. Putting schedules "on hold" or de-emphasizing them may be a device for deferring social conflict. Whatever Indian Time really is, it disrupts the schemes of white men far more than it does those of Indians.

Many Indians who live on reservations not only have difficulty following the dictates of the clock, but also find themselves distracted by a variety of family and ceremonial obligations that often make a full workweek an impossibility. Remarked one friend of the author, "Being an Indian is a full-time job itself." Such traits may have worked a century ago in camp, around the tipi circle, at the hunt, or for ceremonial events, but today in a white man's economy they almost always result in the loss of income and self-reliance. Too many tribes remain heavily dependent on federal funding to support reservation schools, health care, and employment.

Some tribes, however, such as the Mescalero Apaches of New Mexico, have succeeded in avoiding fiscal crises. Led by Wendell Chino, a descendant of Geronimo and one of the shrewdest businessmen anywhere, the Mescalero people enjoy a level of prosperity that would be the envy of almost any other Indian community in the United States.

When Chino first took office in 1953, the tribe's future was bleak at best. Only 1,200 Mescaleros were on the tribal rolls and unemployment on the reservation had soared above 80 percent. Only six Mescaleros had ever attended college. Living conditions were deplorable: most tribe members lived in tents or shacks without electricity or running water; infant mortality was high; and illness was rampant, especially respiratory infections, tuberculosis, and a persistent eye inflammation called trachoma.

All this has now changed. The tribe, with only 500 people at the close of the Indian wars in 1886, numbered more than 3,000 a century later. Today, most reservation residents live in modern homes with electricity and indoor plumbing. The school dropout rate, according to tribal records, is less

Light glows through chinks in the slabs of a newly constructed igloo or snow house, opposite, at the Igloolik Model Community Village at Igloolik, on the Melville Peninsula of the Canadian Arctic, north of Hudson Bay. Until recently, such houses were characteristic winter dwellings of the Iglulik Inuit (Eskimos), who inhabit this region of the Arctic. Like most other Inuit groups, today's Iglulik Inuit favor all-terrain vehicles, right, over traditional dog sleds for travel and hunting.

During the 19th century, Indian peoples from many parts of the nation were forcibly relocated to the so-called Indian Territories in Oklahoma, opposite. Recently, Hopis and Navajos have clashed in court over land originally set aside for the Hopis but claimed by Navajos as part of their traditional tribal realm. Left, Navajos at Keams Canyon, Arizona, protest forced relocation of members of the tribe from disputed territory awarded to the Hopis for their exclusive use.

than five percent; unemployment is less than 40 percent and falling.

Mescaleros now work at a number of tribally owned enterprises, including a game preserve that caters to wealthy sportsmen, a sawmill, a ski lodge called "Ski Apache," and a luxury resort hotel with 250 guest rooms that also boasts an 18-hole golf course, tennis courts, a pool, a spa, and a riding stable. As one hotel employee recently admitted to a reporter for the *New York Times*, "Apaches were known historically as raiders, and we're continuing on in the raiding tradition. We're taking from rich Texans and using their money for our education and health and other facilities for our people."

Few tribes possess a Wendell Chino or a success story similar to that of the Mescaleros, but many are now attempting to promote enterprises that will provide employment and attract dollars to the reservation. One of the most popular and successful enterprises is big-time bingo, a phenomenon that is sweeping Indian country, and, unfortunately, sparking controversy and division within the tribes. More than 100 tribes have established high-stakes bingo games on their reservations since the Florida Seminoles opened the first one in 1979.

It may still be too early to make a judgment about the social and moral effects of legalized gambling on Indian reservations. In some instances, such as the one involving the Mohawks of New York State and nearby Canada, violence has resulted. Elsewhere, gambling may further strain tribal societies that already bear serious intercultural problems. However, two economic factors seem clear: white Americans are gambling more than ever before, and gambling is pumping large sums of money into cash-starved Indian communities.

One such community is the Oneida Indian Reservation located near Green Bay, Wisconsin. Attracting busloads of players from the Twin Cities, Chicago, and Milwaukee, Oneida bingo nets the tribe in excess of $10 million annually. Besides financing housing projects, a modern motel and convention center, scholarships, and similar community services, the money is also targeted for land acquisition, and the Oneidas have systematically bought up property adjoining the reservation as it becomes available, thereby enlarging their holdings.

As one might expect, the land purchases have embroiled the Oneidas in a bitter legal fight with their non-Indian neighbors, especially in the city of Green Bay, which stands to lose a large chunk of its tax base. In addition to land purchases, the tribe has used some of its bingo money to press lawsuits against Wisconsin and New York for past land transactions which the Oneidas believe were unfair.

Thus far the tribe has won almost all the suits they have brought, and others are still pending before the Supreme Court. If their present litigation is successful, the Oneidas are willing to accept land as part of the compensation, but not just any land. "We aren't going to be happy with some worthless piece of swampland," remarked one tribal official. "We have our eye on a high-rise or two in Manhattan, something that is income-producing."

The Oneidas, Mescaleros, and others are working to join the rest of America in its hot pursuit of money, often through the sponsorship of gambling. Another kind of "game," however, has embroiled many tribes in the United States and Canada in an increasingly acrimonious confrontation with their white neighbors and governmental authorities. Native peoples exercise hunting-and-fishing rights granted under treaties now more than a century old, and often hunt and fish outside tribal bounda-

ries without regard to the bag limits or seasons imposed on non-Indians. Indians often view hunting as subsistence activity, a basic necessity rather than a recreation.

Non-Indian sportsmen, sporting associations, and individuals dependent on recreation dollars for their income claim that Indians are depleting already threatened game and fish species by excessive harvesting. They also charge that Indians sometimes engage in these practices just to provoke confrontations, knowing how angry it makes their white neighbors. The Indians, in turn, insist that the fish, ducks, and deer they kill for the table or for seasonal commerce are small compensation for the long-term loss of their land, their culture, and their livelihood.

As Ed Burnstick, a Canadian Indian, lamented at

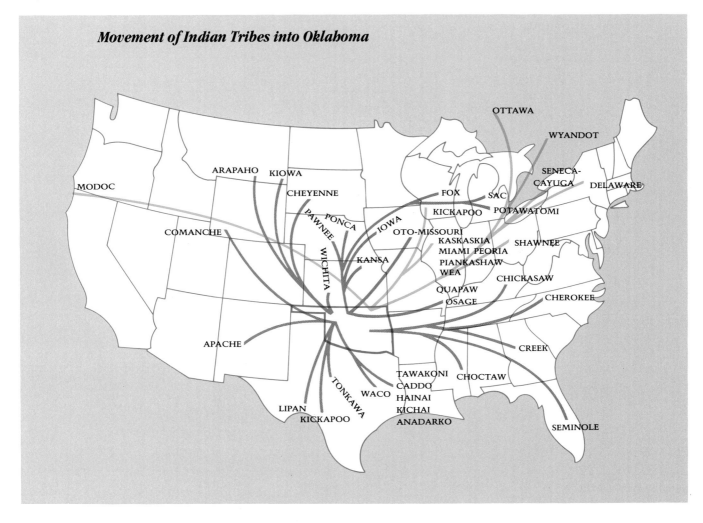

Movement of Indian Tribes into Oklahoma

an international congress in 1977 in Geneva, Switzerland: "We [in Canada] are affected by such laws as the Migratory Bird Act, and yet in our treaties we have fishing and hunting rights. We have court cases where our people have been put in court for shooting ducks to feed their family because it infringed on the Migratory Bird Act. In many areas, however, there are no jobs, and people must rely on hunting and fishing to survive."

When U.S. courts uphold the treaty rights of Indians, tensions are aggravated even further. In Wisconsin, for instance, angry sportsmen have established such organizations as Equal Rights for Everyone and Protect America's Rights and Resources, PARR, whose purpose is to overturn the treaty rights presently enjoyed by the Indians of that state. They seek especially to curtail the right of the Ojibwas to spear walleye pike, a technique the Indians have used each spring since long before contact with the first white man.

Fueled by posters and automobile bumper stickers proclaiming such slogans as "Save a Walleye, Spear an Indian" or "Shoot an Indian, Save a Deer," and by editorials in the national press, the white backlash may be gaining momentum. In 1977, staff writer Richard Barnes editorialized in *Outdoor Life*: "There is a strange mood of guilt and shame abroad in our country. A lot of imprecise thinkers . . . are trying to give the country back to the Indians. I don't agree. Giving Indian tribes the right to wipe out game is an injustice to the rest of us and . . . my tax-paying, license-buying kids are just as entitled to catch fish as old Throwing-the-Bull's freeloading kids are."

Addressing this and other potentially disruptive situations, Gordon McLester, former secretary of the Oneida Nation in Wisconsin, writes, "The problems the Indian people are facing today have not changed much over the past 400 years. They have gotten more sophisticated, that's all."

Indian responses to intercultural dilemmas are also becoming more sophisticated, a capability

A Hopi farmer harvests his painstakingly tended corn crop on the desert floor between Second and Third Mesas, Arizona, below. Most Hopis live in ancient villages atop several mesas in the middle of their north-central Arizona reservation. A man lounges in the shade of a dilapidated roof at Crow Agency, Montana, in the early 1970s, opposite.

born of the activist 1960s and earlier coming-of-age experiences in wartime. Within the tribes themselves, the most heartening outcome of the postwar years may be the Indian cultural renaissance—a tribal Manifest Destiny. It is being achieved through a variety of programs that focus on such areas as tribal languages and lore, historical and ethnographic scholarship, the arts, and traditional crafts such as carving, pottery making, weaving, beadworking, and quill working.

Because many craft workers are dependent upon the income they derive from the sale of their output, most have had to adapt modern technology to traditional crafts in order to stay in business. One young man, a Makah carver in the Pacific Northwest, had been part of a movement among craftspeople to work only in traditional materials using

traditional methods of preparation. Such idealism collapsed, however, when the artists discovered how tedious and time-consuming it was to fell trees and carve masks without metal tools. "Let's face it," the carver remarked in a recent conversation at the visitor center on the Makah Indian Reservation at Neah Bay in Washington State. "I have a wife and kids to support, and I can't afford to be idealistic anymore." He now uses a chain saw to rough out his cedar blocks, which he then dries in his microwave oven—"300 degrees for five or ten minutes is ideal." The use of labor-saving devices makes the artwork no less genuine or "authentic."

Contemporary, independent expression in dance,

Sadly, as street scenes from Phoenix, Arizona, reveal, above and right, drunkenness is common among urban Indians. This blight also affects reservation dwellers. Although tribal leaders strongly encourage treatment programs, alcoholism and substance abuse remain major social and public-health problems. Drivers leaving the Sioux reservation at Pine Ridge, South Dakota, run a gauntlet of markers that pinpoint traffic fatalities, many of them alcohol-related, suffered by members of the tribe.

sculpture, literature, and painting also helps to communicate Indian values and spirit to a wide audience. Fine artists such as Fritz Scholder, Kevin Red Star, Retha Gambaro, and scores of other exciting and creative individuals have gained dedicated, enthusiastic followers who pay top prices for their work. They do this because the work is by very talented artists, however, not simply because it is by Indian artists.

Spurred by the red-power movement, the cultural renaissance, and religious needs, Indians have developed an insatiable appetite for solid facts about their past, rather than accepting the romantic notions that predominated for so long. Knowledge seekers have often turned to museums for assistance in saving languages, for photographs of ancestors, and for information about ceremonies and customs. And as Indian cultural-studies programs flourished on college campuses across the country in the 1970s, the level of interest in museum collections and services increased accordingly, especially on the part of Indians who were anxious to learn the traditional art styles of their tribes so that they could continue or reintroduce this heritage.

Not all museums or curators welcomed this interest in the past, however, fearing that confrontations would be inevitable when Indians began requesting the return of unique or sacred objects. The Smithsonian Institution was no exception— except that as a leader in the museum world, its reaction and response to Indian requests would have tremendous impact across North America.

Despite initial misgivings in 1972, the Smithsonian's Department of Anthropology responded to

Indian requests for access by establishing the Native American Cultural Resources Training Program. It provided funds for tribally selected interns to spend up to six months in residence in Washington conducting research on their tribes not only at the Smithsonian, but also at the National Archives and the Library of Congress. Over a ten-year period, some 90 men and women from 55 tribes participated in the program, which eventually expanded to include other Smithsonian bureaus. At the time of its inception, there were no employees of Indian heritage on the Smithsonian's staff; in recent years there have been a dozen or more, including two curators, JoAllyn Archambault, an anthropologist in the National Museum of Natural History, and Rayna Greene, a folklorist on the staff of the National Museum of American History.

Curators at first feared that this initiative would be a Trojan horse used by Indians to gain access to the collections and to acquire information they needed to demand the return of specimens. The program had an opposite effect. Indian interns not only allowed the archives to copy old family photographs and documents, but some even donated cultural objects to the artifact collections.

The most poignant contribution came from the Tunica-Biloxi tribe of Louisiana, which in 1974 numbered fewer than 100 members and which sent an intern to participate in the research program. Besides obtaining information about Tunica-Biloxi history and culture, the intern was especially anxious to find evidence in government archives that could be used to secure federal recognition for the tribe and thereby obtain a few acres of land for a reservation. Although the Smithsonian had no Tunica-Biloxi artifacts in its collections, the intern did find enough documentary material to enable the tribe to receive federal recognition. In due course, the Tunica-Biloxis also acquired a federal grant of 80 acres for a reservation.

And the story did not end there. A few months after the tribe established occupancy of what had once been part of its ancestral lands, a grave was discovered. In it, along with a skeleton, Indians found a few beads and other items that had been used as trade goods during the Colonial period. After reburying the skeleton, the tribe sent the objects

retrieved from the grave to the Smithsonian so that at last the Tunica-Biloxis would also be represented in the national collections.

The culmination of the Smithsonian's cultural initiatives is to be a new museum on the Mall in Washington, D.C., devoted exclusively to America's Indians. A fortuitous combination of talents and contributions made the project possible, and three individuals, in particular, had the vision and ability to make it happen. One is Congressman Sidney R. Yates of Illinois, who has been one of the foremost friends of the American Indian and the Smithsonian Institution during his lengthy and distinguished legislative career. Another is Smithsonian Secretary Robert McCormick Adams, who felt that the Institution needed to do more than offer a few token gestures or exhibits on behalf of America's Indians. After some years dealing with Native Americans, he observed, "their story takes

From high technology to the high life, from banking to bingo, Indian tribes increasingly involve themselves in business, industry, and entertainment. A bank sign in Tahlequah, Oklahoma, appears in both Cherokee and English, left. Ojibwa activist and Indian rights leader Dennis Banks addresses a group of businessmen in Chadron, Nebraska, near the Pine Ridge Reservation of South Dakota, below left. Workers assemble missile electronics systems at a General Dynamics Corporation plant on the Navajo reservation. The factory grew out of an agreement between tribal chairman Peter MacDonald and the aerospace manufacturer.

on an anguish . . . and becomes a weight one cannot carry."

But the person most responsible for the new museum is the late George Heye, an eccentric oil executive so fascinated by American Indian art that he built a museum—it opened in New York City in 1922—to house his enormous collection, which he acquired, in part, by descending upon remote Indian communities in his chauffeur-driven limousine and buying everything within reach. After Heye's death in 1957, his museum languished and its million or more artifacts fell victim to the same malaise that seemingly had beset the people it honored, a case of out-of-sight and out-of-mind. Finally, after an endless series of lawsuits, political maneuvers, and negotiations with New York State officials, part of Heye's collection is to take its place of honor on the Mall as the National Museum of the American Indian.

But the museum would have remained an impossible dream had not the Smithsonian made a major concession to acquire it—which was to divest itself of some of its Indian skeletal remains. Like the backlash over Indian treaty rights that is proving so detrimental to Indian-white relations today among sportsmen, the "bone issue" took on the same confrontational aspect in the museum world. On the one hand, scientists want to retain Indian skeletal remains in hopes that future technological breakthroughs will allow them to learn even more than they presently know about the diet, illnesses, and lifestyles of tribes in both pre-Columbian and modern times. For their part, Indians want the bones of their ancestors to be returned to the earth so that their spirits can finally enjoy eternal rest.

Groused one unnamed New York anthropologist in a *Washington Post* editorial in October 1988: "All that wandering souls stuff is dramatic for the media. We are doing important work that benefits all mankind, and we're portrayed as grave robbers." And yet, in 1987, on the other side of the issue, Bill Tall Bull, a Cheyenne religious leader, testified before the U.S. Senate: "It is uncivilized . . . savage . . . barbaric . . . inhuman. It is sick behavior. It is un-Christian. It is punishable by law."

Perhaps the Smithsonian's decision to return Indian skeletal remains and funerary objects that

can be specifically identified by tribes will ease tensions and enable museum officials and the Indian community once again to work in harmony, and will ensure that the National Museum of the American Indian will be as dynamic, creative, and vibrant as the people it seeks to honor. As Representative Ben Nighthorse Campbell, an American Indian from Colorado and member of the United States Congress, commented at a ceremony authorizing the new facility, "The museum will symbolize a rebirth for us. Our people across the country know the importance of this."

Culturally, Native Americans fight many good fights and win many victories, but they also suffer numerous defeats. Native craftspeople, for instance, may establish reputations and prosper in cottage industries while larger tribal endeavors fail. Jealousy seems implicated in some cases, and this

Mescalero Apaches own the Inn of the Mountain Gods, left, a resort in the Sacramento Mountains of New Mexico. The brainchild of chairman Wendell Chino, its grounds include an artificial lake stocked from the tribe's hatchery and elk introduced for hunting. The resort complements the tribe's luxury ski lodge. Remarks Chino on his people's place in society, "We've seen the tyranny of the majority. We know we don't have to give in to conventional thinking." Unidentified child on the Mescalero Reservation, right, gapes at pow-wow dancer's finery.

uncomfortable fact of life is reflected in Indian humor. The story is told of a white man and an Indian, each carrying a can of fishing worms. When they reach the stream, the white man looks in his can and sees that his worms are gone, but the Indian has not lost one. "How do you explain that?" the white man asks. "The explanation is simple," replies the Indian. "I'm using Indian worms. Every time a worm tries to crawl out of the can, two others pull it back."

As the person who related this joke explained, a person who tries to succeed on a reservation is often held back by relatives and friends. Those who do become successful, often outside the reservation, may find it difficult to rejoin the traditional community.

One way of overcoming such pressures and restraints is to honor Indian high-school and college graduates in traditional ways. On the Pine Ridge Reservation, for example, each high-school graduate receives not only his or her diploma but also an eagle feather, symbolic of the warrior who counted coup against a worthy opponent.

In 1987 the Northern Cheyennes held a traditional honor ceremony on their Montana reservation for tribal member Tim Wilson, who had recently graduated from Stanford University's medical school. As he is believed to be the first Cheyenne to obtain a degree in medicine, the tribe accorded him honors traditionally reserved for such successful war deeds as counting coup in battle—capturing a horse, for instance. The ceremony, at which Wilson received the Cheyenne name Cause First as well as a medallion confirming him as an honorary chief, attracted Cheyennes from as far as Oklahoma. "This," remarked Jimmie Old Coyote, who con-

Belief in the Future

by Wilma Mankiller
Cherokee Nation Principal Chief

As we approach the 21st century, many native communities face a plethora of social, economic, and political problems. It is difficult for most non-native people fully to understand these problems and how it came to pass that native people find themselves in their current situation.

In order to understand the struggles, the hopes, and the vision of today's native communities, it is instructive to review the treatment of native people from 1492 to the present. Without a doubt, the darkest pages in American history are those that chronicle the story of the taking of the Americas from indigenous people.

Yet despite facing virtually every social indicator of decline, tribal communities and indi-

The first female Chief of the Cherokee Nation of Oklahoma, Wilma Mankiller works at the grass roots for the benefit of all Indians.

vidual people have a tremendous strength, resiliency, and hope for the future. Native people cling tenaciously to a sense of interdependence, to tribal heritage, culture, and traditions. Even in the most troubled tribal community, I hear discussion of plans for the future so that someday we will again have whole, healthy communities for our children and our children's children. The dreams of our people are woven from a tragic past and difficult present. Yet those dreams have the ability to continue to guide our people to hope and work for a positive future. Most of us have a firm belief that 500 years from now there will still be strong tribal communities of native people in the Americas where ancient languages, ceremonies, and songs will be heard.

ferred Wilson's Indian name, "is our recognition of his manhood, of his coming home a full warrior." And, as Gros Ventre curator George Horse Capture explained, "We have adapted an old tradition to honor modern-day achievements. This action bridges the gap between the old and the new."

Many young Indians undergo trials of the spirit and experience defeats: they are often caught between their own tribal universe, with its serious religious foundations, and the white man's glib and acquisitive world. Not only do Indian teenagers suffer from early and heavy exposure to alcohol and drugs, but they experience high suicide rates, well above those of young people in non-Indian communities. Many whites believe that part of the Indians' emotional trauma may stem from a genetic predisposition concerning alcohol. Preliminary research indicates that the metabolism of some substances may differ between people of a particular European heritage and Indians with their Asian origins.

Serious study is under way to outline approaches to culturally acceptable mental-health counseling within the all-important tribal setting. Ethnic solidarity appears to offer healing power for tribal groups, as do both Christian and traditional religious practices and their various amalgamations. Indian communities have begun a shift from ignoring alcoholism to programs of active prevention. The Crow tribe, for instance, has proposed the establishment of an old-style warrior society dedicated to a tribe-wide battle against substance abuse among young people.

There is also evidence that Indians are gaining more experience at bridging the gap between modern and traditional practices. Greater support for higher education within the tribal territory is one important factor. The community college, a recent innovation, has proven effective in attracting and keeping Indians in school. Since the first one was established on the Navajo Reservation in 1969, the Indian community-college system has grown to embrace 21 such institutions across the Far West from Oklahoma to Washington State. Although only two of these schools provide four-year programs, together they enroll nearly 5,000 full-time students.

Tribal community colleges are certainly not typical of American institutions of higher education. The Oglala Lakota College on the Pine Ridge Reservation, for example, enrolls 1,000 students or more, among whom the average age is 30. Almost half of these students never finished high school. To reach out to students living on this enormous reserva-

The sign at Our Lady of the Sioux church in Oglala, South Dakota, advertises bingo, a pastime that has brought cash to many reservations. Since state gambling laws do not apply to the reservations, large jackpots draw gamblers from hundreds of miles away.

A Little Humor

Indian humor has been described as poignant, with a human touch, and even bittersweet. And well it might be, considering the several centuries of cultural domination that Native Americans have experienced. Typically, the Indian humorist aims the message of his or her joke or cartoon directly at the heart rather than going for the jugular. Like the monologues of Will Rogers, the "Cherokee Kid," Indian stories seem designed to arouse the conscience. Many illuminate the prickly no-man's-land between the world of the Native Americans and that of the dominant white culture. During the Vietnam war, one of the jokes that circulated among the troops involved Indian fighting men who were surveyed about U.S. foreign policy. Forty percent said that the United States should get out and leave Vietnam to the Vietnamese. Sixty percent said that the United States should get out of the United States and leave it to the Indians. Members of the governing white culture may not always understand the Indian joke, but the universal function of humor—that of lightening the emotional load—has clearly served the Indian community well.

The TUMBLEWEEDS comic strip at bottom by T.K. Ryan, and that shown opposite bottom, by Steve Sack, another white cartoonist, display empathy with the Indian viewpoint. The other three panels, all by Indian cartoonists and aimed at an Indian audience, tend to poke fun at whites, showing them as outlandish and insensitive to Indian issues.

268

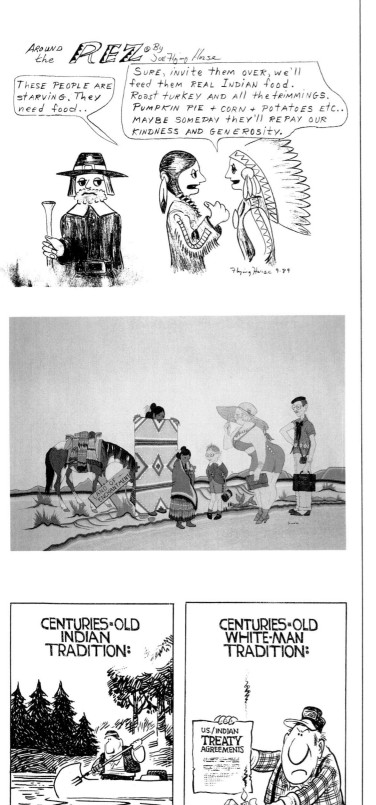

tion—7,000 square miles or roughly three times the size of Rhode Island—the college has nine teaching centers staffed by 33 full-time and 75 part-time faculty members. Even so, it is not uncommon for teachers and students alike to drive hundreds of miles to a campus each week over roads that are more like washboards than highways, or to be trapped overnight on snow-covered roads. Faithfulness and fortitude overcome such operational hitches.

Unfortunately, Indian college graduates still have difficulty finding jobs on their own home reservations. As this group's numbers climb, so does its frustration level. Many reservations are located in areas that lack employment opportunities and, in terms of technological complexity, resemble poverty-stricken hometowns of the rural South during the 1930s and 1940s. Graduates are thus often forced to seek employment elsewhere, thereby contributing to the very "brain drain" from the reservations that the community colleges are working to offset.

Robert Gay, formerly vice president for instruction at the Oglala Lakota College, is not overly upset by the fact that so many Pine Ridge graduates leave the reservation. "We try to teach them to succeed in both worlds. We want to see Indian people become more self-sufficient." His sentiments are echoed by Janine Windy-Boy Pease, president of the Little Big Horn College on the Crow Reservation and past president of the American Indian Community College Association. Pease believes strongly that education should not be tied solely to economics. "Higher education for American Indians should be emphasized for its own sake. We're into placement as much as we can be, but we're not interested in running a relocation program," she points out. "Education has to do with the solidarity of our people, so they can make good decisions and understand who they are." This may be one of the best definitions of what the Indians' cultural Manifest Destiny is all about.

A two-year college located within shouting distance of the Custer battlefield, Little Big Horn has but four full-time faculty members for its 200 or so students, who take courses that stress Crow history, language, and culture as well as mathematics and science. "We tell our students that if they're inter-

George Takes The Gun, below, a respected Crow elder, relates traditional stories to his grand-daughter, Lauren Flatlip. Along with a diploma, a Crow Creek graduate at Flandreau Indian School in South Dakota, right, receives an eagle feather, a symbol of honor from the warrior societies of the past. At Little Big Horn College, Professor Henry Bear Cloud teaches a class in Crow Creative Expression, left. The junior college is on the Crow Reservation in Montana. Native Americans increasingly view education as a means to protect their future.

ested in Western Civilization courses, they can take them on a four-year campus," Pease says. "We feel it's very important for them to know their own culture first." Mathematics and science courses are also offered because of the extreme shortage of Indian teachers in those fields. "I think there are phenomenal things going on in these colleges," Janine Windy-Boy Pease concludes. "They started out of nothing, but I think they are going to make it out of sheer guts."

Law enforcement provides another area of concern for Indians caught between the old ways and the new. Traditionally, Indians evolved various means of dealing with crimes against person and property. Peer pressure and the use of gifts to compensate an aggrieved party were usually sufficient to maintain law and order within the community. Many tribes even had a court system of sorts, whereby tribal elders attempted to resolve disputes in a public meeting in which anyone with an opinion could comment.

Although certain serious crimes such as murder, arson, and grand larceny fall under federal and state laws, tribal courts still exist, and Indian judges continue to mete out a form of justice rooted in tribal values. At present there are some 150 Indian courts on reservations, which hear about 200,000

civil and criminal cases annually. Tribal law codes are generally simple and to the point, as a lawyer helping the Muckleshoot tribe of Washington revise its legal codes recently discovered. Tribal leaders, who wished to cut through his complicated terminology, wanted to establish only three categories of crime involving hunting rights—not so bad, bad, and real bad.

Disputes concerning hunting-and-fishing rights predominate, but the courts can handle a variety of cases providing they involve only tribe members living on reservations. Ironically, as a result of these tribal courts, reservation Indians often find themselves in double jeopardy for criminal offenses, since they can be tried both on and off the reservation for the same crime. A 1988 case in eastern Washington received national attention when a Yakima man was tried in both federal and tribal courts for fishing out of season. His argument that salmon fishing was an integral part of his religion won him acquittal in the tribal court but not in the federal, which sentenced him to five years in prison.

Among some tribes, traditional punishment for someone who has committed a serious crime such as murder against a fellow tribe member might have meant eviction from the village. Banishment was often tantamount to a death sentence in the days of intertribal warfare. Although today federal laws govern those crimes committed on reservations, tribal traditions still persist. In November 1977, on the Rosebud Sioux Reservation in South Dakota, a drunken man killed a neighbor who had tried to stop a fight. Although authorities arrested the killer, the neighbors of the slain man expressed their disapproval in unique but dramatic fashion. The next day they evicted the killer—literally—from their community by placing his house on a flatbed trailer and dumping it on the prairie several miles away.

Tribal communities also care about the improvement of housing. According to Dom Nessi, director of the office of Indian housing in the Department of Housing and Urban Development, or HUD, many reservations now have adequate modern dwellings for their residents. Since passage of the Indian Housing Act in 1961, HUD has built over 70,000 units on Indian reservations. Yet even well-meaning Indians have trouble convincing their older relatives to move into modern structures. Perhaps typical of this dilemma is the story of the successful Santa Clara Pueblo businessman living in Santa Fe who tried to get his elderly aunt to leave her one-room cabin, which lacked plumbing and electricity, and move into a new condominium in his neighborhood. "Would the house have a gas stove and an indoor toilet?" she asked. Of course it would, her nephew said. "If that is the case, then I want to stay here," she replied. "The gas would give me headaches and it will spoil the taste of the food. I prefer the smell and taste of food cooked over a wood-burning stove. I also don't think having an indoor toilet is a good idea. It doesn't seem very sanitary to me." In the end, her nephew laughed and shrugged his shoulders. "I didn't argue with her. Auntie is 80 years old. Who am I to tell her she's wrong and I'm right; I'll probably die of a heart attack before I'm 50."

Modern Indian housing has other potential drawbacks for traditional Indians besides gas stoves and indoor plumbing. Recently, a woman on the Blackfeet Reservation refused to move into her new government-built home, claiming that it was haunted by evil spirits. She wanted a medicine man to bless it. When HUD refused a request for federal funds to pay for the exorcism, the exasperated offi-

Young and old enjoy the 1989 Crow Festival in Montana, below. Colorado Congressman Ben Nighthorse Campbell, a Northern Cheyenne, appears at top right during Oklahoma's Red Earth Festival. Open to Indians of all tribes, Red Earth Festival is the largest pow wow in the United States and includes dance competitions, art,

fashion, and a film festival. At right, one of several com-
peting drumming teams joins the opening-day parade
through downtown Oklahoma City.

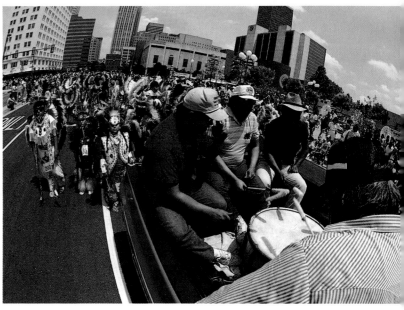

cial who had to deal with the problem saved the day by paying for the ceremony himself—with ten dollars and a pound of tobacco.

Indian parents often worry about how much "Indianness" their children will retain, and how important their culture will be to them as adults. Imagine the anguish of the Hopi potter who returned home after a business trip to see his children watching TV instead of attending a tribal ceremony just a few feet away from their house. "You could look through the windows and see the dancing going on, but the children were ignoring this, sprawled on the floor, glued to the TV."

One of the most visible expressions of Indianness today is the pow wow, which is at once a social gathering, celebration, family reunion, and an occasion for spiritual renewal. Pow wows are a time when babies are named, heroes honored, and friendships renewed. All who appreciate the singing, drumming, and dancing are welcome, Indians and non-Indians alike. Although they may have begun as tribal celebrations, they are now pan-Indian and can be found wherever there are Indians and a drum, from picnic grounds to church halls, from inner cities to remote reservations, from the East Coast to the West and all points in between.

Of concern to all Indians, rural or urban, is a satisfactory definition of who is an Indian. This consideration is complicated by the important trend toward marriage outside the tribe. Intermarriage by Indians with whites and members of other tribes has been so constant over the past 500 years that "purebloods"—individuals who are genetically pure—are now rare in most tribes, and "full bloods," those who are 100 percent Indian, although not necessarily descended from just one tribe, are becoming rare. Today, more and more Indians are marrying non-Indians, an inevitable result of their increasing movement off reservations for educational and employment opportunities. In cities, Indians have little opportunity to meet other Indians, much less members of their own tribe. Thus many marry non-Indians, and the children of such unions are, genetically speaking, only half-Indian. As such intermarrying occurs with increasing frequency, pureblood and full-blooded Indians will soon disappear. Ironically, even militant

Navajo weaving by Isabel John portrays the final day of the Yeibichai healing ceremony. People arrive for the feast as a dance takes place. Over 100 human figures and 44 animals appear in this design.

Indians who fear this outcome and argue for the importance of marriage within the race often fail to practice what they preach. In a conversation with an Indian man who was a militant activist in the 1960s and is now married to a white woman, I asked about his own inconsistency in this matter. He laughed and said, "I fell in love, what else can I say."

One answer to the quandary of defining who is an Indian and who is not, argues Cherokee attorney Joel Thompson, is to end the practice of using racial makeup as a standard of Indianness. "What other people in the world allow their ethnicity to be determined by blood quantum?" he asks. "As long as we allow the white man to determine who is an Indian, we are in trouble. Is being Indian a physical attri-

bute or a state of the mind? We must be allowed to define ourselves, to determine who we are."

Indians can survive into the 21st century and beyond, Thompson argues, if they can hold onto their land and achieve self-determination of their lives and their future. "We must hold onto what defines us culturally and spiritually and combine these values with what it takes to survive within the dominant society. If we have our land and economic development, we will survive. If not, Indians will disappear as a people."

Thompson's Cherokee tribe offers an excellent case in point. Today more than 200,000 Americans claim Cherokee blood, but few of them are full bloods. In fact, within 15 years there may be no living Cherokees on the last federal tribal roll, which

was closed in 1906; the youngest enrolled Cherokee alive in 1990 was more than 80 years old.

Soon there will be only descendants of enrolled Cherokees. "Does that make them any less Cherokee?" asks Evelyn Pickett, senior information specialist for the Bureau of Indian Affairs in Washington, D.C. Of Cherokee descent herself, she fears that one day the government will draw the line, declaring that only people with a quarter or more of Indian blood can be considered Indians. "If it happens, most of the Cherokees alive today would be affected by such a ruling," she points out. "This would be unfair to those people who claim Cherokee blood but do not want or expect services to which tribal membership entitles them. Although most of these people have little real knowledge of their tribe, they are Cherokees and proud of it."

Gordon McLester of the Wisconsin Oneidas provided another perspective on this issue. "I look at the Indian people like a prize fighter who went down, but not for the full count. Maybe that is the way it is supposed to be. Maybe that's one of our gifts to the rest of the world."

McLester explains that whatever the outcome, Indians will always be part of America because of the people themselves. He points out that they believe in their tribal governments; they believe in their tribal ways. "All these people could turn around and walk into the mainstream and then everything in Indian country would dissolve. It's not the amount of your Indian blood, if you dance, if you talk an Indian language, but that you believe in what you are. No legislation can take that away. We are still here, and we will always be here."

One hard-bitten definition of Indianness pulls no punches. A tough-minded Indian commentator put it this way: *The Indians will be those who remain after it becomes very difficult to be an Indian and after all the other Indians have become white men.*

Tribal communities also harbor deep concern about the future of reservations, which are now home to only one Indian out of four in the United States. Will there be a place for the reservation in the 21st century? After all, they are the artificial creations of white men. How long will the federal government continue to assign them special status when they serve so few Indian people, even though such reservations are usually guaranteed by treaty obligations? The current population of the Flathead Reservation in Montana, for example, is only 16 percent Indian, the result of intermarriage and land sales to non-Indians, who bought their land from Indian allotment holders. Similarly, on the Umatilla Indian Reservation in Oregon, Indians make up only 40 percent of the total population.

For Indians, it is not a question of economic efficiency. To them it is immaterial how many people

Beaded sneakers, below, were made by Effie Tybrec, a Sioux. "Grandmother Gestating Father and the Washita River Runs Ribbon-like" was created by the late Caddo-Kiowa artist T.C. Cannon in 1975.

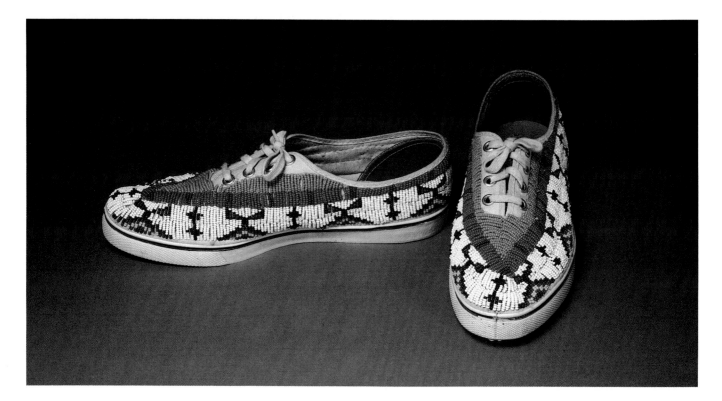

live on the reservation permanently. What is important is that a reservation exists, a haven from the pressure of the dominant society. As one Indian friend remarked, "When I hit that dirt road, I feel like I have come home. I am surrounded by friends and relatives, by people who speak my language, by people who could care less who or what I am in the white world." His sentiments were echoed by Potawatomi Marty Kreipe: "We move around, leave the res, [but] we come back at pow-wow times or celebrations. Then we need our own things just as much as in the past. Maybe we need them more. Underneath it hasn't changed that much, not at all."

Another Indian put it more bluntly: "All Indians eventually return to the res, either upright or in a box." Maybe the white reformers and religionists, though generally for all the wrong reasons, did something beneficial by providing safe havens for the tribes, hideaways where Indians could heal the wounds of old battles. Here they could also work toward the day when they could win new triumphs on their own terms.

Where will Indians find themselves 1,000 years after the arrival of Columbus? Perhaps a clue to the answer may reside in the words of humorist Will Rogers, who was of Cherokee descent. As he liked to joke, "My forefathers didn't come over on the *Mayflower*, but they met the boat."

It would be sad indeed if these great people, whose ancestors welcomed the first visitors to the New World 500 years ago, often with warmth and friendship, were to be lost to the American experience. In greeting the newcomers, Indians launched a tradition that has become the hallmark of the United States: this land continues to welcome immigrants from all over the world. What if there were no longer Indians here to "meet the boat." Could the nation survive if it failed to make tolerance and fair play work for the tribal peoples who embody America's first reality, the enduring spirit of the land itself?

Hopi eagle-gatherer stands on the Kachina Bluffs of the Hopi Reservation. Golden eagles are captured for an age-old rain ritual. Clouds in the distance are viewed as kachinas, supernatural guardians.

Index

A

Adams, Hank, 247
Adams, Robert McCormick, Secretary of the Smithsonian Institution, 262, 264
Alaskan Indians, 19, 73, 74, 253
Alcatraz Island, 229-230, 243
Alcoholism and drug abuse, 89, 140, 245, 260, 266
Aleuts, 19, 54, 55-56, 69, 72, 85, 87, 253
Allotment, 137, 187, 211, 215-219, 233, 234, 236
American Indian Movement (AIM), 239, 243, 247-248
Amherst, Lord Jeffrey, 98
Apaches, 19, 37, 48, 80, 83, 148, 150, 181-182, 185, 255; Chiricahua, 181-182, 183, 241; Mescalero, 256, 265; White Mountain, 180
Appalachians, 100, 101, 128, 134, 135
Arapahos, 17, 19, 26, 153, 157, 158, 159, 168, 169, 212, 213, 214
Arawaks, 43
Arikaras, 64, 94, 169, 223
Art and artists, Indian, 28, 159, 166, 180, 183, 199, 203, 213, 214, 232, 248, 261, 264, 272, 274. *See also* Crafts
Assimilation, as federal policy, 187, 195, 207, 214-215, 243; Indians' attitudes toward, 211, 230-231, 234, 237, 243, 274
Assiniboines, 65, 80, 169
Athapascans, 31
Atkin, Edmund, 95
Aztecs, 33, 42, 46

B

Bahamas, 27, 41
Banks, Dennis, 239, 247, 263
Bannocks, 19
Baranov, Aleksandr, 69, 72, 85
Battles and fights: Fallen Timbers, 121, 123, 129; Fetterman Fight, 157, 163, 164; Grattan Massacre, 157; Horseshoe Bend, 131, 133; Little Bighorn (Custer's Last Stand), 157, 168, 169-171, 172; Sand Creek Massacre, 153-154, 159; Thames, 131, 132; Tippecanoe, 130; Wounded Knee Massacre, 195-200, 217, 218, 220, 221, 223; Wounded Knee II, 239, 247, 248
Bellecourt, Clyde and Virgil, 247

Beothuks, 40
Big Foot (Spotted Elk), 195, 200, 218, 221
Bingo, 256, 267
Black Hawk, 134, 140, 144-146
Black Hills (SD), 169, 170
Black Kettle, 151, 153, 154
Blackfeet Confederacy, 23, 28, 59, 64, 151, 211, 214; Blackfoot, 26
Bloods, 24, 182
Blue Jacket, 120
Bodmer, Karl, 124, 144-147
Boone, Daniel, 100
Boudinot, Elias, 152
Bozeman Trail, 160, 162, 163
Braddock, Edward, 90, 95
Bradford, William, 27, 63
Brant, Joseph, 93, 96, 106, 112, 114, 117-118, 123; Molly, 96
Brown, Dee, *Bury My Heart at Wounded Knee*, 13, 245
Bureau of Indian Affairs, 137, 164-165, 167, 207, 208, 219, 222, 233, 234, 239, 243, 247, 253, 254, 275
Businesses, tribal-owned, 239, 256, 263, 265. *See also* Bingo

C

Caddos, 276
Californian Indians, 32-33, 149-151, 178, 207
Canada, 19, 21, 29, 32, 36, 51, 56, 82, 84, 87, 93, 97, 108, 118, 119, 130, 132, 139, 157, 171, 179, 180, 222, 230, 247, 255, 256, 257-258; government policy toward Indians, 21, 26, 182-184
Canadian Indians, 51, 182-184, 257-258
Captain Jack, 178-179
Caribbean Indians, 43, 47, 76
Carlisle Indian Industrial School, 187, 195, 196, 199, 216, 219-220. *See also* Education
Carrington, Henry B., 160-163
Carroll, Henry, 200-206
Carson, Christopher "Kit", 176, 179
Carver, John, 70
Catlin, George, 57, 143
Cayugas, 86
de Champlain, Samuel, 52, 82, 86
Chatto, 181-182
Cherokees, 19, 28, 97, 112-114, 123, 124, 131, 134, 137, 142-144, 148, 149, 152, 175, 212, 254, 263, 266, 268, 274-276; Trail of Tears, 139, 144
Cheyennes, 19, 31, 147, 151, 153-154, 157, 158-163, 168, 169-172, 200-206, 209, 212, 214, 216, 264, 265; Northern Cheyennes, 171-172, 200-206, 264, 265, 266, 272; Southern Cheyennes, 159

Chickasaws, 19, 114, 123, 134, 142, 144, 149, 151, 152
Chino, Wendell, 255, 256, 265
Chivington, J.M., 153-154
Choctaws, 19, 114, 123, 131, 133, 134, 137, 140, 142, 144, 148, 149, 151, 152, 223, 225
Christianity, Indian, 25, 29, 75, 110, 143, 237, 266
Chumashes, 75
Citizenship, U.S., 215, 220
Claims, settlement of, 71, 229, 245, 253, 256-257, 253
Clark, George Rogers, 116; William, 128
Cleveland, Grover, 216
Cody, William F. "Buffalo Bill", 169, 207, 209, 211, 223
Collier, John, 231-234, 237-238, 254
Columbia River, 17, 19, 188
Columbus, Christopher, 27, 41-44, 60, 101
Comanches, 31, 147, 148, 150, 157, 158, 167, 203, 205, 214, 234
Congress, Continental, 109, 112, 118; United States, 109, 118, 125, 143-144, 151, 164, 176, 211, 215, 219, 220, 234, 237, 245, 247, 253, 264
Constitution, U.S., 91, 123
Coronado, Francisco, 47, 56, 60-61
Cortés, Hernán, 42, 46, 59, 76
Crafts, adaptation of modern technology, 252, 259-260; basket weaving, 33, 75; beadworking, 80, 276; carving and woodworking, 19, 40, 57, 71, 79, 259-260; grass weaving, 85; metalworking, 46, 77, 89; pottery, 34, 38, 253; traditional, 259-260; weaving, 77, 89, 231, 274; Indian Arts and Crafts Board, 233
Crazy Horse, 31, 160, 162-163, 169, 170, 171, 241
Creeks, 19, 64, 97, 114, 122, 123, 129, 131-133, 134, 135, 142, 144, 146, 148, 149, 152, 240, 241
Crees, 19, 64-65, 80, 133, 182
Crook, George, 176
Crows, 20, 21, 22, 23, 24, 34, 35, 145, 166, 168, 169-171, 266, 270, 272
Custer, George Armstrong, 34, 168-171

D

Dakota Territory, 154, 157, 163, 169, 171, 191, 195
Dancing, traditional, 29, 34, 37, 38, 59, 147, 180, 207, 225, 229, 233, 252, 265, 272, 274
Deer, Ada, 236, 243
Delawares (Lenni Lenape), 32, 66, 109, 118, 129, 144, 148, 150, 203
Delaware Prophet, the, 98

Delegations, Indian, 23, 92-93, 140, 164, 165-169, 176, 182
Deloria, Vine, Jr., *Custer Died for Your Sins*, 245, 248
Demographics, Indian: population figures, 12, 26-28, 34, 43, 47, 151, 251; intermarriage, 47, 69, 72, 74, 85, 96, 143, 146, 218, 234, 243, 274, 276
Densmore, Frances, 26, 35, 38
Disease and epidemics, 27, 47, 55, 57-59, 70, 87, 112, 147, 172, 176, 178, 179, 230, 239, 255
Dodge, Henry Chee, 235, 237
Dogribs, 19
Dragging Canoe, 112
Duke, Doris, 35
Dull Knife, 31, 171-172

E
Eagle-Horn, Chauncey, 223
Education of Indians, 70, 112, 137, 142, 239, 248, 269-270; federally sponsored, 195, 196, 215, 219, 237, 253; graduates, high school and college, Indian, 237, 265-266, 269; reservation community college system, 35, 266-270
Eisenhower, Dwight D., 238
England: colonialism, 27, 47, 51, 52-55, 63-64, 68, 69, 70-71, 73-76, 84, 86, 87, 89, 90, 91, 92-93, 94-101, 184; Revolutionary War and afterward, 105, 106, 109, 114, 116, 117, 118-119, 120, 123, 124, 125; War of 1812, 127, 128, 130, 132, 133, 135
Eskimos. *See* Inuit

F
Fetterman, William J., 163
Firearms, 51, 60, 62-65, 89, 98, 147, 148, 172, 174
Five Civilized Tribes, 144, 216, 234. *See also* Cherokees, Chickasaws, Choctaws, Creeks, and Seminoles
Flatheads, 64, 276
Food and diet, 28, 32; New World crops, 44; hunger and famine, 56, 160; food rationing, 191, 192, 207
Forts: Laramie (WY), 157, 160; Pitt (PA), 98; Ross (CA), 56, 72, 93; Wayne (IN), 123
France, 47, 51-52, 59, 69, 82, 84-87, 89, 90, 91, 92, 93, 94, 95, 97, 98, 99, 128, 134, 184
Franklin, Benjamin, 91, 104, 117

G
Gall, 168, 169-170
Gay Heads, 71
Gay, Robert 269
George, Chief Dan, 242

Geronimo, 182, 255
Ghost Dance religion, 190-200, 214, 217-218
Grant, Ulysses S., 152, 164-167
Great Lakes, 56-57, 119
Great Plains, 59, 60
Greenland, 19, 28, 31, 56
Gros Ventres, 16, 26, 159, 243, 266

H
Haidas, 19
Hampton Normal and Agricultural Institute, 196, 237. *See also* Education
Harding, Warren G., 214
Harmar, Josiah, 120
Harrington, John P., 26, 35-36
Harrison, Wm. Henry, 129-130, 135
Hayes, Ira, 229
Head Chief, 200, 206
Hendrick (Tiyanoga), 93, 94, 96
Heye, George, 264
Hidatsas, 28, 64, 147
Hispaniola, 27, 43, 44, 47, 69
Hopis, 19, 32, 34, 37, 60, 80, 180, 229, 256, 259, 275, 278
Horse Capture, George P., 13, 16, 26, 243-244, 266
Horses, in Indian culture, 31, 44, 60-65, 150, 157, 179
Houmas, 242
Housing, Indian, 110, 111, 255; modern, 244, 256, 271, 274; traditional, 19, 235, 255
Hudson Valley, 86, 89, 109
Hurons, 79, 82, 85-87, 91

I
Indian studies programs, 230, 243, 269. *See also* Education
Indian Territory, 133, 171, 172, 180, 218, 256
Intertribal warfare, 59, 170
Inuit (Eskimos), 19, 28, 30-31, 38, 51, 55-56, 85, 253, 255
Iowas, 29
Iron Teeth, 172
Iroquois Confederacy, 19, 82, 86-89, 91, 93, 95-97, 108, 109-112, 118
Ishi, 207-211

J
Jackson, Andrew, 131-133, 134, 135, 144
Jamestown Colony, 52, 55, 75-76
Jay, John, 118
Jefferson, Thomas, 127, 129, 134
Johnson, Andrew, 160
Johnson, William, 95, 96, 97, 106, 109
Joseph, Chief, 177, 179-180, 182, 190
Josephy, Alvin, Jr., *Now That the Buffalo's Gone*, 13

K
Kansa tribe, 29, 140
Kickapoos, 144, 148, 149
Kiowa-Apaches, 158, 212
Kiowas, 147, 187, 212, 213, 276
Kirkland, Samuel, 106, 110-112
Klamaths, 238
Kodiak Island, 55, 69
Kreipe, Marty, 278
Kutchins, 19
Kutenais, 17
Kwakiutls, 19

L
Labrador, 51
Land acquisition by Indians, 233, 253, 256
Languages, Indian, 28, 32, 34, 71, 112, 137, 142, 208, 225, 232, 263, 269
Law enforcement, Court of Indian Offenses 205, 211-214; police, tribal, 193, 194, 206, 207, 211, 214; tribal, 270-271
Legislation, federal, affecting Indians, 137, 157, 253-254
Lincoln, Abraham, 94, 152, 234
Little Crow, 152
Little Turtle, 120-123
Little Wolf, 171-172
Lost Colony, 53, 55
Louisiana Purchase, 126, 128, 134
Luiseños, 248

M
Mahicans, 92
Makahs, 259
Mandans, 29, 64, 128, 144
Manifest Destiny, 127-128, 134, 147, 148, 179
Mankiller, Wilma, 266
Marshall, John, 144
Martínez, María, 38, 253
Massachusetts Bay Colony, 73
Massasoit, 70
Mayas, 33, 59
McDonald, James L., 137-141
McGillivray, Alexander, 122, 123
McIntosh, William 131, 142
McKenney, Thomas L., 137-141
McLester, Gordon, 259, 276
Means, Russell, 239, 247, 248
Medicine Crow, Joseph, 20, 23, 34-35, 169
Menawa, 131, 133, 142
Menominees, 134, 236, 238-239, 243
Mestizos, 47
Métis (mixed-bloods), 80, 182
Mexico, 19, 26, 28, 29, 33, 36, 44, 46, 57, 59, 76, 78, 83, 139, 148, 149, 150, 181, 182, 233,
Miami Confederacy, 19, 118, 120-123, 144

Miles, Nelson A., 180, 182
Mingos, 101
Missions and missionaries: American, 106, 187; French, 86-87; Spanish, 47-49, 72, 73, 77-78, 80, 82, 83, 148-149; others, 74, 85
Mississippi River (Valley), 89, 91, 118, 128, 134, 135, 139, 140, 141, 144, 146
Missouri River (Valley), 64, 124, 128, 144, 163
Mitchell, George, 247
Modocs, 178-179, 180
Mohawk Valley, 96, 117
Mohawks, 82, 86, 92-93, 94, 96-97, 106, 108, 110, 112, 114-115, 117, 129, 241, 256
Mojaves, 32
Montezuma, 46, 76
Montreal, 89
Mooney, James T., 27, 192, 212-213
Morgan, Jacob Casimera, 234-237
Motion pictures, 240-242
Muckleshoots, 271
Museums and archives, 26, 35-36, 38, 261-264

N
Naiche, 182, 183
Narragansetts, 70-71, 129
National Museums of the American Indian (New York and Washington, D.C.), 36, 262-264
Nationalism, Indian, during War of 1812, 128-132
Native American Church of North America, 25, 214, 233-234
Navajos, 19, 44, 48, 60, 77, 80, 83, 150, 158, 176, 179, 225, 231, 232, 234-237, 240, 250, 256, 274
Neamathla, 135
Netherlands, 51, 66, 86, 87, 89
New Amsterdam, 66, 89
New England Indians, 52-53, 64, 70-71, 73, 129
New France, 51-52, 59, 87, 89, 93, 97
New Netherland, 89
New Spain, 27, 51, 59, 61, 76
Newfoundland, 40, 41, 51
Nez Percés, 19, 62, 64, 150, 151, 177, 178, 179-180, 182, 190, 219
Nighthorse Campbell, Ben, Congressman, 264, 272
Nipmucs, 71

O
Oakes, Richard, 247
Occupations: farming, 19, 28, 30, 33, 72, 73, 110, 143, 176, 181, 188, 191, 193, 259; fishing, 19, 247, 257-258, 271; herding, 176, 179, 237; hunting, 19, 30, 37, 72, 87, 183, 257-258, 271

Ohio River (Valley), 91, 100, 118, 119
Ojibwas, 17, 26, 98, 133, 216, 244-245, 247, 258, 263
Oklahombi, Joseph, 223
Omahas, 29, 144, 203
de Oñate, Juan, 47, 49, 79
Oneidas, 86, 106, 108, 110-112, 118, 152, 222, 256-257, 259, 276
Onondagas, 86, 112, 222
Ontario, 85, 112, 182
Opechancanough, 52, 55
Organizations, Indian, 201, 231, 236, 243, 245, 248. See also American Indian Movement (AIM) and red power movement
Osages, 29, 147
Osceola, 143, 146
Otos, 29
Ottawas, 98-101, 118, 144
Overland Trail, 150

P
Pacific Northwestern Indians, 89, 151, 178, 188
Paiutes, 19, 190, 217
Pan-Indianism, 230, 244-245
Parker, Ely S., 149, 152, 164
Parker, Quanah, 31, 203, 205, 214-215, 234
Passamaquoddies, 222
Pawnees, 91, 147, 164, 232
Pease, Janine Windy-Boy, 269-270
Penn, William, 66, 93
Peorias, 101, 144
Pequots, 129
Peter the Great, 55
Peyote, 28, 203, 233-234
Pickett, Evelyn, 275-276
Piegans, 24, 64-65, 147, 182. See also Blackfeet Confederacy
Pilgrims, 52, 55, 57, 70, 74
Pimas, 229
Pizarro, Francisco, 42
Plains Indian Museum, 244
Plains Indians, 30, 31, 56, 60, 63, 104, 147, 151, 157, 158-160, 234
Plymouth Colony, 27, 53, 55, 57, 63, 74
Pocahontas, 68, 75
Pocanets, 129
Pomos, 72
Poncas, 29, 164, 172, 176
Pontiac, 98-101
Pope, John, 152, 158-160
Popé, 80
Potawatomis, 118, 129, 144, 164, 278
Pow wows, 17, 38, 225, 252, 272-273, 274
Powhatan, 55, 68, 75
Powhatan Confederacy, 19, 52, 55, 68, 75-76
Pratt, Richard H., 196, 216, 219

Proclamation of 1763, 101
Pueblo Indians, 47-49, 61, 78-83, 94, 231, 234
Pueblos: Acoma (NM), 49, 78, 80; San Ildefonso (NM), 36, 38, 253; San Juan (NM), 80; Santa Clara (NM), 36, 38, 271; Shongopavi (AZ), 180; Taos (NM), 48, 253
Puritans, 57, 63, 70, 71, 73, 110
Pushmataha, 134

Q
Quapaws, 29
Quebec, 36, 52, 84

R
Raleigh, Sir Walter, 53, 55
Red Cloud, 160-164, 165, 169
Red Jacket, 116, 152
Red power movement, 229-230, 239, 243, 247-248
Religion and spirituality, traditional, 24-26, 31, 32, 37, 71, 94, 180, 183, 207, 212, 214, 231, 233, 235, 253, 266, 271, 278. See also Sun Dance
Religious liberty, for Indians, 207, 231, 233, 237, 248
Religious movements, traditionalist, 98, 129-131, 187-190
Relocation, voluntary, federal program, 238, 243
Remington, Frederic, 65, 79, 157, 200
Removal, forced, as federal policy, 135-137, 139, 141-146, 149, 150, 171, 178, 182, 236
Reservation, role of in Indian culture 234, 278
Reservations: Allegany (NY), 111; Blackfeet (MT), 211, 271; Buffalo Creek (NY), 112; Cattaraugus (NY), 111; Colville (WA), 216; Crow (MT), 35, 171, 231, 259, 269, 270; Flathead (MT), 218; Fort Belknap (MT), 26, 243; Fort Berthold (ND), 188; Fort Thompson (SD), 24; Hopi (AZ) 259, 278; Makah Indian (WA), 260; Menominee (WI), 236; Mescalero (NM), 265; Navajo (UT, AZ, NM), 36, 219, 250, 263, 266; Northern Cheyenne (MT), 200; Omaha (NE), 176; Oneida (NY), 256; Pine Ridge (SD), 191, 193-195, 200, 220, 247, 248, 260, 263, 265, 267-269; Rosebud Sioux (SD), 191, 193, 206, 225, 244, 247, 271; Standing Rock (ND, SD), 194, 206, 207; Umatilla (OR), 276; Walker River (NV), 190; Wind River (WY), 26; Zuni (NM), 36
Reservations, federal policy of, 150, 151, 154, 163, 176, 177, 179, 191, 207, 216
Rio Grande (Valley), 44, 47-48

Robinson, Paul A., 71
Rogers, Will, 268, 278
Rolfe, John, 68, 75
Roosevelt, Franklin Delano, 233
Ross, John, 143, 152
Royer, Daniel F., 193
Running Crane, 211, 214
Russia, 55-56, 69-73, 78, 85, 93

S
Sac and Fox, 134, 140, 144-146, 147, 164
Salishes, 242
Sampson, Will, 240, 241
Sanpoils, 188
Santa Fe, 36, 51, 80, 253, 271
Seminoles, 19, 135, 143, 144, 146, 152, 256; Black Seminoles, 143; Oconees, 146; Yamasees, 19, 146
Senecas, 86, 106, 111, 112, 116, 117, 149, 152, 164. *See also* Iroquois Confederacy
Sequoyah (George Guess), 137, 142
Seventh Cavalry, of U.S. Army, 168-170, 194-200, 217
Shawnees, 101, 120, 121, 128-130, 144, 148, 150, 203
Sherman, William T., 162
Shoshones, 19, 57, 64, 65
Siberia, 19, 27, 28, 31, 54, 55, 60
Silverheels, Jay, 241
Sioux (also Dakotas or Lakotas), 19, 23, 29, 31, 34, 61-62, 63, 134, 154, 157, 158-164, 166, 167, 168, 169-171, 172, 187, 190-200, 211, 216, 220, 229, 232, 244-245, 267, 276; Brule, 167; Crow Creek, 270; Hunkpapa, 206; Miniconjou, 195-200, 218, 221; Oglala, 160, 247; Santee, 57, 152, 158, 200; Wahpeton, 62; Yankton, 207
Sitka, 69, 72
Sitting Bull, 31, 160, 168-171, 179, 194-195, 206, 207, 211, 217
Skolaskin, 188
Slaves and slavery: African, 43, 47, 128, 134, 135, 143, 146, 152, 196; Indian, 27, 43, 46, 49, 56, 76, 77, 83, 178
Smith, Captain John, 52, 55, 68
Smithsonian Institution, 18, 38, 179, 261-264; Bureau of American Ethnology, 26, 27, 35, 36, 192, 212; National Anthropological Archives, 13, 36; Native American Cultural Resources Training Program (intern program), 13, 36, 38, 262
Smohalla, 188-190
de Soto, Hernando, 47, 60
Southwest, 60, 148, 150, 251
Southwestern Indians, 47, 60, 80, 147-148, 233

Spain, 27, 33, 41, 42, 43, 44-49, 51, 53, 60-61, 76-84, 89, 92, 93, 94, 97, 105, 114, 122, 123, 125, 128, 134-135, 147-149, 179, 181, 210
Spokanes, 19
Spotted Eagle, Chris, 242
Spotted Tail, 165, 167, 187
Squanto, 53-55, 74
St. Clair, Arthur, 120
St. Lawrence Valley, 52, 86
Standing Bear, 172, 176
Sun Dance, 13, 17, 24-26, 233
Supreme Court, 140, 143, 144, 220, 253, 257

T
Tainos, 27, 41
Taylor, N.G., 160
Tecumseh, 128-131, 132
Tekakwitha, Catherine (Kateri), 82
Tenskwatawa, 129-130, 131
Termination, federal policy of, 236, 237, 238-243
Tewas, 36, 38, 80
Thawengarakwen (Honyery Doxtator), 112
Thompson, Joel, 254, 274-275
Timucuas, 43
Tipis, 31, 62, 104, 154, 167, 171, 193, 197, 212, 213, 252
Tlingits, 19, 69, 72, 85
Tohono O'odams, 48
Trade between whites and Indians, 86, 124, 148
Trade, Indian, 56, 59, 60, 64
Treaties, between whites and Indians, 66, 109, 118, 123, 142, 144-145, 150, 151, 164, 176, 179, 257-258; Treaty of Canadaigua, 108; Treaty of Fort Jackson, 131, 135; Treaty of Fort Laramie, 162, 163, 168, 169, 245; Treaty of Fort Wayne, 129; Treaty of Greenville, 121, 123
Treaty of Paris 118, 119, 120
Truman, Harry S, 238
Tunica-Biloxi, 262
Tuscaroras, 86, 106, 108, 110-112

U
University of California, Berkeley, 208, 230, 243
Urban Indians, 244-245, 247, 260, 274
Utes, 19, 21, 148, 150, 167, 214, 223; Southern Utes, 36

V
Vikings, 41, 51

W
Wades-In-Water, 211, 214
Wampanoags, 53, 55, 70
Wampum, 108, 111

Wanapams, 188
Wappingers, 89
Walks-Over-Ice, Carson, 20, 21, 24-25
War: Civil, 152, 157, 158, 164; Indians for the Union, 149, 152; for the Confederacy, 152; French and Indian, 90, 91, 95-97; King George's, 91; King Philip's, 71; King William's, 91; Korean, 20; Lord Dunmore's (1774), 101; Mexican, 148; Pequot, 71; Queen Anne's, 91; Revolutionary, Indians and British, 106, 112, 114, 129; Indians and Patriots, 106, 112, 118; Vietnam, 20-21, 24, 26, 268; War of 1812, 125, 127, 128, 130-133, 135; World War I, 220-225, 231; World War II, 20, 22, 229, 232, 237, 243, 244; "code talkers," 225, 232
War and military service, in Indian culture, 18, 20, 21, 24, 166, 222; counting coup, 180, 200
Warren, Dave, 36, 38
Washington, D.C., 23, 137, 140, 160, 164, 165, 167-168, 176, 179, 189, 214, 239, 247, 248, 262, 264
Washington, George, 90, 95, 116, 123, 125
Watie, Stand, 152
Wayne, Anthony, 121, 123
West Indies, 41, 43
Wheeler-Howard Act of 1934, 233, 234, 237
White, Jim, 243
White Man Runs Him, 34, 168
Williams, Roger, 73
Winnebagos, 29, 134, 199, 232
Winthrop, John, 73
Wovoka, 190, 193, 214, 217
Wyandots, 118, 121, 144

Y
Yahis, 210-211
Yakimas, 19, 62, 150, 271
Yanas, 208, 210
Yates, Sidney R., Congressman, 262
Yellow Bird, 195, 197, 200
Yellow Thunder, Raymond, 247
Young Hawk, Joe, 223
Young Mule, 200-206
Yukis, 31

Z
Zunis, 19, 36

Acknowledgments

Author's Acknowledgments
All writers must acknowledge their reliance on others, and I am in debt to many. I am especially grateful to my friends in the Indian community, particularly those who took the time to read and comment on all or part of this book, including Evelyn Pickett, Michael Doss, George Horse Capture, Ada Deer, and Gordon McLester. Special thanks are also due to the Reverend F.P. Prucha, S.J., my mentor and friend, who first introduced me to the field of American Indian scholarship; to Robert M. Kvasnicka, who did much of the archival and library research for this book; and to Jan Shelton Danis, who provided considerable editorial assistance. Finally, I wish to thank my wife, Susan, and my sons Joseph, Paul, and Peter, who have shared many of the experiences reflected in this book and who with me cherish our American Indian friends.

Herman J. Viola,
Falls Church, Virginia, 1990

Herman J. Viola, a native of Chicago, a U.S. Navy veteran, a graduate of Marquette University in Milwaukee, Wisconsin, and a Smithsonian historian, is currently director of the Institution's Quincentennial program and exhibit, *Seeds of Change*. Previously head of the Smithsonian's National Anthropological Archives, he has traveled widely among American Indian peoples, is an honorary member of several tribes, and prizes numerous friendships of long standing with many Native Americans. He is also the author of Smithsonian Books' *Exploring the West*.

Guest Essayists
Russell Bourne, the only non-Indian guest essayist in this volume, has nurtured a lifelong enthusiasm for the tribal history of his native New England and for the testimony of the land itself. A founding father of Smithsonian Books in 1976, he is the author of the recently published *The Red King's Rebellion: Racial Politics in New England 1675-1678*.

Ada Deer, a nationally recognized Indian leader and member of the Menominee tribe of Wisconsin, has gained extensive experience in public service and government. From 1974-76, she served as chairwoman of her tribe, and in 1989 was unanimously elected to lead the Native American Rights Fund, or NARF, the nation's largest Indian legal rights organization.

George Horse Capture, of Gros Ventre heritage, was born in 1937 on the Fort Belknap Indian Reservation in Montana. A U.S. Navy veteran and the father of four children, he earned his B.A. in anthropology from the University of California, Berkeley and his M.A. in history from Montana State University, Bozeman. Since 1979 he has served as curator of the Plains Indian Museum, part of the Buffalo Bill Historical Center, Cody, Wyoming. He teaches American Indian history and culture, and participates in numerous ceremonies.

Wilma P. Mankiller has served since 1987 as the elected Principal Chief of the Cherokee Nation of Oklahoma. Her long commitment to community organization has promoted the cultural, social, and economic advancement of her tribe. The basis of Chief Mankiller's philosophy is empowerment of the people at the local level.

Rennard Strickland is a scholar of Osage-Cherokee heritage who grew up in eastern Oklahoma and has written extensively about Native American life, law, and culture. Previously a law school dean, he is currently Director of the American Indian Law and Policy Center of the University of Oklahoma. Strickland is also a filmmaker, and has been curator of a number of Native American history and art exhibitions. He served as editor-in-chief for the revision of Cohen's *Handbook of Federal Indian Law*, and at present is helping to create an understanding of the contemporary legal and cultural rights of native peoples.

Special Thanks
Carolyn J. Margolis—Project Coordinator, National Museum of Natural History's Quincentenary Program
Gary Avey—Publisher, *Native Peoples* magazine, Phoenix, Arizona
Joseph Medicine Crow—Historian and Tribal Elder, Crow Indian Reservation, Montana
Kay-Karol—Conservator, Buffalo Bill Historical Center, Cody, Wyoming
Dennis Sanders—Hardin, Montana
Geri Sanders—Hardin, Montana
Dave Warren—Special Assistant for Applied Community Research (SI)

Research Assistance
Richard Ahlborn, Department of Social and Cultural History, NMAH; Joallyn Archambault, Department of Anthropology, NMNH; Kathleen Baxter, NMNH/NAA; Debra Berke, Department of the Interior Museum; Tim Bernardis, Librarian, Little Big Horn College, Crow Agency, Montana; Andrew Bird-In-Ground, Crow Indian Reservation; Lydia T. Black, Department of Anthropology, University of Alaska, Fairbanks; Robin Blair Bolger, George Eastman House; Barbara Booher, Superintendent, Custer Battlefield National Monument; John E. Carter, Curator of Photographs, NSHS; Ed Castle, photographer, Washington, D.C.; Mrs. John Clymer, Teton Village, Wyoming; Nita Cochran, Administrative Assistant, Cherokee Tribe; Dale Connelly, Still Pictures Branch, NA; Cathy Creek, NMNH/NAA; Mary Kay Davies, Anthropology Library, NMNH; Mary Davis, MAI; Sharon Dean, MAI; Jim Flatnus, Geography and Map Division, LC; Paula Fleming, NMNH/NAA; Jocelyn Costa Garner, Crow Agency, Montana; Charles T. Gehring, New York State Library, Albany; Terry Geesken, Film Stills Archives, Museum of Modern Art; Rayna D. Green, American Indian Program, NMAH; Father Alexander Guay, Mission Saint-François-Xavier, Caughnawaga, Quebec, Canada; Judith Hallet, National Geographic Society; Jonathan Heller, Still Pictures Branch, NA; Elizabeth Holmes, Assistant Registrar, BBHC; J. Christopher Horak, George Eastman House; Harry Hunter, Division of Armed Forces History, NMAH; Donald Jackanicz, Civil Reference Branch, NA; Ellen Jamieson, MAI; Robert Kvasnicka, Archival Publications and Accessions Control Staff, NA; Deborah Lawson, *Native Peoples* magazine; Dr. Thomas Lewis, Red Lodge, Montana; Jenny Little Coyote, Northern Cheyenne Indian Reservation, Montana; Judith Luskey, NMAfA, SI; Cesare Marino, Handbook of North American Indians, NMNH; Mary Ellen McCaffrey, NMAH, OPPS; Douglas C. McChristian, Chief Historian, Custer Battlefield National Monument; Magdalene Medicine Horse, Archivist, Little Big Horn College, Crow Agency, Montana; Joann Meide, Reference Librarian, Assistant Professor, Eastern Montana College, Billings; Laura Nash, MAI; Mary Noonie, MAI; Arthur Olivas, Museum of New Mexico, Santa Fe; Howard Paine, National Geographic Society; Janine Windy-Boy Pease, President, Little Big Horn College, Crow Agency, Montana; Laura Peers, Washington State University, Pullman; Monique Pelletier, Bibliothèque Nationale, Paris; Fred Pernell, Still Pictures Branch, NA; Felicia Pickering, Department of Anthropology, NMNH; Evelyn Pickett, Bureau of Indian Affairs; Richard A. Pierce, History Department, University of Alaska, Fairbanks; Mardell Plainfeather, Park Ranger, Plains Indian Historian, Custer Battlefield National Monument; Craig Reynolds, Smithsonian Institution Press; Mayda Riopedre, Anthropology Library, NMNH; Joanna C. Scherer, Handbook of North American Indians, NMNH; Peter Schmid, Photograph Curator, Marriott Library, University of Utah, Salt Lake City; Catherine Scott, SI Libraries; Barbara H. Shattuck, National Geographic Society; Reverend Harvey Stewart, Lodge Grass, Montana; William Stewart, Crow Indian Reservation, Montana; Sha-Nice Stokes, SI Libraries; George Takes The Gun, Crow Indian Reservation, Montana; Adams Taylor, MAI; Robert Tenequer, Editor *Smithsonian Runner*, Native American newsletter; Ted Teodoro, NYPL; Marty Vestecka-Miller, Assistant to the Curator, NSHS; Carson Walks-Over-Ice, Crow Indian Reservation, Montana; Wilcomb Washburn, Director, Office of American Studies, SI; Melissa Webster, Assistant Curator, BBHC; John C. Weiser, Time-Life Books; Ray Williamson, Office of Technology Assessment, United States Congress; Tim Wilson, Northern Cheyenne Reservation, Montana, and St. Paul, Minnesota.

Organizations
Bureau of Indian Affairs, Washington, D.C.; Colorado Historical Society; Denver Art Museum; Denver Public Library; Denver Federal Complex, NA; Deseret News, Salt Lake City, Utah; Embassy of Canada; Embassy of the Netherlands; Indian Health Service; Ladies' Prayer Meeting Group, Crow Agency, Montana; Marriott Library, University of Utah; Montgomery County (Maryland) Library Phone Reference Service; Native American Rights Fund; Salt Lake Tribune, Salt Lake City, Utah; Utah State Historical Society, Salt Lake City.

Orion Books/Crown Publishers, Inc.
Carl Apollonio; Peter A. Davis; Betty A. Prashker; Deborah Rowley; Michelle Sidrane; Steve Topping; James O'Shea Wade.

Suppliers
Jerry Benitez, Stanford Paper Company; Paul Blossey, The Lanman Companies; Bruce B. Cunningham, The Lanman Companies; Mary Devaux, Phil Jordan and Associates, Inc.; Ronald Harlowe, Harlowe Typographers, Inc.; Don Herdtfelder, The Lanman Companies; Kim Hilling, Lindenmeyr Paper; Bob Jillson, Holliston Mills, Inc.; Phil Jordan, Phil Jordan and Associates, Inc.; Pete Jurgaitis, Lehigh Press Lithographers; Emily Kendall, Phil Jordan and Associates, Inc.; John King, R.R. Donnelley & Sons Company; Harry T. Knapman, II, The Lanman Companies; Barbara Manis, Holliston Mills, Inc.; Cliff Mears, R.R. Donnelley & Sons Company; Eileen McDonald, The Lanman Companies; Jessie Renshaw, Stanford Paper Company; Julie Schieber, Phil Jordan and Associates, Inc.; Steve Smith, Harlowe Typographers, Inc.; Mannie Tobie, Phil Jordan and Associates, Inc.; Steve True, Lindenmeyr Paper; Joseph Vicino, Harlowe Typographers, Inc.; Ed Watters, The Lehigh Press, Inc.

Picture Credits

The following are abbreviations used to identify Smithsonian Institution sources and other collections. Negative numbers appear in parentheses.

Smithsonian Institution (SI): NAA National Anthropological Archives; NMAA National Museum of American Art; NMAfA National Museum of African Art; NMAH National Museum of American History; NMNH National Museum of Natural History; NPG National Portrait Gallery.

Other Sources: BBHC Buffalo Bill Historical Center, Cody, WY; JAM Joslyn Art Museum, Omaha, NE; LC Library of Congress, Washington, DC; MAI Museum of American Indian, Heye Foundation, NY; NA National Archives, Washington, DC; NGA National Gallery of Art, Washington, DC; NSHS Nebraska State Historical Society, Lincoln, NE; NYPL New York Public Library, NY; TGI The Thomas Gilcrease Institute of American History and Art, Tulsa, OK.

Front Matter: p. 1 NSHS; 2-3 "Visions of Yesterday," by William R. Leigh, 1944, Woolaroc Museum, Bartlesville, OK; 4-5 "Earth Knower," by Maynard Dixon, ca.1932, photo by M. Lee Fatherree, collection of The Oakland Museum, bequest of Dr. Abilio Reis; 6-7 "The Mirage," by Thomas Moran, 1879, Stark Museum of Art, Orange, TX; 8-9 Awa Tsireh, MAI; 10-11 "The Emergence of the Clowns," by Roxanne Swentzell, 1988, photo by Tamea Mikesell, collection of The Heard Museum, Phoenix; 14-15 Edward Curtis, NMNH/NAA (76-4128).

Real Americans: p. 16 MAI; 16-17 John Running; 18-19 Phil Jordan and Assocs., Inc.; 20T Dane Penland/SI; 20B Dennis Sanders/Hardin Photo; 21 Dane Penland/SI; 22 Dennis

Sanders/Hardin Photo; 23 NMNH/NAA (52818); 24T NMNH/NAA (56814); 24B Dennis Sanders/Hardin Photo; 25 American Museum of Natural History, NY; 26 NMNH/NAA (4305-A); 27 NMNH/NAA (55300); 28 Kal Muller/Woodfin Camp Inc.; 29L John Running; 29R Christine Keith; 30 NA; 31 NA (126-ARA-2-235); 32 MAI (24275); 32-33 Susanne Page; 34 MAI, photo by Rosamond Purcell; 35 Stephen Trimble/DRK PHOTO; 36,37 John Running; 38 "Pearlene," by Nora-Naranjo Morse, photo by Mary Fredenburgh; 39 J.B. Diederich/Contact Stock/Woodfin Camp & Assocs.

Landfalls: pp. 40-41 Bibliothèque Nationale, Paris; 41 Newfoundland Museum, photo courtesy Glenbow Museum, Calgary, Canada; 42 National Archives of Canada (c-116116); 43T The Pierpont Morgan Library, NY (MA 3900, f.100); 43B "Spanish Cruelties," engraving by Bartolomé de las Casas, photo by Ed Castle; 44L David Cavagnaro; 44R André Thevet, *Les singularités de la France antarctique autrement nommée Amérique et de plusieurs terres et îles découvertes de notre temps.* Paris: Le Temps, 1982, photo by Ed Castle; 45 John Running; 46L Museo de América, Madrid; 46R American Museum of Natural History, NY, Dept. of Library Services (3691) (2); 47 *Lienzo de Tlaxcala,* ed. by Coronel Prospero Cahuantzi, Mexico: Liberia Anticuaria, 1939, photo by Ed Castle; 48L Denver Art Museum; 48R Thomas Wiewandt; 49 Randy A. Prentice; 50T National Archives of Canada (10,000/1546 [1854]; 50B National Maritime Museum (1048); 51 LC (LC-7365); 52T LC (LC-USZ62-51971); 52B NMNH/NAA (81-818); 53 LC, map collection; 54T American Museum of Natural History, Dept. of Library Services, NY, (336697); 54B Royal Library, Humlegarden; 55 Wolfgang Kaehler; 56 TGI; 57 Science Museum of Minnesota; 58 MAI, photo by Rosamond Purcell; 59 Fray

Bernardinode Sahagun, *General History of the Things of New Spain*; 60 Bob Waterman/West Light; 60-61 Thomas Wiewandt/DRK PHOTO; 62T NMNH/Dept. of Anthropology; 62B MAI; 63T "The Buffalo Hunt," by John Innes, Luxton Museum, Glenbow-Alberta Inst., 1974, Tom McHugh/Photo Researchers, Inc.; 63B NMNH/Dept. of Anthropology; 64 "Indian Women Moving Camp," by Charles M. Russell, BBHC; 65 "Ghost Riders," by Frederic Remington, BBHC.

Cultures in Collision: pp. 66-67 "Penn's Treaty with the Indians," by Edward Hicks, TGI; 67 The New-York Historical Society; 68 from *Captain John Smith Works*, 1608-1631, NMNH/NAA; 69 "Pocahontas," after engraving by Simon van de Passe, NPG, gift of Andrew W. Mellon; 70 Haffenreffer Museum of Anthropology, RI; 71 Dartmouth College Library, NH; 72 Abrams Photo/Graphics; 73 art by de Mafras, photo by Caughey, California State University, State Library, Chico (21,717); 74-75 NYPL, Rare Books and Manuscripts Div., Astor, Lenox and Tilden Foundations; 75,76 MAI; 77 Denver Public Library, Western History Dept.; 78 "Indian Encampment on Lake Huron," by Paul Kane, 1845, Art Gallery of Ontario, Toronto; 79T "Evening on a Canadian Lake," by Frederic Remington, 1905, courtesy Saint Louis Art Museum, private collector; 79B MAI; 80 courtesy Royal Ontario Museum, Toronto (972.306.2); 81 Provincial Archives of Manitoba, Canada; 82T "Catherine Tekakwitha," by Father Claude Chauchetière, photo by Jacques Turcot, Mission Saint-François-Xavier, Caughnawaga, Quebec; 82B LC (LC-USZ62-33987); 83 LC (LC-USZ62-57966); 84 Lael Morgan, 1974, National Geographic Society; 85T "Aleksandr Baranov," after Mikhail Tikhanov, Lime Stone Press, University of Alaska, Fairbanks; 85B *Crossroads of Continents,* William W. Fitzhugh and Aaron Crowell, 1988, SI; 86 "Aleut Hunting," by Mikhail Tikhanov, 1817, *Crossroads of Continents,* William W. Fitzhugh and Aaron Crowell, 1988, SI; 87 "Inhabitants of the Aleutian Islands," by Louis Choris, 1816-1817, *Crossroads of Continents,* William W. Fitzhugh and Aaron Crowell, 1988,

SI; 88 American Museum of Natural History, NY, Dept. of Library Services (121545); 89 MAI.

End of the Beginning: pp. 90-91 "The Defeat of General Braddock," by E.W. Deming, State Historical Society of Wisconsin; 92 LC (LC-762-73350); 94 LC (LC-USZ62-14987); 94-95 New York State Library, Albany, photo by Deborah A. Bryk; 96-97 "Johnson Hall," by E.L. Henry, collection of Albany Institute of History & Art; 97 "Sir William Johnson," by John Wollaston, collection of Albany Institute of History & Art, gift of Laura Munsell Tremaine; 98 LC (LC-USZ62-14142); 99T "The Baffled Chiefs Leaving the Fort," by Frederic Remington, The Eiteljorg Museum of American Indian and Western Art, Indianapolis, gift of Harrison Eiteljorg; 99B NYPL, Rare Books and Manuscripts Div.; 100-101 from *THE OLD WEST: The Frontiersmen*, 1977 Time-Life Inc., detail from portrait "Scenes in the Life of Daniel Boone," Victor Nehlig, The Filson Club, Louisville, KY, photo by Henry Beville; 102-103 LC (LC-USZ62-51066).

A New Nation: p. 104 "Benjamin Franklin," by J. Elias Haid, 1780, after Cochin portrait, LC (LC-USZ62-45185); 104-105 "The destruction of tea at Boston Harbour," by N. Currier, 1840, LC (LC-USZC4-523); 106T "Samuel Kirkland," by Augustus Rockwell, Hamilton College, Clinton, NY, photo by Marianita Peaslee; 106B MAI, photo by Rosamond Purcell; 107 "Colonel Guy Johnson," by Benjamin West, NGA, Andrew W. Mellon collection; 108L New York State Museum, Albany; 108R art by Gerry Embleton, Canadian Park Service, Ottawa; 109 New York State Library, Albany, photo by Deborah A. Bryk; 110 "Niagara Falls from Below," by Thomas Davies, New-York Historical Society; 111TL "A Mohawk Village in Central New York," 1780, NYPL; 111BL art after J.F. Lafitau, 1724, NYPL; 111TR, BR Michael Schwarz; 112 "Captain Cole," by William John Wilgus, Yale University Art Gallery, gift of de Lancey Kountze, photo by Michael Agee; 113TL Michael Schwarz; 113TR Newberry Library, Chicago; 113B Michael Schwarz; 114 "Joseph Brant," by George Romney, 1775, National Gallery of Canada, Ottawa; 114-115 "Massacre of Wyoming," 1778, LC (LC-USZ62-38111); 116L "Sagoyewatha," by Charles Bird King, Albright-Knox Art Gallery, Buffalo, NY, Gift of The Seymour H. Knox Foundation, Inc. 1970; 116R MAI; 117 art by G.F.J. Frentzel, 1776, LC (LC-USZ62-46076); 119 "Fort Harmar in 1790," after Joseph Gilman, New-York Historical Society; 120 "Battle of Fallen Timbers," by Rufus Zogbaum, Ohio Historical Society; 121T *The National Archives of the United States*, Herman J. Viola, NY, 1984, Harry N. Abrams, Inc.; 121B "The Treaty of Greenville, 1795," Chicago Historical Society; 122 Massachusetts Historical Society; 124 "The Trading Store," 1840, from R.M. Ballantyne's *Hudson Bay . . .* ,London, 1979, courtesy Hudson's Bay Company Archives, Provincial Archives of Manitoba, Canada; 125 "Beaver Hut on the Missouri River," by Karl Bodmer, TGI.

Indian Destiny Sealed: pp. 126-127 "A View of New Orleans," Boqueto de Woieseri, 1803, Chicago Historical Society; 127 *The National Archives of the United States*, Herman J. Viola, NY, 1984, Harry N. Abrams, Inc.; 128 "York," by Charles M. Russell, 1908, Montana Historical Society, photo by J. Smart; 129 from the collection of Chief Henry Lookout, on loan to SI, photos by Charles Rand; 130 "Prisoners after Dudley's Defeat in 1813," Cincinnati Historical Society; 131T Field Museum of Natural History, Chicago (A93851.1c); 131B "Tenskwatawa, The Prophet," by Henry Inman after Charles Bird King, NPG; 132T "Death of Tecumseh," LC (LC-USZC4-1518); 132B NMAH; 133 "A Scene on the Frontiers as Practiced by the Humane British and their Worthy Allies," LC (LC-USZC4-1589); 134 "Push-ma-ta-ha," by Henry Inman, private collection; 135 William L. Clements Library, University of Michigan; 136 NYPL; 136B "Se-Quo-Yah," by Charles Bird King, American Museum of Natural History, Dept. Library Services, NY (319770); 137 *Native Peoples*, 1989, Phoenix, photo by Christopher Nyerges (Woodenturtle); 138-139 "The Trail of Tears," by Robert Lindneux, 1942, Woolaroc Museum, Bartlesville, OK; 140 "Black Hawk and His Son Whirling Thunder," by John W. Jarvis, 1833, TGI; 141 photo by Alexander Gardner, NMNH/NAA (690-B); 142 "United States Marines Penetrating the Everglades," by John Clymer, 1944/45, NA (127-G-10H); 143T "Osceola," by George Catlin, NPG; 143B courtesy William Katz, *Black Indians, a Hidden Heritage*, Atheneum, 1986, NY; 144L "Mató-Tópe, Mandan Chief," by Karl Bodmer, JAM; 144R "Omaha Boy," by Karl Bodmer, JAM; 145L "Chan-Chä-Uiá-Teüin, Teton Sioux Woman," by Karl Bodmer, JAM; 145R "Massika, Sauk Man," by Karl Bodmer, JAM; 146 "Bison Dance of the Mandan Indians," by Karl Bodmer, JAM; 147T "Pioch-Kiäiu, Piegan Blackfeet Man," by Karl Bodmer, JAM; 147B "Péhriska-Rúhpa, Hidatsa Man," by Karl Bodmer, JAM; 148 NMNH/NAA (906-B); 149 NMNH/NAA (741-A); 150 photo by Lloyd Rule, Denver Art Museum; 151 Colorado Historical Society; 153 "Sand Creek Massacre," by Robert Lindneux, Colorado Historical Society; 154-155 photo by Benjamin Franklin Upton, 1862, Minnesota Historical Society.

Loss of the West: pp. 156-157 NYPL Print Collection; 156 "Conjuring Back the Buffalo," by Frederic Remington, private collection; 158 Eastern Montana College Library, Special Collections Division; 159T LC (LC-USZ62-44084); 159B Kansas State Historical Society, Topeka; 160 from *Cheyennes and Horse Soldiers*, William Y. Chalfant, 1989, University of Oklahoma Press, art by Roy Grinnell; 161T "The Fetterman Fight," by Charles M. Russell, 1922, BBHC; 161B NMNH/NAA (2860-W); 162 NMNH/NAA (3689); 163 NMNH/NAA (3686); 164 Cumberland County Historical Society, Carlisle, PA; 165 NA (111-B-4669); 166 MAI; 167 Eastern Montana College Library, Special Collections Division; 168L NA (111-SC-82572); 168R NMNH/NAA (44821-A); 169 NMNH/NAA (3409-B); 170-171 "After the Battle," J.K. Ralston, collection of Stella A. Foote, Custer Battlefield National Monument, photo by Dennis Sanders/Hardin Photo; 172 Scott Rutherford; 173 NA (111-SC-82968); 174-175 NMNH/Dept. of Anthropology, NMAH/Division of Armed Forces History, photo by Ed Castle; 176-177T NMNH/NAA (43201); 176-

177B NMNH/NAA (2987-B-12); 177 Russell D. Lamb; 178T courtesy Museum of New Mexico (1816); 78B courtesy Museum of New Mexico (3242); 179 Michal Heron/Woodfin Camp & Assocs.; 180 Marty Cooper/Peter Arnold, Inc.; 181T NMNH/NAA (42189-F); 181B "Fertility Symbols," Waldo Mootzka, TGI; 182 NA (111-SC-102833); 183 MAI; 184 NMNH/NAA (56477); 184-185 Tom Danielsen.

Era of Internal Exile: p. 186 John A. Anderson, NSHS; 187 MAI; 188 NA (75-PA-8-8); 188-189 Jim Brandenberg/DRK PHOTO; 190-191 NMNH/NAA (56630); 191T MAI, photo by Rosamond Purcell; 191B, 192 John A. Anderson Collection, NSHS; 193 Fr. Eugene Buechel, NSHS; 194 NA (75 1P-1-34); 195 LC (4391-B); 196T NMNH/NAA (54799); 196B NA (75-EXP-2B); 197 NA (75-EXC-6A); 198, 199L NYPL; 199R art by Angel De Cora, from *The Middle Five: Indian Boys at School*, 1900, by F. La Flesche; 201 NA (75-M-1-3); 202 Archives & Manuscripts Div., Oklahoma Historical Society; 203T Denver Art Museum; 203B MAI (3/3612A); 204-205 TGI (4336.3854); 205 Denver Public Library, Western History Dept.; 206T John A. Anderson Collection, NSHS; 206B NMNH/NAA (I-2892); 207 Denver Public Library, Western History Dept.; 208T BBHC; 208-209 Stimson Collection, 1919, Wyoming State Archives, Museums and Historical Dept., Cheyenne; 209T Melinda Berge/DRK PHOTO; 210 BBHC; 211 NMNH/NAA (3195-A); 212 NMNH/Dept. of Anthropology, photo by Ed Castle; 213T NMNH/NAA (P-4-B); 213B, 214 NMNH/Dept. of Anthropology, photo by Ed Castle; 215 NMNH/NAA (55298), photo by James Mooney; 216 NMNH/Dept. of Anthropology; 217 NMNH/NAA (1659-C); 218 NA (111-SC 85682); 219 George Trager, NSHS; 220 NMNH/NAA (3200-B-2); 221T NMNH/NAA (3200-B-15); 221B NMNH/NAA (76-15359); 222 NMNH/NAA (86-4132); 223 NMNH/NAA (3198); 224 Jim Brandenberg/Woodfin Camp & Assocs.; 226-227 Abrams Photo/Graphics.

Red Power: p. 228 UPI/Bettmann Newsphotos; 229 AP/Wide World Photo; 230-231 courtesy Wheelwright Museum of the American Indian, Sante Fe, NM; 232T NA (75-N-Misc-115); 232B "First Furlough," by Quincy Tahoma, 1943, MAI; 233 NA (127-GR-137-69889-A); 234 Jerry Jacka; 235T courtesy Museum of New Mexico (9866); 235B Amon Carter Museum, Laura Gilpin Collection, 1981, Fort Worth, TX; 236T Bruce M. Fritz, photographer, *Capital Times*; 236B collection of Ada Deer; 238,239 UPI/Bettmann Newsphotos; 240 "Lone Ranger," George Eastman House, Palladium Entertainment Inc.; 241T "Broken Arrow," Museum of Modern Art/Film Stills Archives, 1950 Twentieth Century-Fox Film Corporation, all rights reserved; 241B "The White Buffalo," Museum of Modern Art/Film Stills Archives, 1977 Dino De Laurentiis Corp., all rights reserved; 242R "Little Big Man," Museum of Modern Art/Film Stills Archives, 1970 CBS Inc., photo courtesy CBS Inc.; 242L "Chris Spotted Eagle," photo by Robert Marc Friedman; 244,246 Don Doll S.J.; 249 "Last Indian with American Flag," by Fritz Scholder, collection of Mr. and Mrs. Edward Blumenfeld.

Horizons: pp. 250-251 Roger Wolken/Tony Stone Worldwide; 252 Thomas Wiewandt; 253 Jerry Jacka; 254,255 R. Klingholz/Focus/Woodfin Camp & Assocs.; 256 Dan Budnick/Woodfin Camp & Assocs.; 257 Phil Jordan and Assocs., Inc.; 258 Martin Rogers/Woodfin Camp Inc.; 259 John Running; 260T Abrams Photo/Graphics; 260B Allen Russell/Profiles West; 261 Abrams Photo/Graphics; 262 Allen Russell/Profiles West; 263 Kim Newton/Woodfin Camp & Assocs.; 264-265 Scott Rutherford; 266 Cherokee Nation Communication; 267 Allen Russell/Profiles West; 268T J. Hasteen, *Navajo Times*, 2-15-90; 268B T.K. Ryan, 7-16-70, Reprinted with special permission of North American Syndicate, Inc.; 269T "Around the Rez," by Joe Flying Horse, 9-89, *The Lakota Times*; 269C "Land of Enchantment," by Woodrow Crumbo, Philbrook Museum of Art, Tulsa; 269B "Centuries-Old Indian Tradition/Centuries-Old White Tradition," by Steve Sack, reprinted with permission of the *Star Tribune*, Minneapolis; 270T Dilip Mehta/Contact Stock/Woodfin Camp & Assocs.; 270B Dennis Sanders/Hardin Photo; 271T Jim Cartier/Photo Researchers Inc.; 272-273 Dane Penland/SI;

273T,B Allen Russell/Profiles West; 274-275 art by Isabel John, 1984, courtesy American Federation of Arts, from *Lost and Found Traditions: Native American Art 1965-1985*, NY, American Federation of Arts and University of Washington Press, 1986, photo by James Milmoe; 276 art by Effie Tybrec, 1982, courtesy American Federation of Arts, from *Lost and Found Traditions: Native American Art 1965-1985*, NY, American Federation of Arts and University of Washington Press, 1986, photo by Bobby Hansson; 277 "Grandmother Gestating Father and the Washita River Runs Ribbon-like," by T.C. Cannon, 1975, from the collection of Nancy & Richard Bloch, photo by Tony Vinella; 278-279 Susanne Page.